FOREW

The **Hidden Inns** series originates from the enthusiastic suggest of the popular **Hidden Places** guides. They want to be directed to traditional inns "off the beaten track" with atmosphere and character which are so much a part of our British heritage. But they also want information on the many places of interest and activities to be found in the vicinity of the inn.

The inns or pubs reviewed in the **Hidden Inns** may have been coaching inns but have invariably been a part of the history of the village or town in which they are located. All the inns included in this guide serve food and drink and some offer the visitor overnight accommodation. A full page is devoted to each inn which contains a coloured photograph, full name, address and telephone number, directions on how to get there, a full description of the inn and its facilities and a wide range of useful information such as opening hours, food served, accommodation provided, credit cards taken and details of entertainment. **Hidden Inns** guides however are not simply pub guides. They provide the reader with helpful information on the many places of interest to visit and activities to pursue in the area in which the inn is based. This ensures that your visit to the area will not only allow you to enjoy the atmosphere of the inn but also to take in the beautiful countryside which surrounds it.

The **Hidden Inns** guides have been expertly designed for ease of use and this guide is the first to be printed in full colour. **The Hidden Inns of Yorkshire** is divided into six chapters each of which is laid out in the same way. To identify your preferred geographical region refer to the contents page overleaf. To find a pub or inn and details of facilities they offer simply use the index to the rear of the guide or locator map at the beginning of each chapter which refers you, via a page number reference, to a full page dedicated to the specific establishment. To find a place of interest, again use the index to the rear of the book or list found at the beginning of each chapter which will guide you to a descriptive summary of the area that includes details of each place of interest.

We do hope that you will get plenty of enjoyment from visiting the inns, pubs and places of interest contained in this guide. We are always interested in what our readers think of the inns or places covered (or not covered) in our guides so please do not hesitate to write to us. This is a vital way of helping us ensure that we maintain a high standard of entry and that we are providing the right sort of information for our readers. Finally if you are planning to visit any other corner of the British Isles we would like to refer you to the list of Travel Publishing guides to be found at the rear of the book.

Travel Publishing

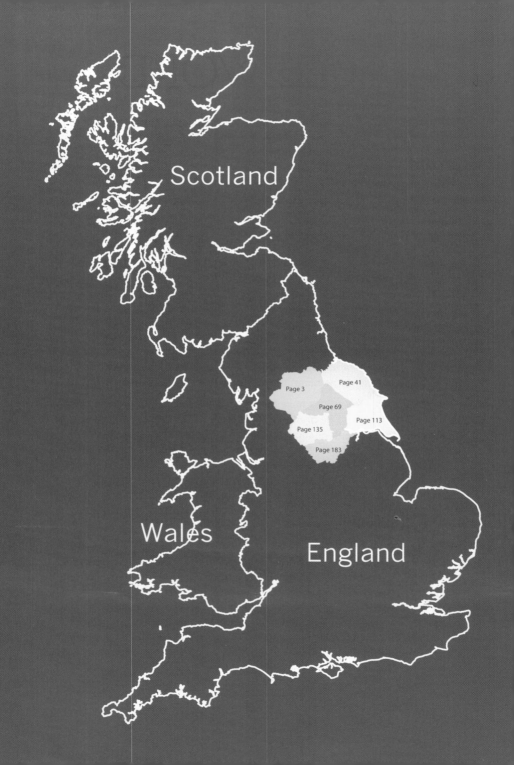

THE HIDDEN INNS OF
YORKSHIRE

By Peter Long

Regional Hidden Places

Cambs & Lincolnshire
Chilterns
Cornwall
Derbyshire
Devon
Dorset, Hants & Isle of Wight
East Anglia
Gloucs, Wiltshire & Somerset
Heart of England
Hereford, Worcs & Shropshire
Kent
Lake District & Cumbria
Lancashire & Cheshire
Lincolnshire & Nottinghamshire
Northumberland & Durham
Sussex
Thames Valley
Yorkshire

National Hidden Places

England
Ireland
Scotland
Wales

Hidden Inns

East Anglia
Heart of England
Lancashire & Cheshire
North of England
South
South East
South and Central Scotland
Wales
Welsh Borders
West Country
Yorkshire
Wales

Country Living Rural Guides

East Anglia
Heart of England
Ireland
North East of England
North West of England
Scotland
South
South East
Wales
West Country

Published by: Travel Publishing Ltd, 7a Apollo House, Calleva Park, Aldermaston, Berks, RG7 8TN

ISBN 1·904·43406·1

© Travel Publishing Ltd

First published 2000, second edition 2003,

Printing by: Ashford Colour Press, Gosport

Maps by: © Maps in Minutes ™ (2003)
© Crown Copyright, Ordnance Survey 2003

Editor: Peter Long

Cover Design: Lines & Words, Aldermaston

Cover Photograph: The Old Horn Inn, Spennithorne, North Yorkshire

Text Photographs: © www.britainonview.com

CONTENTS

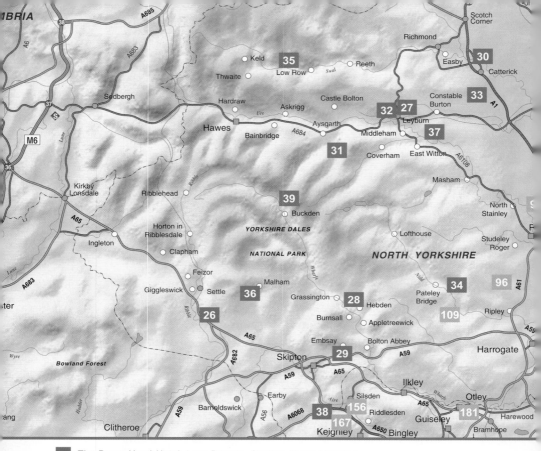

Please note all cross references refer to page numbers

THE YORKSHIRE DALES

The Yorkshire Dales, one 11 National Parks in England and Wales, is an area rich in farmland, high moorland and deep valleys. The predominant limestone found here gives rise to many of the area's interesting geological features, including waterfalls, potholes and disappearing rivers. Considered by many to be the most appealing and beautiful region in the country, the Yorkshire Dales have been receiving increasing numbers of visitors since the arrival of the railways in the 19th century though many of the settlements date back to the Bronze and Iron Ages. With the large industrial areas of Yorkshire and nearby Lancashire close to hand, the Dales are easily accessible but, with so much open countryside, visitors are able to avoid the more popular attractions and enjoy the beauty of the region in solitude.

The largest of the northern Dales, Swaledale is also one of the grandest and it has a rugged beauty that is in contrast to the pretty and busier Wensleydale to the south. It is this dale's sheep, the Swaledale, with their characteristic black faces, white muzzles and grey speckled legs, which have been adopted as the symbol for the National Park. The valley of the River Ure, Wensleydale, is, perhaps, the one that most people associate with the Yorkshire Dales. One of the longer dales, it is a place of green

PLACES OF INTEREST

Appletreewick 5	Hawes 13
Askrigg 5	Hebden 13
Aysgarth 5	Horton in
Bainbridge 6	Ribblesdale 14
Bolton Abbey 6	Ingleton 14
Buckden 7	Keld 15
Burnsall 7	Leyburn 16
Castle Bolton 8	Lofthouse 16
Catterick 8	Low Row 16
Clapham 8	Malham 17
Constable	Masham 18
Burton 9	Middleham 18
Coverham 9	Pateley
Earby 10	Bridge 19
Easby 10	Reeth 19
East Witton 10	Ribblehead 20
Embsay 11	Richmond 20
Feizor 11	Ripley 21
Giggleswick 11	Settle 22
Grassington 12	Skipton 23
Hardraw 12	Thwaite 24

pastureland grazed by flocks of Wensleydale sheep, lines of drystone walls and, of course, this is where the famous cheese is made. Further south again, is Wharfedale, a spectacular valley that is home to one of the National Park's most famous features, the Strid, where the River Wharfe charges through a narrow gorge just to the north of Bolton Abbey. To the east lies Nidderdale, a charming valley that was dubbed 'Little

Kisdon Force, Swaledale

Switzerland' by the Victorians as its upper reaches are steep and wooded with the River Nidd flowing through narrow gorges. To the west is Ribbledale that is overlooked by the famous Three Peaks of Whernside, Ingleborough and Pen-ghent, and that is also home to a spectacular stretch of the famous Settle-Carlisle Railway. Finally, there is Airedale, the valley of the River Aire, where, near the river's source, can be found the extraordinary limestone landscape around Malham Tarn. Further downstream lies Skipton, an ancient market town and "Gateway to the Dales" that is often many people's first experience of this glorious region of Britain.

The Yorkshire Dales provide the perfect setting for walking with at least 1,000 miles of public footpaths and ancient trackways, along with miles of bridleways. The **Pennine Way**, Britain's first long distance footpath, is some 270 miles in length and particularly inviting for ramblers in part or as a whole. The much shorter **Dales Way**, from Leeds to Lake Windermere in Cumbria, takes in old textile villages and the towns of West Yorkshire before heading through the western section of the Dales and on into Lancashire. There is also the **Trans Pennine Trail** that not only runs right across the country from east to west but also has a variety of extra, small diversions for those wishing to build up thirsts with shorter walks.

APPLETREEWICK

This peaceful village, which is known locally as Aptrick, lies between the banks of the River Wharfe and bleak moorland and is overlooked by the craggy expanse of **Simon's Seat,** one of Wharfedale's best loved hilltops.

Just to the north of Appletreewick lie **Parcevall Hall Gardens**, a wonderful woodland garden that includes many varieties of unusual plants, shrubs and tress along with rock gardens, terraces, streams and reflective pools. Though the 16 acre gardens are high above sea level, (which provides the visitor with splendid views), many of the plants still flourish in these beautiful, peaceful surroundings.

ASKRIGG

Recorded in the *Domesday Book* as 'Ascric', this once important market town lies on the edge of land that was designated by the Normans as a hunting forest and, although it has been a centre for trading for centuries, it did not receive its market charter until 1587. However, with the rise in importance of Hawes, further up the dale, the market here lapsed in the 19th century but, in the cobbles near the old market cross, can still be found a bull-ring to which a bull was attached by a long chain and set upon by dogs – a favourite Tudor spectator sport. During the 18th century, Askrigg was a thriving town with several prosperous industries, cotton was spun in a nearby mill, dyeing and brewing took place here and it was also a centre for hand-knitting.

However, the town is particularly famous for clock-making that was introduced here by John Ogden in 1681. This now sleepy and quaint town was also one of the first places in the Dales to be supplied with electricity when, in 1908, the local miller harnessed the power of Mill Gill Beck.

Askrigg's popularity as a tourist destination dates back to the days of Turner and Wordsworth when the chief attractions here were the two waterfalls – **Whitfield Gill Force** and Mill Gill Force – that can be reached by taking one of the various footpaths that radiate out of the village.

AYSGARTH

This village is famous for the spectacular **Aysgarth Falls**, where the River Ure

Aysgarth Falls

thunders through a rocky gorge and drops some 200 feet over three huge slabs of limestone that divide the wonderful, natural feature into the Upper, Middle and Lower Falls. They provided a perfect location for the battle between Robin Hood and Little John in Mel Gibson's film *Robin Hood, Prince of Thieves* while Hardraw Force, further up Wensleydale, was also used as a location for the film. Housed in a late 18th century mill that drew off water from the falls, the **Yorkshire Museum of Horse-Drawn Carriages** has a collection of nearly 60 Victorian coaches.

Semer Water, Bainbridge

Also close to the falls is the **Church of St Andrew**, home of the Jervaulx Treasures – a vicar's stall that is made from the beautifully carved bench ends salvaged from the abbey. Aysgarth is the home, too, of the Yorkshire Dales National Park Visitor Information Centre.

BAINBRIDGE

At the time of the Norman Conquest, this area of Upper Wensleydale was a hunting forest, known as the Forest and Manor of Bainbridge, and the village was established around the 12th century as a home for 12 foresters. One of their duties was to show travellers the way through the forest and, should anyone still be out by nightfall, a horn was blown to guide them home. This ancient custom is still continued between the Feast of Holy Rood (27 September) and Shrove Tuesday when the present horn is blown at 9 pm.

Just to the east of Bainbridge is Brough Hill (private) where the Romans built a succession of forts known collectively as Virosidum. First excavated in the late 1920s, they now appear as overgrown, grassy hummocks but much more visible is the Roman road that strikes southwestwards from Bainbridge and was part of their trans Pennine route to Lancaster. This ancient route passes close to the isolated lake of **Semer Water**, one of Yorkshire's only two natural lakes, which stretches for half a mile in length and teems with wildfowl. To the north the lake is drained by the River Bain, which, at little more than two miles long, is the shortest named river in England.

BOLTON ABBEY

The main attraction here is undoubtedly the substantial ruin of **Bolton Priory**, an Augustinian house that was founded in 1155 by monks from Embsay. After the

Bolton Abbey

Tower, once the principal hunting lodge in the Forest of Barden that was rebuilt in the 15th century as a fortified dwelling by the 'Shepherd Lord', Henry Clifford. The tower is now in ruins, albeit impressive ruins.

Dissolution of the Monasteries the priory was sold to the 2nd Earl of Cumberland, Henry Clifford, and it has since passed into the hands of the Dukes of Devonshire, the Cavendish family. The 14th century priory gatehouse, **Bolton Hall**, is the present Duke's shooting lodge. Visitors walking to the priory ruins from the village pass through a hole in the wall that frames one of the most splendid views of the romantic ruins.

In and around this beautiful village there are some 75 miles of footpaths and nature trails, skirting the riverbanks and climbing up on to the high moorland. Upstream from the priory ruins, however, lies one of the most visited natural features in Wharfedale, a point where the wide river suddenly narrows into a confined channel of black rock through which the water thunders. This spectacular gorge is known as the **Strid** because, over the centuries, many heroic (or foolhardy) types have attempted to leap across it as a test of bravery.

Further upstream again lies **Barden**

BUCKDEN

The village is an excellent starting point for those wanting to climb **Buckden Pike** (2,302 feet), which lies to the east, and the route to the summit takes in not only superb views but also several waterfalls.

Designated in Norman times as one of the feudal hunting forests, **Langstrothdale Chase** was governed by the strict forest laws. Just to the south of the village, which lies on the eastern edge of the Chase, can be seen an old stone cross which was used to mark the forest boundary.

BURNSALL

It is not just the sturdy 12th century church that draws visitors to Burnsall but also its bridge. Today, this typical Dales' bridge of five stone arches is the start of the annual **Classic Fell Race** that takes place on a Saturday towards the end of August. Over the years, the flood waters of the River Wharfe have washed away the arches on several occasions but the villagers have always replaced them as this is the only crossing point for three miles in each direction.

CASTLE BOLTON

Although this little village, with its row of cottages on either side of the long village green, is dwarfed by the huge castle, both the village and the church pre-date the great fortification. **Bolton Castle** has dominated mid-Wensleydale for more than six centuries and is one of the major tourist attractions in the area as not only is it a magnificent example of a medieval castle but it also provides stunning views over the dale. Down the centuries, the castle has played its part in the history of the area and the country and, along with connections with the Pilgrimage of Grace and Richard III, Mary, Queen of Scots was a reluctant visitor here when she was imprisoned in the castle between 1568-69 and, during the Civil War, Royalists were besieged here. Today, this luxurious fortified manor house is still occupied by a direct descendant of the 1st Lord Scrope and, following major conservation work in 1995, it remains one of the country's best preserved castles. Visitors can tour the halls, galleries and state apartments, see the dungeons and study the numerous tableaux that bring history to life. The castle gardens are also well worth taking the trouble to explore.

CATTERICK

Ever since the time of the Romans, when the settlement was known as 'Cataractonium', Catterick has been associated with the armed forces and, located on the Roman highway between London and Hadrian's Wall, is the garrison that also stands close to the place where Paulinus, Bishop of York, baptised 10,000 Christians in the River Swale. Today, the large army camp is some way from the village to the west but there are many reminders of Catterick's military connections. The village's connections with Nelson are not so obvious but it was Alexander Scott, vicar of Catterick in 1816, who was at Nelson's side when he died at the Battle of Trafalgar. Also, the Admiral's sister-in-law, Lady Tyrconnel, lived at nearby **Kiplin Hall**, a beautiful Jacobean country home famed for its wonderful interior plasterwork and medieval fishponds. The hall also contains many mementos of Nelson and Lady Hamilton and on display in the Blue Room is a folding library chair from the Admiral's cabin on *HMS Victory*.

CLAPHAM

By far the largest and most impressive building in this village is **Ingleborough Hall**, once the home of the Farrer family and now a centre for outdoor education. One member of the family, Reginald Farrer, was an internationally renowned botanist and he was responsible for introducing many new plant species into this country. Many examples of the plants that he introduced can still be found in the older gardens of the village while in the hall's gardens there is a particularly pleasant walk, the **Reginald Farrer Nature Trail**, which leads from Clapham to nearby Ingleborough Cave.

Packhorse Bridge, Clapham

Though the whereabouts of **Ingleborough Cave** have been known for centuries, it was not until the 19th century that exploration began. One of these early explorers, geologist Adam Sedgwick, is quoted as saying "we were forced to use our abdominal muscles as sledges and our mouths as candlesticks," which gives an excellent indication of the conditions the early potholers had to endure. Today's visitors to the caves see only a small part of the five miles of caverns and tunnels but, fortunately, this section is easily accessible and particularly spectacular. As well as exotic cave formations and illuminated pools there is **Eldon Hall Cavern**, home to a vast mushroom bed! Just above the cave, on the southern slopes of Ingleborough, is **Gaping Ghyll Hole**, which is, at 365 feet deep, 450 feet long and 130 feet wide, the grandest and largest pothole in Britain and is also part of the same underground limestone system as Ingleborough Cave. It's a great favourite with potholers, who come to admire the main chamber that is similar in size to York Minster, and at both the spring and August Bank Holiday weekends a winch is erected, allowing the descent of the hole in a bosun's chair.

CONSTABLE BURTON

Constable Burton Hall Gardens are particularly famous for the fine terraced gardens that were designed and developed by Mrs Vida Burdon between 1932 and 1976. Featuring a collection of Maples planted beneath ancient yew trees, the gardens also have a fabulous display of daffodils in early spring and extensive shrubbery and roses. The fine Georgian house, which provides an elegant backdrop to the gardens and surrounding 18th century parkland, was designed by John Carr and has remained in the same family, the Wyvills, since 1768. The house is not open to the public.

COVERHAM

Situated beside the River Cover, in little visited Coverdale, this village is perhaps best known for the ruins of Coverham Abbey that was built in the late 1200s and of which only some decorated arches and a Norman gateway remain. Close by is **Braithwaite Hall** (National Trust), a remote 17th century stone farmhouse built with stones from the abbey, on some of which effigies from the old buildings can still be seen. The hall is noted for fine original features that include fireplaces, panelling and an oak staircase. Also in the village is a delightful walled garden, the **Forbidden Garden**, which includes a grotto with an underground labyrinth of chambers and passages.

EARBY

Though the Yorkshire Dales are thought of as a once thriving textile producer, lead mining was for many centuries also an important industry. Housed in an old grammar school, which was founded in 1591 by Robert Windle, is the **Museum of Yorkshire Dales Lead Mining**, opened in 1971. This large collection has been put together by several local interest groups who began their work in 1945 when the Earby Mines Research Group was formed within the Earby Pothole Club. The museum, which has limited opening times, has many excellent displays including mine tubs, photographs, mine plans, small implements, mining machinery and miners' personal belongings.

EASBY

This small hamlet, on the banks of the River Swale, is home to the delightful and romantic remains of **Easby Abbey**, which was founded here in 1155 by Roald, Constable of Richmond Castle. The order of monks who resided here were of more modest leanings than the Cistercians and, as a result, the buildings possessed none of the grandeur of Rievaulx and Fountains, but the riverside

setting is a common feature to all. Easby Abbey's most notable feature is its replica of the Easby Cross, a Saxon cross dating from the 9th century, and the extensive ruins can be reached by a pleasant riverside walk that is well signposted from Richmond.

EAST WITTON

A quiet and attractive village, which was once an important market centre, East Witton sits beside the confluence of the Rivers Cover and Ure.

To the west of the village lie the graceful ruins of **Jervaulx Abbey**, one of the very few privately owned Cistercian abbeys and one of the great sister houses to Fountains Abbey. The name Jervaulx is a French derivation of Yore and Vale and it was founded in 1156 by monks who came over from France following the Norman Conquest. These strictly disciplined monks, who followed a regime of silence, prayer, study, contemplation and manual labour, also saw the abbey grow wealthy from sheep rearing and horse breeding and, before the Dissolution, Jervaulx owned vast areas of Wensleydale. However, the monks were forbidden to eat the soft cheese that they produced at the abbey and so they sold it for a profit and the origins of the world-famous Wensleydale cheese were born. Though in ruins, Jervaulx is among the most evocative of Yorkshire's many fine abbeys and the grounds in which it stands have been transformed into beautiful gardens with the crumbling walls providing interesting backdrops for the sculptured trees and colourful plants and shrubs.

EMBSAY

The village is home to the **Embsay Steam Railway**, based at the small country station built in 1888. As well as taking a scenic steam train journey to the end of the line at Bolton Abbey, a couple of miles away, visitors can see over 20 locomotives, both steam and diesel, and railway carriages. Special events are arranged throughout the year and opening times vary, though the trains run every Sunday. Embsay also became part of the textile industry but today one of its old mills has been converted into **Embsay Crafts** where a wealth of crafts, including glass painting, furniture making and parchment craft, can be seen.

Long before the days of railways, Embsay was home to an Augustinian priory, founded in 1130. However, for some reason the monks found life difficult here and, in 1145, they crossed Embsay Moor and moved to what is now Bolton Abbey. Those choosing to walk over the moor to the north of the village should take care as the area is peppered with old coal pits and disused shafts. However, the view from **Embsay Crag** (1,217 feet high) is well worth the effort of climbing.

FEIZOR

Feizor dates back to monastic times when it lay on the well-trodden route from Kilnsey to the Lake District that was used by the monks of Fountains Abbey. Although both Fountains Abbey and Sawley Abbey had possessions in this area, there are few reminders of those times today. However, the **Yorkshire Dales Falconry and Conservation Centre**, set in these dramatic limestone surroundings, does bring visitors to Feizor. The first privately owned falconry centre in the north of England, its aim is to educate and make the public aware of the number of the world's birds of prey that are threatened with extinction and through their successful captive breeding programmes to safeguard the birds' future for generations to come. Visitors here have the chance to see many of the centre's birds in flight during the demonstrations and, along with the vultures, eagles, hawks, falcons and owls, there is also the chance to see 'Andy', an Andean Condor with a massive wingspan of 10½ feet!

GIGGLESWICK

This ancient village, which stands on the opposite bank of the River Ribble from Settle, is home to several interesting buildings including the 15th century Church of St Alkelda and the well-known Giggleswick School.

Just to the north of the village is the famous **Ebbing and Flowing Well**, one of many in the area that owe their unusual name to the porous nature of the limestone that causes there to be sometimes water flowing and sometimes not.

GRASSINGTON

One of the best-loved and most popular villages within the Yorkshire Dales National Park, Grassington in many ways typifies the Dales' settlement with its bustling cobbled market square and charming main street that reflects its role as a traditional working centre. Grassington's origins go back many centuries and there was certainly a Bronze Age settlement here while the remains of an Iron Age village have been found, a Celtic field system lies on nearby **Lea Green** and the village was mentioned in the *Domesday Book*. The settlement seen today, which is now part of the estate of the Duke of Devonshire, has narrow streets lined with attractive Georgian buildings and is a delight to wander around.

Linton Falls, Grassington

Housed in two 18th century lead miners' cottages, in Grassington Square, is the **Upper Wharfedale Folk Museum** that contains many exhibits and displays relating to the lives of the people of the Dale and the trades they plied. Throughout the year, there were many festivals and holidays observed by the dales people and one, the **Feast Sports**, still takes place here on a Saturday in October. Among the many traditional events that are carried out there is the tea cake eating race, where children have to eat a tea cake then race to the other end of the field. **Wharfedale**, the valley of the River Wharfe, is, at 70 miles, the longest of the Yorkshire Dales and runs from the river's source on **Cam Fell** to Cawood where it joins the River Ouse. It is one of the most spectacular and most varied of the Yorkshire Dales and no one who sees the river charging through the narrow gorge at The Strid, near Bolton Abbey, will deny that the power of the river is to be respected.

There is much to see in Wharfedale and a variety of landscapes to discover. It is not surprising that it has, over the years, inspired many of Britain's poets, writers, and painters: Coleridge and Wordsworth were taken with its beauty while Ruskin enthused about its contrasts and Turner painted several scenes that capture something of the dale's history and mystery.

HARDRAW

Located in a natural amphitheatre of limestone crags, **Hardraw Force** is the

Hardraw Force

tells the fascinating story of how man's activities have helped to shape the landscape of the Dales. Providing interesting historical details on domestic life, the lead mining industry, hand-knitting and other trades as well as archaeological material, the museum covers many aspects of life in the Yorkshire Dales from as far back as 10,000 BC.

Another local industry was rope-making and at **The Hawes Ropeworkers**, next door to the museum, visitors can still watch the skilled art of rope-making. Wensleydale's most famous product, after its sheep, is its soft, mild cheese, and at the **Wensleydale Creamery** visitors can sample this delicacy and learn about its history through a series of interesting displays. With a museum, viewing gallery of the production area, cheese shop, gift shop and licensed restaurant, there's plenty here for the cheese lover to enjoy.

HEBDEN

To the east of this quiet hamlet are the wonderful **Stump Cross Caverns** that were discovered in 1858 by lead miners working nearby and have been open to the public ever since. Exploration since then has extended the network of caverns to over four miles in length and, along with revealing a fantastic collection of stalactites, stalagmites and unusual rock formations, animal bones dating back over 90,000 years have also been found inside. Along with touring the caverns, which are open all year,

highest, unbroken, above ground waterfall in England, and, due to an undercut in the cliff, the breathtaking 98 foot cascade can be viewed from behind – as both JMW Turner and William Wordsworth so famously did. Best seen after heavy rain as, generally, the quantity of water tumbling over the rocks is not great, the falls have, on two separate occasions, in 1739 and 1881, frozen solid in a near 100 foot icicle. The amphitheatre also provides superb acoustics, a feature that has been put to great effect in the annual brass band competitions that were begun here in 1885 and that have recently been revived. Access to the falls is through the lovely old Green Dragon pub.

HAWES

Housed in the former railway station is the **Dales Countryside Museum** that visitors can take in the displays and exhibitions in the visitor centre, where there is a gift shop and a tea room.

HORTON IN RIBBLESDALE

The oldest building here is the 12th century **St Oswald's Church** that still shows signs of its Norman origins in the chevron designs over the south door. Inside, peculiarly, all the pillars lean to the south and, in the west window, there is an ancient piece of stained glass showing Thomas à Becket wearing his bishop's mitre.

This village is the ideal place from which to explore the limestone landscape and green hills of Upper Ribblesdale. To the east lies **Pen-y-ghent** (2,273 feet), one of the famous **Three Peaks.** For particularly energetic visitors to Horton, the demanding Three Peaks Challenge is organised by the Pen-y-ghent Café. The 24-mile hike takes in not only Pen-y-ghent but also the other two peaks, Ingleborough and Whernside, and those completing the trek within 12

hours qualify for membership of the Three Peaks of Yorkshire Club. The whole of this area has been designated as being of Special Scientific Interest, mainly due to the need to conserve the swiftly eroding hillsides and paths.

INGLETON

Mentioned in the *Domesday Book* – the name means 'beacon town' – Ingleton is certainly one of the most visited villages in the Yorkshire Dales and is particularly noted as being the gateway to the Three Peaks. From as long ago as the late 18th century, Ingleton has been popular with walkers as well as being famous for the numerous caves and other splendid scenery that lies close by, though some of these sights are more accessible than others. Though Ingleton is no longer served by a railway, the village is still dominated by the railway viaduct that spans the River Greta. The river, which is formed here by the meeting of the Rivers Twiss and Doe, is famous for its salmon leaps. Also of interest in the village is the parish **Church of St Mary** that lies on a hill overlooking the river. Although the tower dates from the 13th century the rest of the church was constructed in 1887 but its most prized possession, an elaborate font, dates back to around 1150.

The **Ingleton Waterfalls** have been delighting

Pen-y-ghent

Ingleborough

on its summit, including the remains of a tower built by a local mill owner. The land encompassing the mountain is now the **Ingleborough National Nature Reserve,** known for its wildlife as well as its geology and, in particular, the limestone pavements and other features unique to this rockbed.

visitors since 1885 and the footpath walk, considered by many to be the most scenic waterfall walk in England, takes in **Pecca Falls** and Hollybush Spout along with Thornton Force, which tumbles 40 feet into a pool surrounded by a natural amphitheatre. Along with the waterfalls, there are also potholes in the area including **Alum Pot**, which is 292 feet deep and down which Alum Pot Beck cascades. However, it is the nearby network of caverns, known as **White Scar Cave**, which is particularly popular. Discovered in 1923, the caves feature Britain's longest show cave along with two waterfalls and superb stalactites. The cave remains at the same temperature throughout the year (8°C) and there are guided tours all year round.

Of all the natural features to be seen from Ingleton, the most famous is **Ingleborough**, at 2,375 feet the middle of the Three Peaks, which shadows both the village and the surrounding area. As well as offering fine views, on a clear day, there are also several interesting features

KELD

The little cluster of stone buildings that make up this village stand beside the infant River Swale. For lovers of green woodlands and breathtaking waterfalls, this village is definitely well worth a visit and it has also managed to retain an impression of being untouched by modern life. Backed by rugged Cotterby Scar, **Wain Wath Force** can be found alongside the road towards Birkdale while Catrake Force, with its stepped formation, can be reached from the village's main street. However, Kidson Force, the most impressive waterfall in Swaledale, can be reached most easily of all – by taking a gentle stroll of less than a mile from the village along a well-trodden footpath. For serious walkers, though, Keld is the most important crossroads in northern England as here the south-to-north **Pennine Way** and the east-to-west **Coast to Coast Footpath** intersect.

LEYBURN

The main market town and trading centre of mid-Wensleydale, Leyburn is an attractive town with a broad market place lined with handsome late Georgian and Victorian stone buildings.

In the unusual **Violin Making Workshop** visitors have the rare opportunity to see an ancient and fascinating craft that has changed little down the centuries. The traditional tools and methods used by such master craftsmen as Stradivari are still employed here and the workshop is open every day during the high season. Close by, other craftsmen are at work at **The Teapottery** where witty and unique teapots are created and then put on sale in the showroom. Not surprisingly, the workshop has a tea room and, naturally, the tea is served in their own astonishing teapots.

Both children and adults will enjoy the **Beech End Model Village**, a unique experience where visitors can 'drive' cars down the village streets and out into highly detailed countryside, press a button to see inside a perfect scale model of a house or shop and also hear the sounds of village life. Equally enchanting is the **Teddy Bear Workshop** where traditional Teddy Bears are designed and hand-crafted in small limited editions for collectors around the world.

As it flows down its valley, the River Ure is fed by a series of smaller rivers and becks, many of which have their own charming dale. Among these are **Coverdale**, the home of some of England's finest racecourse stables, peaceful Bishopdale, with its ancient farmhouses, and remote Cotterdale, with its striking waterfall. Most famously, Wensleydale, along with Swaledale and the area around Thirsk, are commonly referred to as Herriot Country since it was this region of fells and friendly villages that provided many of the locations for the television series *All Creatures Great and Small*. Based on the working life of vet, Alf Wight (1916-95), the stories recount the working life of dalesfolk between the 1930s and the 1960s with much humour and affection.

LOFTHOUSE

Close to this village, in the heart of Nidderdale, lies **How Stean Gorge**, a spectacular limestone gorge that is up to 80 feet deep in places, through which the Stean Beck flows. Narrow paths with footbridges cut into the steep-sided ravine guide visitors along the gorge where the waters rush over the large boulders below. However, there are also many sheltered areas of calm water where fish hide under the rocks. As well as taking a stroll up this fascinating path, visitors can also step inside Tom Taylor's Cave and, along the walk, marvel at the wide variety of plant life that grows in this steep ravine.

LOW ROW

During the Middle Ages, the track along the hillside above this small village formed part of the Corpse Way, along which relays of bearers would carry the deceased in a large wicker basket to Grinton church for burial. The journey could take up to two days to complete and, along the route, the large stone slabs where they rested their heavy burden can still be seen.

Just on the edge of the village lies **Hazel Brow Organic Farm and Visitor Centre**, a family-run farm in the heart of glorious Swaledale that provides all

Malham Cove

that is needed for an interesting and entertaining day out. Down by the river there are the internationally famous hay meadows while, higher up, is the heather-clad moorland that is home to a flock of hardy Swaledale sheep. At lambing time children can bottle feed the lambs and there are also ponies to ride, calves to feed and different activities and demonstrations throughout year.

MALHAM

This pretty village of farms and cottages is one of the most visited places in the Yorkshire Dales though it is not the charming stone-built dwellings that visitors come to admire but the spectacular limestone scenery that lies just to the north.

To the north of the village lies the ancient glacial grandeur of **Malham Cove**, a 300 foot limestone amphitheatre that forms the most spectacular section of the mid Craven Fault; as recently as the 1700s, a massive waterfall, which was higher than Niagara Falls, cascaded over its edge! These days the water disappears through potholes at the top, called water sinks, and reappears through the cavern mouth at Aire Head near the village. A steep path leads to the limestone pavement at the top, with its characteristic clints and grykes, where water has carved a distinctive natural sculpture through the weaknesses in the limestone.

Just to the east lies the equally inspiring **Gordale Scar**, a huge gorge carved out by glacial melt water with an impressive waterfall leaping, in two stages, from a fissure in its face. Also nearby is another waterfall known as

Janet's Foss beside which is a cave where Janet, a friendly fairy, is said to have lived. To the north again is Malham Tarn, a glacial lake that by way of an underground stream is the source of the River Aire. The tarn, England's highest freshwater lake, lies at the centre of the **Malham Tarn Estate** (National Trust), some 7,200 acres of open limestone country that also includes Malham Tarn House, where such famous names as Ruskin, Darwin and Charles Kingsley (author of *The Water Babies*) found inspiration. Back in the village, at Townhead Barn, there is an interpretive centre, along with an exhibition of farming in the Dales.

MASHAM

The wealth of this market town by the River Ure was built on sheep, and the sheep fairs held in the town in the 18th and 19th centuries were among the largest in the country. In September the Masham Sheep Fair revives those heady days, giving visitors the chance of seeing many rare breeds of sheep and goats as well as witnessing events such as dog agility and sheep racing!

However, today, the town is famed for its beer and it boasts two celebrated breweries – **Theakston's** and **Black Sheep**, both of which can be visited.

Away from the breweries there are several other buildings of note in Masham including the 15th century Church of St Mary, whose spire dominates the town.

MIDDLEHAM

Famous for its castle, the childhood home of Richard III, and its thriving racehorse training industry, Middleham is an enchanting little town with some handsome Georgian architecture that, despite its small population, boasts its own Mayor, Corporation and not one but two market places. Rising high above the town are the magnificent remains of **Middleham Castle** (English Heritage), whose 12th century keep was the largest in the north of England. Visitors to the castle today can take in the magnificent views of the keep from the oak viewing gallery and also learn more of the castle's history and

Druid's Circle, Masham

its influence on the surrounding area through the small exhibition here. Above the castle lies **William's Hill**, the site of Middleham's first castle, a Norman motte and bailey fortification.

Middleham is often referred to as the 'Newmarket of the North', as nearly 500 racehorses are stabled in and around the town and strings of them can be seen walking through the town on their way to the training gallops on Low Moor. It was the monks of Jervaulx Abbey who founded this key industry and, by the late 18th century, races were being run across the moorland and the first stables established. Since then the stables have produced a succession of classic race winners while one local trainer, Neville Crump, trained three Grand National winners in the space of just 12 years. On Good Friday each year **Middleham Stables Open Day** takes place, when all the town's yards open their doors to visitors and various equine events are held on Low Moor.

PATELEY BRIDGE

Considered by many to be one of the prettiest towns in the Dales, Pateley Bridge is perfectly situated as a base from which to explore Upper Nidderdale. Despite its compact size, the town is remarkably well connected by roads that have been here since the monastic orders established trade routes through Pateley Bridge for transporting their goods. Among the quaint and pretty buildings, the oldest is St Mary's Church, a lovely ruin dating from 1320 and from where

there are some fine panoramic views. Another excellent vista can be viewed from the aptly named **Panorama Walk**, part of the main medieval route from Ripon to Skipton.

The award-winning **Nidderdale Museum** is housed in one of the town's original Victorian workhouses and presents a fascinating record of local folk history.

The valley of the River Nidd, **Nidderdale**, is a typical Yorkshire dale with drystone walls, green fields and pretty stone villages; it was christened 'Little Switzerland' by the Victorians, as the upper reaches are steep and wooded, with the river running through gorges. It is this natural beauty that draws many people to the dale and there are several remarkable features that are well worth exploring. Walkers revel in the dale's wide variety of landscape and birdwatchers will twitch with delight at the prospect of spotting a number of species of duck as well as Brent geese and whooper swans.

REETH

Considered to be the capital of Upper Swaledale, this small town was once a centre of the lead mining industry, which served the town well for many years until competition from abroad gradually caused its decline. Along the top of the green is High Row, with its inns, shops and outstanding Georgian architecture, which reflects the affluence of the town in the 18th century when the trade in lead and in wool was booming. Also here, housed in what was once the old Methodist Sunday School, is the **Swaledale Folk Museum**, which tells how the local mining, farming and craft industries have shaped the lives of those living in this beautiful dale. Reeth is also noted for its variety of craft shops and, close to the green, is the **Reeth Craft Workshops** where a range of hand-crafted goods, including furniture and exquisite animal models, can be seen and purchased.

The town is strategically sited at the point where the Arkle Beck joins the River Swale and from here, running northwards, is the small and remote valley – **Arkengarthdale**.

RIBBLEHEAD

Lying close to the source of the River Ribble is an impressive structure, the **Ribblehead Viaduct**, which was built to carry the Settle-Carlisle Railway. Opened in 1876, after taking five years to construct, its 24 arches span the dark moorland and it is overlooked by Whernside. A bleak and exposed site, the viaduct is often battered by strong winds that have been known to stop a train literally in its tracks.

RICHMOND

The former county town of Richmondshire, which still survives as a parliamentary constituency today, Richmond has a long and distinguished history that dates back to 1071 when Alan Rufus, the 1st Earl of Richmond, built a castle here. The site of the fortification, 100 feet up on a rocky promontory with the River Swale flowing below, was not only imposing and well chosen but also gave rise to the name of the town that grew up around the castle – 'riche-mont' or 'strong hill'. **Richmond Castle** (English Heritage) was the first Norman castle in the country to be built, from the foundations upwards, in stone. The keep rises to over 100 feet in height and has walls that are 11 feet thick, and the cliff beyond the fortification makes this an impregnable defence.

Much of the town seen today dates from the Georgian period

Ribblehead Viaduct

Richmondshire Museum

Westwards from this historic town lies **Swaledale**, which is, for many, the loveliest of the Yorkshire Dales and it runs through countryside that ranges from the dramatic lower dale with its steep-sided wooded hills to the austere upper reaches and a landscape where nearest neighbours can be several miles away. Today, one of the key features of the dale are the **Swaledale Sheep** that can easily be recognised by their black faces, white muzzles and grey speckled legs. Introduced into the area as late as the 1920s. The sheep have to cope with extremely wild weather and their hardiness is typified by the warmth and durability of their wool. Not surprisingly, the Swaledale ram has been adopted as the emblem of the Yorkshire Dales National Park.

RIPLEY

Still very much an estate village, Ripley is a quiet and pretty place with cobbled streets, a castle, a wonderful hotel and an interesting history. This title was granted to Thomas Ingilby in the 1300s, for killing a wild boar in Knaresborough Forest that was charging at Edward III, and it remains with the family today. The magnificent **Ripley Castle** has been

and later, and one of the most notable buildings is the grand **Culloden Tower**, just off the town green, which was erected in 1747 by the Yorke family, one of whose members had fought at the Battle of Culloden the previous year. Unlike most follies, the interior of this three-storey tower is elaborately decorated in the rococo style; it is now in the care of the Landmark Trust. Richmond is also home to England's oldest theatre, the **Georgian Theatre Royal**, which was built in 1788 by the actor and manager Samuel Butler.

For a complete insight into the history of this attractive and interesting town, and the surrounding area, the **Richmondshire Museum** covers many aspects of life in Swaledale. In the converted 12th century Church of the Trinity is the town's other museum, the **Green Howards Museum**, which relates over 300 years of history of the North Riding's Infantry.

home to the family since 1325 and, open to the public, it is set in an outstanding Capability Brown landscape with lakes, a deer park and an avenue of tall beeches over which the attractive towers can only just be seen. Visitors to the castle can see the fine Georgian and Tudor rooms, the Civil War armour in the Knight's Chamber and a secret priest's hole that was discovered by accident in 1964. Outside, the walled garden contains the National Hyacinth Collection as well as rare fruits and vegetables, while the recently restored hothouses are home to a tropical plant collection.

SETTLE

This small, delightful and unspoilt market town, which received its charter in 1249 from Henry III, still retains a lively weekly market (on Tuesdays) as well as some quaint old buildings. A busy stopping place in the days of the stagecoach, when travellers journeying between York and Lancaster and Kendal called in here, Settle is most closely associated with the railways and, in particular, it is the home of the famous **Settle-Carlisle Railway**, a proudly preserved reminder of the great railway

days. England's greatest, historic, scenic route, the railway passes through lowland valleys before climbing into the dramatic landscape of the Pennines on its route northwards to Carlisle. One of the last great mainline railways to be built, the 72 miles of track were first opened to passenger rains in 1876 but its construction took place in the midst of great controversy and even greater cost, in both money and lives. It was dubbed 'the line that should never have been built', and in the churchyard at Chapel-le-Dale over 100 of the workers and miners who laboured under the most adverse conditions lie buried. Today, modern trains still thunder over the 21 viaducts, through the 14 tunnels and over the numerous bridges for which these workers gave their lives. Along with the scheduled regular services, there are also special excursions on certain days along with charter trains organised by various operators throughout the country.

Preston's Folly, Settle

The town is dominated by one of the railway's huge viaducts as well as the towering limestone cliffs of **Castleberg Crag** while Settle's architecture is equally striking – being mainly Victorian sandstone buildings that were built at the height of the railway age. These include the arcaded Shambles (originally the butcher's slaughterhouses), the French-style Town Hall and the Music Hall, while Settle's oldest building, **Preston's Folly**, is an extravaganza of mullion windows and Tudor masonry that is named after the man who created this anomalous fancy and impoverished himself in the process. In Chapel Street is the **Museum of North Craven Life**, which gives a historical, topographical and geological background to the area and tells the story of the local farming traditions through a series of imaginative displays. The features of the surrounding countryside are equally interesting and, in particular, there is the fascinating **Victorian Cave** that was discovered in 1838 by Michael Horner. Although the instability of the rock in the area has caused the cave and the surrounding land to be closed to the public, the cave has yielded some interesting finds including Roman relics, Stone Age artefacts and 120,000-year-old mammoth bones.

SKIPTON

Often called the Gateway to the Dales, Skipton's origins can be traced to the 7th century when Anglian farmers christened it Sheeptown. The Normans decided to build a castle here to guard the entrance to Airedale and Skipton became a garrison town. One of the most complete and best-preserved medieval castles in England, **Skipton Castle**, home of the Cliffords, was begun in 1090 and the powerful stone structure seen today was devised in 1310 by Robert de Clifford, the 1st Earl of Skipton. The Cliffords were a fighting breed and, throughout the Middle Ages, wherever there was trouble a member of the family was sure to be found. The 8th Lord Clifford, Thomas, and his son John were both killed while fighting for the House of Lancaster during the War of the Roses. Later, George Clifford, Champion to Queen Elizabeth I and a renowned sailor, fought against the Spanish Armada and, as well as participating in many voyages of his own, he also lent a ship to Sir Walter Raleigh. However, it is thanks to Lady Anne Clifford that visitors to Skipton can marvel at the castle's buildings. Following the ravages of the Civil War, from which the castle did not escape, Lady Anne undertook a comprehensive restoration programme and, though little of the original Norman stonework remains, much of the work of the 1st Lord Clifford still stands. Adjacent to the castle, at the top of the High Street, lies the parish **Church of the Holy Trinity** that was originally built in the 12th century and replaced in the 1300s. There is a wealth of interest inside the building, which has been topped by a beautiful oak roof since the 15th century.

The **Leeds and Liverpool Canal**, which flows through the town, provided a cheap form of transport as well as linking Skipton with the major industrial centres of Yorkshire and Lancashire. The first of three trans Pennine routes, the 127-mile canal has 91 locks along the full length as well as two tunnels, one of which is over a mile long. Though used well into the 20th century, the canal lost its freight trade and fell into disuse in the 1960s. Today, the canal basin, behind the town centre, is busy with pleasure craft and boat journeys can be taken along a section in the direction of Gargrave. The towpath was also restored at the same time as the canal and there are a number of pleasant walks that include a stretch along the cul-de-sac Spring Branch beside the castle walls.

A walk around the town is also worthwhile and there are many interesting buildings to be found here. One, in particular, is the Town Hall that is now also the home of the **Craven Museum**. Dedicated to the surrounding area, it has many interesting displays relating to the geological and archaeological treasures that have been found locally, including a piece of Bronze

Craven Museum, Skipton

Age cloth that is considered the oldest textile fragment in the country. Closer to the present day, there are displays of furniture illustrating the fine craftsmanship that went into even the most mundane household item and farming exhibits that reflect the changing lives of many of the people who lived off the surrounding land. The museum is open all year except Tuesdays and winter Sundays.

THWAITE

Surrounded by a dramatic landscape that includes Kisdon Hill, Great Shunnor, High Seat and Lovely Seat, this tiny village has ancient origins and, like so many places in Swaledale, its name is derived from the Nordic language, in this case 'thveit', meaning 'a clearing in the wood'. However, the woodlands that once provided both shelter and fuel for the Viking settlers have long since gone.

Thwaite

a curious natural feature of closely packed vertical stone stacks rising from some unseen, underground base to the level of the road. The narrow road from Thwaite across the Buttertubs Pass is not for the faint-hearted driver as only a flimsy post and wire fence separates the road from a sheer drop of near Alpine proportions. It is, perhaps, more satisfying to cross the pass in the opposite direction, from Hawes, as when the summit of the pass is reached there are stupendous views of Swaledale.

To the southwest of the village, on the road to Hawes in Wensleydale, lies **Buttertubs Pass**, one of the highest and most forbidding mountain passes in the country. The Buttertubs themselves are

THE BOARS HEAD HOTEL

9 MAIN STREET, LONG PRESTON, NR SKIPTON,
NORTH YORKSHIRE BD23 4ND
TEL: 01729 840217

Directions: Long Preston is adjacent to the A65, north of Skipton and three miles south of Settle.

Dating back to the 16th century, **The Boars Head Hotel** is a large and impressive public house serving great food, drink and hospitality. The interior boasts comfortable seating amid attractive surroundings. The non-smoking dining room seats 30, while other dining areas include the lovely beer garden. Children are welcome at this friendly pub, where the menu includes traditional favourites, modern dishes and daily specials. Wednesday night is curry night, while on Thursday evenings sirloin steaks are a speciality. The Sunday carvery (also available on

Bank Holidays) is a sumptuous feast at a very reasonable price. Booking required Friday to Sunday.

There is a choice of three real ales (Tetleys, Bombardier and Flowers IPA) plus a good range of draught keg bitter, lager, cider, stout, wines, spirits and soft drinks. Licensees Ivan and Linda have been here since September 2002, having spent 12 years in the trade. Their families have held various celebrations here and it remains a hub of the community. There's occasional live music on a Saturday night, a fun quiz Sunday evenings, and a function room for small gatherings.

The four en suite guest bedrooms come in a range of sizes to suit different numbers of guests. Each is individually decorated with taste and style, and are supremely comfortable. A full English breakfast is included in the rate.

- Mon 17.00-23.00; Tues-Sat 11.00-23.00; Sun and Bank Hol 12.00-22.30
- Tues-Fri and Bank Hol Mon 12.00-14.30, 18.00-21.00 ; Sat-Sun 12.00-21.00 (Sunday and Bank Holiday carvery 12.00-18.00)
- £ All major
- 4 rooms en suite
- Off-road parking
- Special themed nights, quiz night Sun, occasional live entertainment
- @ ivan-linda@huff.fslife.co.uk
- ? Giggleswick 4 miles, Settle 3 miles, Skipton 7 miles, Ribblesdale 2 miles, walking, horse riding, fishing, bird watching

THE BOLTON ARMS

MARKET PLACE, LEYBURN, NORTH YORKSHIRE DL8 5BW
TEL: 01969 623327 FAX: 01969 624927

Directions: Leyburn lies at the junction of the A684 (Northallerton-Hawes) and the A6108 (Ripon-Richmond)

Rachel Lambie and her friendly, attentive staff offer all guests at **The Bolton Arms** a warm welcome and genuine hospitality. Set in the charming market place of Leyburn, this traditional stonebuilt pub is impressive and welcoming. Dating back to the late 18th century, the pub took its name from the local Lord of the Manor of the time and boasts a long history of providing good food and drink to weary travellers.

The décor and furnishings are pure quality – many people visit specially to see the magnificent stone fireplace and surround, a real eye-catcher that stands several feet high, and stay to enjoy the range of well-kept ales available – John Smith cask and up to three changing guest ales – along with a good selection of draught keg bitters, lagers, cider, stout, wines, spirits and soft drinks. The bar is spacious and attractive, with exposed beams and stone walls, subtle lighting and comfortable seating in a relaxed ambience.

Meals are served every lunchtime and Monday to Saturday evening, in the upstairs non-smoking dining room, downstairs or outside in the delightful walled garden or patio area. There's a range of hearty and delicious favourites on the menu and blackboard specials. The Sunday carvery is justly popular.

Rachel, ably assisted by her parents Lynda and Roy, has given this gracious inn a new lease of life since becoming leaseholder here in February 2003, and goes from strength to strength in providing excellent food, drink and hospitality. Children are welcome at this friendly family-run pub.

- Mon-Sat 11.00-23.00; Sun 12.00-22.30
- Mon-Sat 12.00-14.00, 18.00-20.00; Sun 12.00-16.00
- All major
- Off-road parking, patio area, walled garden
- Jazz evenings Tues from 8 pm; occasional quiz nights and other entertainments
- Jazz evenings Tues from 8 pm; occasional quiz nights and other entertainments

THE CLARENDON HOTEL

HEBDEN,NR GRASSINGTON,SKIPTON,NORTH YORKSHIRE BD23 5DE
TEL: 01756 752446

Directions: From Grassington take the B6265 3 miles east to reach Hebden.

The Clarendon Hotel is a spectacular-looking inn which began life as a farmhouse and went on to become an alehouse and then, in the 18th century, a coaching inn on the Skipton–Grassington–Pateley Bridge–Harrogate route. Occupying a scenic location in the heart of the Yorkshire Dales, ideal for walkers, the exterior is bedecked with ivy and the forecourt contains picnic tables, perfect for a relaxing drink or meal on fine days.

Inside, all is pristine and traditional, comfortable and welcoming. The no-smoking dining area seats 20.

This Free House boasts three real ales – Timothy Taylor Best, Tetleys and a changing guest ale – together with a good selection of draught lagers, cider, stout, wines, spirits and soft drinks.

Leaseholders John and Rachel have been here since 2002. A local couple, Rachel is experienced in the catering business, having cooked at two local establishments for 19 years before taking over here. She is renowned in the area for her delicious food, and creates freshly prepared and delicious dishes. Guests choose from the ever-changing blackboard menu from a range of home-made specialities including meat and potato pie, curries, joint of lamb and more. The hotel enjoys a growing reputation for serving fine steaks, and fish-lovers and vegetarians are also catered for.

- 🕐 Tues-Sun lunch 12.00-15.00, Tues-Sat evening 18.00-23.00; Sun evening 18.00-22.30
- 🍴 Tues-Sun 12.00-14.00; Tues-Thurs 18.00-20.30, Fri-Sat 18.00-21.00; Sun 18.00-20.00
- £ Visa, Mastercard, Switch, Delta, Amex, Access, Eurocard, Solo
- 🛏 3 en suite rooms
- Ⓟ Patio area, off-road parking
- @ www.yorkshirenet.co.uk/stayat/clarendonhotel/index.htm
- 🎵 Mid-week quiz once a month – please ring for details
- ❓ Stump Cross Caverns, Grassington 3 miles, Appletreewick 3 miles, Settle 13 miles, Skipton 12 miles, Harrogate 18 miles, fishing, walking

THE ELM TREE INN

5 ELM TREE SQUARE, EMBSAY, SKIPTON,
NORTH YORKSHIRE BD23 6RB
TEL: 01756 790717

Directions: 1 mile northeast of Skipton off the B6365

Formerly a coaching inn, set on the Skipton–Pateley Bridge route, **The Elm Tree Inn** enjoys a long tradition of great service and hospitality. The inn boasts décor and furnishings that happily marry tradition with modern comfort, creating a cosy and friendly feel to the place.

The five real ales on tap include Tetleys and Keighley brewery Goose Eye's No Eye Deer, along with rotating guest ales chosen from a list of over 50 possible contenders. These are complemented by a good range of lagers, cider, stout, wines, spirits and soft drinks.

Excellent food is available every day at

lunch and dinner, with a selection of traditional and more modern favourites prepared by the inn's professional cooks. The good range of dishes on the menu and specials board includes haddock, Yorkshire gammon, salmon and dill lasagne and much more, as well as a good selection of snacks, sandwiches and salads. Booking required Friday, Saturday and Sunday. There are no-smoking dining areas, and children are welcome.

Tenants Janet and Chris, have been here since May of 2003. Chris is also a driver on the steam engines at the nearby Embsay Steam Railway, which runs for a few miles along a very scenic journey.

Two comfortable and welcoming en suite guest bedrooms – a double and a twin – are available all year round. The tariff includes a hearty full English breakfast.

- 🕐 Mon-Sat 11.30-15.00, 17.30-23.00; Sun 12.00-15.00, 19.00-22.30 Sat,Sun & Bank Hols May-Sept 11.30-23.00
- 🍴 Daily 12.00-14.00, 18.00-21.00
- £ Visa, Mastercard, Switch, Delta, Eurocard, Solo
- 🛏 2 guest rooms en suite
- 🅿 Beer garden, off-road parking, patio area
- 🎵 Quiz night Mondays from 9 p.m.; occasional live entertainment, themed food nights, cocktail evenings – please ring for details
- ❓ Embsay Steam Railway, Bolton Abbey, Skipton 1 mile, Malham Cove 10 miles, Settle 15 miles

THE FARMER'S ARMS

CATTERICK BRIDGE, BROMPTON ON SWALE, RICHMOND,
NORTH YORKSHIRE DL10 7HZ
TEL: 01748 818062

Directions: Close to where the B6271 meets the A6136 at Catterick Bridge

A former coaching inn dating back in parts to the mid-1700s, **The Farmers Arms** is very pleasing to the eye, inside and out. The exterior is a large and impressive stonebuilt structure. The interior is equally gracious and extensive, with the attractive bar and lounge having exposed beams, and a bright, stylish conservatory dining area.

Handily placed just a stone's throw from Catterick racecourse, this fine inn has a long tradition of providing great food and drink. Two real ales – Tetley Imperial and John Smith's – are augmented by a very good range of draught keg bitters, lagers, cider, stout, spirits, wines and soft drinks. Meals are served at lunch and dinner in the bar, lounge, beer garden or non-smoking conservatory dining area, which seats 32. Booking is advised for Friday and Saturday evenings. The extensive menus include such mouth-watering creations as medallions of beef, rack of lamb, pork fillet, Oriental stir-fry beef, Andalusian chicken, seafood melody and trout fillet. There's also a vegetarian, children's and dessert menu. Parties and group bookings are happily catered for.

At present there are two guest bedrooms, a double and a twin, both en suite and with their own separate entrance. The tariff includes a delicious and hearty breakfast – ideal to set guests up for a day's walking or sightseeing. Due for completion in late 2003, is a 40-room hotel with leisure facilities including a swimming pool, spa and beauty salon.

- 🕐 Summer: Mon-Fri 11.00-15.00, 18.00-23.00; Sat 11.00-23.00; Sun 12.00-22.30; Closed Mondays during winter.
- 🍴 12.00-14.00, 18.00-21.00
- 💷 Visa, Mastercard, Delta, Switch, Eurocard, Solo
- 🛏 2 rooms en suite *Due for late 2003:* 40-room hotel including leisure facilities
- Ⓟ Off-road parking, beer garden
- @ ouldfield@aol.com
- ❓ Catterick racecourse (1 mile), Northallerton 9 miles, Richmond 5 miles

THE FOX & HOUNDS INN

WEST BURTON, NR LEYBURN, NORTH YORKSHIRE DL8 4JY
TEL: 01969 663111 FAX: 01969 663279

> **Directions:** Off the B6160 7 miles west of Leyburn, 3 miles south of Aysgarth Falls (A164).

In the centre of this unspoilt, picturesque village, **The Fox & Hounds** is a traditional Wensleydale pub of immense charm. Andrew and Jayne Landau and their staff provide a warm, friendly welcome in this fine refurbished pub, where low oak beams contribute to an olde-worlde scene in the bar and (non-smoking) dining room. Traditional Yorkshire fare, all prepared and cooked on the premises, is served in both areas – the extensive choice of daily specials are in demand at lunchtime, and a light-bites menu at lunchtime and a full menu is served in the evening, when the popularity of the place makes booking advisable. Hand-pulled ales include Black Sheep, Tetleys and a changing guest ale to quench guests' thirst, and

there's a good range of bitters, lagers, cider, stout, wines, spirits and soft drinks. Picnic tables at the front of the pub overlook the pretty village green. Children are welcome, as are well-behaved dogs.

For visitors staying overnight there are six comfortably appointed and attractively decorated guest bedrooms (3 Diamonds ETB), all en suite, with every facility guests could expect. Two of the rooms are located on the ground floor and special one night breaks are offered. A hearty breakfast is included in the tariff. Guests are welcome to join in the fun of the regular quiz nights, music nights and karaoke sessions.

The village of West Burton is one of the prettiest in all of Wensleydale; it lies in a conservation area and is best known for its large and beautiful village green.

- 🕐 Summer: Mon-Sat 11.00-23.00; Sun 11.00-22.30; Winter: Mon-Sat 11.00-15.00, 18.00-23.00; Sun 11.00-15.00, 18.00-22.30
- 🍴 Summer: 12.00-21.00; Winter: 12.00-14.00, 18.30-21.00
- £ Visa, Mastercard, Switch, Delta
- 🛏 6 rooms en suite
- Ⓟ Off-road parking
- 🎵 Live music, karaoke, quiz nights
- ❓ Leyburn 7 miles, Aysgarth 3 miles, Bolton Castle 6 miles

THE GOLDEN LION HOTEL

MARKET PLACE, LEYBURN, NORTH YORKSHIRE DL8 5AS
TEL: 01969 622161 FAX: 01969 623836

Directions: Leyburn lies at the junction of the A684 (Northallerton-Hawes) and the A6108 (Ripon-Richmond)

A traditional family hotel, **The Golden Lion** lies on the broad market place of Leyburn. Dating from 1765, the impressive exterior includes excellent green and gold ironwork and large bay windows. Anne Wood's fine hotel offers facilities usually associated with larger establishments. The 15 tasteful and comfortable en suite guest bedrooms (doubles, twins, family and single rooms) have tv, telephone, radio and tea-making kit, and a lift to the upper floors eases access for guests with disabilities, for whose needs many of the rooms have been adapted. The tariff includes a delicious breakfast, and special breaks are available.

In the 70-cover restaurant, murals of Dales scenes by local artist Lynn Foster

provide a pleasant backdrop to good wholesome Yorkshire fare freshly prepared from local ingredients. Diners can choose between a la carte and fixed-price menus, or something lighter from the informal bar snack menu. Among the favourites are home-made beef and Guinness pie, braised lamb and roast beef. There's also a tempting Sunday dinner menu, and children's meals. Booking is required Friday and Saturday evening, and Sunday lunchtime.

Three real ales – Theakstons, Black Sheep and a changing guest ale – are available in the oak panelled bars, together with a range of draught keg bitters, lagers, wines, spirits and soft drinks.

Anne and her dedicated and hard-working team provide excellent service and hospitality to all their guests.

- 🕐 Mon-Sat 0.800-23.00; Sun 0.800-22.30
- 🍴 12.00-14.00, 18.30-21.00 (restaurant 19.00-21.00)
- £ All major
- ⊖ 15 rooms en suite
- Ⓟ Car park, function room
- @ e-mail: annegoldenlion@aol.com www.thegoldenlion.co.uk
- ❓ Aysgarth Falls 8 miles, Middleham Castle 2 miles, Jervaulx Abbey 4 miles

THE GREYHOUND INN

HACKFORTH,BEDALE,NORTH YORKSHIRE DL8 1PB
TEL: 01748 811415

Directions: Hackforth is a couple of miles north of the A684 (Bedale – Leyburn road) and 1½ miles west of the A1 (south of Catterick), via unnumbered roads.

The Greyhound Inn is a charming country coaching inn occupying a scenic location. Once a farmhouse, built between 1710 and 1720, it was later an alehouse and then a coaching inn. There was once a smithy and stabling to the rear. Superior inside and out, this hidden jewel is large and impressive. Whitewashed and attractive outside, with a patio area with picnic tables to the front and a lovely, well-kept beer garden to one side, the interior is traditional and welcoming, with a wealth of bygone memorabilia and other homely touches.

The McKinlay family have lived in the village, across from the inn, for 23 years. When the opportunity arose in April of 2002, they bought the premises. This fine inn remains very much a family concern, with Gwen and Duncan at the helm ably assisted by their daughters Nicola and Andrea – both chefs – and their son Robert, who looks after the bar.

Three ales are on tap – John Smiths, Black Sheep and Theakstons Best – are complemented by a good choice of lagers, cider, stout, wines, spirits and soft drinks.

Nicola and Andrea create an impressive range of delicious home-cooked meals at lunch and dinner. Guests choose from the menu or specials board from a selection of delicious dishes. The no-smoking restaurant seats 36. Children welcome. Booking required at weekends.

Sights and attractions in the area include walking in the Yorkshire Dales, game and course-fishing, the East Coast, Lake District and urban centres of York, Durham and Ripon, among others.

- Mon 19.00-23.00, Tues-Sat and Bank Hols 12.00-15.00, 19.00-23.00; Sun 12.00-15.00, 19.00-22.30
- Mon 19.00-23.00, Tues-Sun 12.00-15.00, 19.00-22.00
- Visa, Mastercard, Switch, Delta, Access, Eurocard, Solo
- Off-road parking, beer garden, patio area
- 4 rooms en suite
- Catterick 2 miles, Richmond 5 miles, Northallerton 8 miles, Ripon 20 miles, Thirsk 15 miles, Yorkshire Dales

THE HALF MOON INN

FELLBECK,PATELEY BRIDGE,NORTH YORKSHIRE HG3 5ET
TEL: 01423 711560 FAX: 01423 712548

Directions: Fellbeck is situated 2 miles northeast of Pateley Bridge on the B6265.

Fellbeck is a tiny hamlet, a mile or so to the north of Brimham Rocks, which rarely appears on maps but is well worth seeking out for **The Half Moon Inn**. A fully licensed hostelry since the 1700s, the exterior is impressively handsome, with a wide forecourt and hanging baskets adorning the frontage. Inside there's everything you could hope for in a traditional Dales inn, with subtle colours and features such as the wood-burning stove in an eye-catching brick surround, exposed beams and low ceilings, and a rounded, brickbuilt bar. The real fires add to the cosy and welcoming ambience in winter, while all year round there's genuine hospitality and great food and drink.

As a Free House there can be as many

as four real ales on tap, including Black Sheep and changing guest ales. There's also a good selection of draught keg bitters, lagers, cider, stout, wines, spirits and soft drinks.

Excellent food is served at lunch and dinner-time every day, with guests choosing from a menu and specials board of delicious home-made dishes. Children are very welcome.

The pub's rural location – standing in open countryside with lovely panoramic views – has made it a popular base for holiday-makers. Six letting rooms are available in converted former farm buildings next door to the inn. All have baths and showers, and three have a kitchen, bedroom and lounge area. Guests can stay on a B&B or self-catering basis – please ring for details. There's a wealth of sights and attractions in the area just waiting to be discovered and explored.

Mon-Fri 11.00-15.00, 17.00-23.00; Sat 11.00-23.00; Sun 12.00-22.30

Mon-Sun 12.00-14.00, 19.00-21.00

Visa, Mastercard, Switch, Delta, Amex, Eurocard, Solo

6 en suite guest bedrooms

Off-road parking; shooting and horse-riding can be arranged via the inn

colin@halfmooninn.fsnet.co.uk

Brimham Rocks 1 mile, Pateley Bridge 2 miles, Ripon 10 miles, Harrogate 12 miles, coarse fishing.

THE KING'S HEAD

GUNNERSIDE, RICHMOND, NORTH YORKSHIRE DL11 6LD
TEL: 01748 886261

> **Directions:** From Reeth, take the B6270 west to reach Gunnerside

This small, traditional pub is tucked away in the pretty Swaledale village of Gunnerside, located on the B6270 to the west of Reeth. A Free House, **The Kings Head** has been in the capable hands of Steve Stewart and Sam Mealing for several years and, together with excellent chef Alan Lee and their friendly, conscientious staff, run a welcoming, comfortable, well-kept pub. The pub began life in the late 17th century as a blacksmith's; the smithy reputedly brewed his own beer as a sideline, and in the 18th century it became a coaching inn. Much of its olde worlde charm remains, the most dominant feature being the superb stone fireplace. The décor and furnishings throughout are cosy and comfortable, enhancing the relaxed and welcoming ambience of this fine inn.

Here at this Free House, guests – and

the inn is popular with locals and visitors alike - can enjoy a choice of up to four real ales, the regular being the locally brewed Black Sheep and the others being guest ales. There are also a number of lagers and ciders available, together with a good selection of wines, spirits and soft drinks.

Excellent food is available at lunch (12.00-14.30) and dinner (19.00-21.00). The regular printed menu is complemented by blackboard specials. The specialities include home-made soups, steak and ale pie, cottage pie and sausage hot-pot. Only the freshest locally-produced ingredients are used by chef Alan to produce tempting dishes such as wholetail Whitby scampi, beef curry, Cumberland sausage and Wensleydale-stuffed chicken breast. At lunch there are light meals as well as more substantial fare. Children welcome.

🕐 Summer: Mon-Fri 11.00-15.00, 18.00-23.00; Sat 11.00-23.00; Sun 12.00-22.30; Winter: Tues-Sat 11.00-15.00, 18.00-23.00; Sun 12.00-15.00, 18.00-22.30

🍴 12.00-14.30, 19.00-21.00

🎵 Quiz night every fortnight, Sundays from 8.30 pm

❓ Reeth 4 miles, Richmond 14 miles

THE LISTER ARMS HOTEL

MALHAM, NR SKIPTON, NORTH YORKSHIRE BD23 4DB
TEL: 01729 830330 FAX: 01729 830323

Directions: From Skipton, take the A65 to the B6265 to reach Malham.

Dating back to the early 1700s and named after the first Lord of Ribblesdale, Thomas Lister, **The Lister Arms Hotel** occupies a scenic position in the heart of the Dales. This impressive stonebuilt building is large and distinctive. The interior is tasteful and stylish, with polished wood floors, exposed beams and other traditional features happily rubbing shoulders with modern touches such as subtle lighting, clean lines and classic furnishings. Brothers Andrew and Johnathan Ditchfield have been here as owners since 1987. They bring a wealth of experience to maintaining the pub's reputation for great food, drink, and accommodation. They and their conscientious, friendly, attentive staff offer every guest the highest standard of service and hospitality.

- Mon-Sat; 12.00-23.00 Sun 12.00-22.30 (winter weekdays closed 15.00-18.30)
- 12.00-14.00 & 19.00-21.00 every day
- £ Visa, Mastercard, Switch, Delta, Amex, Diners, Eurocard, Solo
- 9 guest rooms en suite
- @ info@listerarms.co.uk www.listerarms.co.uk
- ? Malham Cove, Gordale Scar, Malham Tarn, Settle 5 miles, Skipton 10 miles

There's always a minimum of six real ales on tap at this fine inn. Regulars include Timothy Taylor Landlord, Marstons Pedigree and Jennings Cumberland ale, together with changing guest ales, a traditional hand-pulled cider and a good selection of lagers, wines, spirits and soft drinks.

Food is served at lunch and dinner every day. Guests can choose from a range of traditional and innovative dishes.

There are nine comfortable en suite guest rooms available all year round. All are tastefully decorated and furnished. There is also a brand-new self-contained cottage to the rear of the hotel, built traditionally with exposed beams, flagstone floors and other attractive features and set in its own garden. The cottage sleeps eight, and is available for weekly lets or long weekend breaks.

THE OLD HORN INN

SPENNITHORNE,NR LEYBURN,NORTH YORKSHIRE DL8 5PR
TEL: 01969 622370

Directions: From Leyburn, take the A684 2 miles southeast to Spennithorne.

The Old Horn Inn is a real hidden gem, but once found is never forgotten. Located in a picture-postcard setting, the premises dates back, in parts, to the 16th century and is set in lower Wensleydale, commanding superb views of the dale. Pristine and handsome, the exterior is covered in ivy and features picnic tables for al fresco drinking and dining when the weather is fine.

The interior boasts lots of style and charm, with exposed beamwork, open fires and other homely traditional touches adding to the cosy and welcoming ambience.

Catherine and Des have been here as owners since May of 2002. They and their friendly, attentive staff offer all their guests a warm welcome and genuine hospitality. Catherine is a self taught chef, creating superb dishes including specialities such as home-made steak and kidney pie with home-made gravy. The menu and specials board boast contemporary and traditional dishes, all cooked to order and using the freshest ingredients, locally sourced whenever possible.

Three ales are on tap – Black Sheep, John Smiths and a changing guest ale – together with a good range of lagers, cider, stout, wines, spirits and soft drinks.

The surrounding area is rich in outstanding natural beauty, and this marvellous inn has two quality (3 Stars AA) en suite guest rooms available all year round. Both are doubles, and there are discounts for stays of more than one night. Sights and attractions in the locality include Bolton Castle, Jervaulx Abbey and Aysgarth Falls, as well as the bustling centres at York and Ripon.

- Tues-Sat and Bank Hols 12.00-15.00, 18.30-23.00; Sun 12.00-15.00, 18.30-22.30; open all day Sat in summer
- Tues-Sun and Bank Hols 12.00-14.00 (14.30 in summer), 19.00-21.00 (18.30-21.00 in summer)
- Parking
- 2 en suite rooms
- Quiz every other Sunday; occasional live entertainment
- www.downourlocal.com/theoldhorninn
- Leyburn 2 miles, Middleham 2 miles

THE WHITE LION AT KILDWICK

PRIEST BANK ROAD, KILDWICK, NR SKIPTON,
NORTH YORKSHIRE BD20 9BH
TEL: 01535 632265 FAX: 01535 637539

Directions: Look for the Kildwick sign off the main Skipton–Keighley road (A629).

The White Lion at Kildwick is an impressive inn opposite the church in this picturesque village on the north bank of the River Aire. Leaseholders Duncan and Elaine Jamieson, ably assisted by their son Andrew, are likeable hosts who have between them a wealth of experience in offering guests fine ales, great food and genuine hospitality. Behind the handsome stone frontage, the look is charmingly old-fashioned, with old beams, exposed stone, dark wood panelling and rustic furniture all contributing to the inviting, traditional atmosphere. A minimum of three real ales – Tetley Bitter, Tetley Mild and a changing guest ale - are available along with a good choice of draught keg lagers, cider, stout, wines,

spirits and soft drinks.

In the restaurant, where horse brasses, pewter tankards and old prints adorn the walls, diners have a plentiful choice of dishes. The main menu is supplemented by the specials board. The chef's speciality is his tempting fish dishes. Booking advised Friday to Sunday. Children welcome.

For anyone wishing to prolong their stay in the area – and this part of the county rewards further exploration – there are three en suite rooms (a double and two family rooms) for Bed & Breakfast accommodation.

The Church of St Andrew, opposite the inn dates mainly from the 14th and 15th centuries. The village lies on the River Aire and on the Leeds & Liverpool Canal, no longer used commercially but popular with pleasure craft.

- 🕐 Mon-Sat 11.00-23.00; Sun 12.00-22.30
- 🍴 Mon-Sat 12.00-14.00, Sun 12.00-15.00; Mon-Thurs 18.00-20.30, Fri-Sat 18.00-21.00, Sun 16.30-20.00
- 💷 Visa, Mastercard, Access, Switch, Delta, Amex, Eurocard, Solo
- 🛏 3 en suite rooms
- 🅿 Patio area, off-road parking
- 🎵 Quiz night Weds
- ❓ Keighley 5 miles, Skipton 5 miles, Ilkley 10 miless

THE WHITE LION INN

CRAY, NR BUCKDEN, SKIPTON, NORTH YORKSHIRE BD23 5JB
TEL: 01756 760262 FAX: 01756 761024

> **Directions:** 1 mile off the B6265 Skipton-Grassington road. Take the 6160 towards Buckden. Cray is a small hamlet 1½ miles northwest of Buckden.

The White Lion Inn is the highest pub in Wharfedale and was built between 1635 and 1650. Formerly a drovers' hostelry, the inn has been sensitively and tastefully restored to its traditional glory, and boasts exposed beams, open log fire and stone-flagged floors. Debbie and Kevin, owners since June of 2001 offer warm hospitality.

Well known for the excellent quality of the food, Debbie oversees all the cooking and dishes can be chosen from the printed menu or daily specials boards. Wholesome and plentiful, the specialities include home-made steak and mushroom pie and filled giant Yorkshire puddings. Meals can be taken in the non-smoking dining room, in the bar area, outside in the attractive garden, or beside the cascading Cray Gill, which runs past the inn. Booking is essential on Fridays, Saturdays and Bank Holidays.

The choice of hand-pulled real ales, which is featured in the Good Beer Guide, Good Pub Guide, AA Pub Guide, Good Britain guide and others, includes changing guest ales. There is also a good range of lagers, cider, stout, spirits, wines and soft drinks.

The excellent accommodation comprises eight en suite guest bedrooms, one of which is in a traditional miner's cottage opposite the inn. Families are welcome, and a travel cot and baby monitor are available. Special breaks available throughout the year – ring for details.

- 🕐 Mon-Sat 11.00-23.00; Sun 12.00-22.30
- 🍴 Mon-Sun 12.00-14.00 and 17.45-20.45 (last orders for food 20.30)
- £ Visa, Mastercard, Switch, Delta, Eurocard, Solo
- 🛏 8 rooms en suite
- Ⓟ Car parking, beer garden, children welcome
- @ e-mail: admin@whitelioncray.com www.whitelioncray.com
- ❓ Wensleydale 10 miles, Swaledale 10 miles, Grassington 10 miles, Hawes 8 miles, Skipton 20 miles, Jervaulx Abbey 10 miles, Bolton Castle 12 miles, Aysgarth Falls 15 miles, caving, pot-holing, rock-climbing, fishing, pony-trekking

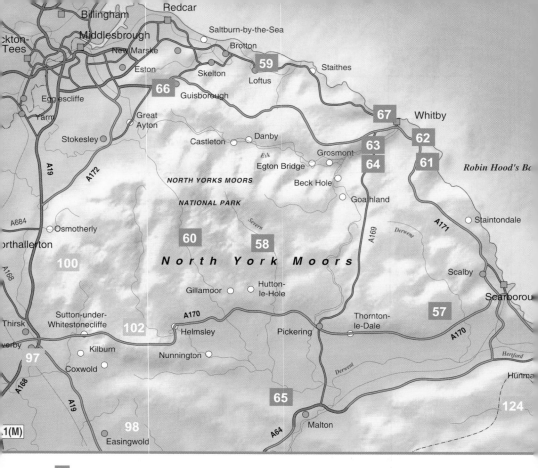

Please note all cross references refer to page numbers

THE MOORS, THE HERITAGE COAST AND THE VALE OF PICKERING

Some 40 miles across and about 20 miles deep, the North York Moors National Park encompasses a remarkable diversity of scenery: moorland, woodland and dales. There are great rolling swathes of moorland rising to 1,400 feet above sea level that are stark and inhospitable in winter; still, wild and romantic in summer; and, in the autumn, they are softened by a purple haze of flowering heather. Almost one fifth of the area is woodland and most of it is managed by Forest Enterprise, which has established many picnic sites and forest drives. Just as the Yorkshire Dales have large areas of moorland, so the North York Moors have many dales, including Eskdale, Ryedale and Farndale but there are more than a hundred in all. Cut deep into the great upland tracts, the dales are as picturesque, soft and pastoral as anywhere in Yorkshire. To the west lies the mighty bulk of the Cleveland Hills while to the east are the rugged cliffs of the Heritage Coast.

Settlements are few and far between in the North York Moors: indeed, there may have been more people living here in the Bronze Age (1500- 500 BC) than there are now, judging by the 3,000 or so 'howes' (burial mounds) that have been discovered. Also scattered across these uplands is a remarkable collection of medieval stone crosses. There are more than 30 of them and one, the **Lilla Cross,** is reckoned to be the oldest Christian monument in northern England.

PLACES OF INTEREST

Two spectacularly scenic railways wind their way through this enchanting landscape. The Middlesbrough to Whitby route, called the Esk Valley Line, runs from west to east following the course of the River Esk and passing through a succession of delightful villages. The vintage steam locomotives of the North York Moors Railway start at Pickering and run northwards for 18 miles through Newton Dale to join the Esk Valley Line at Grosmont. The dramatic route through this glacial channel was originally engineered by George Stephenson himself.

Whitby Abbey

A considerable stretch of the Heritage Coast, which was so designated in 1979, is encompassed within the National Park boundary and along this coastline, from Staithes to Filey, is some of the most striking coastal scenery in the country. There are high cliffs, rocky coves, miles of sandy beaches and a scattering of picture postcard fishing villages. This coastline is famous for its connections with Captain James Cook, one of the country's greatest navigators and seafarers. The family moved to Great Ayton when James was eight years old but by the age of 16 he had left home and moved to Staithes before finally becoming a naval apprentice in Whitby where he learnt his seafaring skills.

BECK HOLE

This pretty little hamlet lies on the route of the **North Yorkshire Moors Railway** that was constructed in the 1830s and was designed by the great engineer George Stephenson. Initially, the trains were made up of stage coaches placed on top of simple bogies that were pulled by horses. At Beck Hole, however, there was a 1 in 15 incline up the line to Goathland so the carriages had to be hauled by a complicated system of ropes and water-filled tanks. Charles Dickens was an early passenger on this route and wrote a hair-raising description of his journey. The precipitous incline caused many accidents so, in 1865, a 'Deviation Line' was blasted through solid rock and although the gradient is still one of the steepest in the country, at 1 in 49, it did open up this route to steam trains. The original 1 in 15 incline is now a footpath, so modern walkers will understand the effort needed to get themselves to the summit, let alone a fully laden carriage.

Every year, Beck Hole plays host to the **World Quoits Championship**, a game that appears to have originated in Eskdale and involves throwing a small iron hoop over an iron pin set about 25 feet away.

CASTLETON

Spread across the hillside above the River Esk, Castleton is a charming village that at one time was the largest settlement in Eskdale and it still has a weekly market and a station on the scenic **Esk Valley Railway** that runs between Whitby and Middlesbrough. Its amber-coloured **Church of St Michael and St George** was built in memory of the men who fell in World War I and inside there is some fine work by Robert Thompson, the famous 'Mouseman of Kilburn': the benches, organ screen and panelling at each side of the altar all bear his distinctive 'signature' of a crouching mouse.

DANBY

Danby is home to **The Moors Centre** that provides an excellent introduction to the North York Moors National Park. It is housed in Danby Lodge, a former shooting lodge that is set in 13 acres of riverside, meadow, woodland, formal

North York Moor, Nr Danby

gardens and picnic areas. Visitors can either wander on their own along the waymarked, woodland walks and nature trails or join one of the frequent guided walks. Inside the lodge various exhibits interpret the natural and local history of the moors; there's a bookshop stocked with a wide range of books, maps and guides, and a tea room serving refreshments.

EGTON BRIDGE

This little village, which lies tucked around a bend in the River Esk, plays host each year to the famous **Gooseberry Show**, which was established in 1800 and is held on the first Tuesday in August. The show attracts entrants from all over the world who bring prize specimens along in an attempt to beat the current record of 2.18oz for a single berry.

The village itself is dominated by the massive **Church of St Hedda** that was built in 1866 and has a dazzling roof painted blue with gold stars while the altar incorporates some distinguished Belgian terracotta work.

FILEY

With its six mile crescent of safe, sandy beach, Filey was one of the first Yorkshire resorts to benefit from the early 19th century craze for sea bathing and its popularity continued throughout Victorian times; this little town has always prided itself on being rather more select than its brasher neighbour just up the coast, Scarborough. Included in the list of distinguished visitors to the resort there is Charlotte Brontë, Jenny Lind

(the 'Swedish Nightingale'), the composer Frederic Delius and the actress Dame Madge Kendall while, before World War I, the Mountbatten family enjoyed holidays here. Inevitably, modern times have brought the usual scattering of amusement arcades, fast food outlets and, from 1939 to 1983, a Butlin's Holiday Camp capable of accommodating 10,000 visitors. But Filey has suffered less than most seaside towns and with its many public parks and gardens still retains a winning, and rather genteel, atmosphere. The town's famous sands were used, in 1910, for the now famous Blackburn flying school and it was here that the first fatal aviation crash involving a passenger took place. However, Filey's greatest claim to fame is the naval battle that took place off its shores in 1779 between the American privateer, John Paul Jones, and the Royal Navy. Though a stronger force, the Navy was defeated by the American, who went on to become known as the Father of the American Navy.

Until the Local Government reforms of 1974, the boundary between the East and North Ridings ran right through Filey: the town lay in the East Riding while the parish church and graveyard in the North. This curious arrangement gave rise to some typically dry Yorkshire humour. If a resident of Filey town admitted that they were feeling poorly, the response might well be "Aye, then tha'll straightly be off t'North Riding" – in other words, the graveyard.

Despite the fact that there is no harbour at Filey, it was once quite a busy fishing port and occasionally a few cobles

– direct descendants of the Viking longships that arrived here more than a thousand years ago – can still be seen beached on the slipways. Filey's parish church, the oldest parts of which date from the 12th century, is appropriately dedicated to St Oswald, the patron saint of fishermen, and the Fishermen's Window here commemorates men from the town who died at sea.

Housed in a lovely old building that dates back to 1696, the **Filey Museum** has numerous displays on the history of the town as well as items on the seashore, fishing and the town's lifeboat. Just to the north of the town, the rocky promontory known as **Filey Brigg** strikes out into the sea and this massive mile-long breakwater of calcareous gritstone protects the town from the worst of the North Sea's winter storms.

GILLAMOOR

A pleasant little village that is well worth a visit to see its very rare, and very elegant, four-faced sundial that was erected in 1800 and also to enjoy the famous **Surprise View**. This is a ravishing panoramic vista of Farndale, with the River Dove flowing through the valley far below and white dusty roads climbing the hillside to the heather-covered moors beyond.

GLAISDALE

This picturesque village lies at the foot of a narrow dale beside the River Esk and **Arncliffe Woods** are just a short walk away. The ancient stone bridge here was built in around 1620 by Thomas Ferris,

Mayor of Hull who, as an impoverished young man, had lived in Glaisdale and had fallen in love with Agnes Richardson, the squire's daughter. To see Agnes, Ferris had to wade or swim across the river and he swore that if he prospered in life he would build a bridge here. Fortunately, he joined a ship that sailed against the Spanish Armada and captured a galleon laden with gold. Tom returned to Glaisdale a rich man, married Agnes and later honoured his promise by building what has always been called the **Beggar's Bridge** or Lovers' Bridge.

GOATHLAND

Some 500 feet high up on the moors, Goathland became 'Aidensfield', the main location for the television series

North York Moors Railway, Goathland

Heartbeat. Earlier visitors mostly came in order to see **Mallyan Spout**, a 70-foot high waterfall locked into a crescent of rocks and trees. These early visitors were also interested in Goathland's rugged church and the odd memorial in its graveyard to William Jefferson and his wife. The couple died in 1923 within a few days of each other, at the ages of 80 and 79, and chose to have their final resting place marked by an enormous anchor.

In the award-winning **Goathland Exhibition Centre** is the full explanation of the curious tradition of the **Plough Stots Service** that is performed in the village every January. It is said to be an ancient ritual for greeting the new year that originated with the Norsemen who settled here more than a thousand years ago. 'Stots' is the Scandinavian word for the bullocks that dragged a plough through the village, followed by dancers brandishing 30-inch swords. This pagan rite is still faithfully observed but with the difference that nowadays Goathland's young men have replaced the stots in the plough harness. The Exhibition Centre can also provide information on the many walks in the area including one of the oldest thoroughfares in the country, **Wade's Way**. The village lies on the route of the North Yorkshire Moors Railway and **Goathland Station** has a newly refurbished tea room, with authentic furniture and artefacts that take visitors back to the age of steam, while recent additions include a cattle dock and coal drops.

GREAT AYTON

This appealing village, set around the River Leven, is an essential stopping point for anyone following the **Captain Cook Country Tour**, a 70-mile circular trip taking in all the major locations associated with the great seafarer. Cook's family moved to Great Ayton when he was eight years old and he attended the little school that is now the **Captain Cook Schoolroom Museum**. The museum first opened in the 1920s and the exhibits here relate to Cook's life and to the 18th century village in which he lived.

The Great Ayton of today is very different from the village that James Cook would have known. Now a pleasant place with the two spacious greens of High and Low Green, with the River Leven flowing through it, this now conservation area was, in the 18th and 19th centuries, home to much industrial activity, including weaving, tanning, brewing and tile making. Situated in a secluded position on Low Green is the 12th century **Church of All Saints**, where James, along with his family, came to worship. Still medieval in structure, the original tower and western portion of the nave were demolished in the late 19th century to make more room for burials.

Standing proudly on High Green is the **James Cook Sculpture**, which depicts the great man at the age of just

16, looking towards Staithes. Unveiled in 1997, it was created by the internationally renowned sculptor Nicholas Dimbleby and it commemorates the life of James Cook along with the contribution that the village made to his development.

Duncombe Park

An altogether more impressive monument can be found to the southeast of Great Ayton on Easby Moor. At 60 feet high, the giant obelisk of local sandstone that is the Captain Cook Monument is visible for miles around; it was erected by Robert Campion, a Whitby banker, in 1827.

GROSMONT

This quiet village's name is derived from 'gros mont' – the French for big hill – and it was here that the Normans built a castle. Although the castle is no longer in existence, **Grosmont Station**, the terminus of the North Yorkshire Moors Railway, is very much in evidence and has been restored to the British Railway's style of the 1960s. Passengers can visit the locomotive sheds at the station.

HELMSLEY

Situated on the banks of the River Rye, at the edge of the North York Moors National Park, Helmsley is one of North Yorkshire's most popular and attractive towns. Its spacious market square is typical of the area but the striking Gothic memorial to the 2nd Earl of Feversham, which stands in the square, is not. An astonishingly ornate construction, it was designed by Sir Giles Gilbert Scott and looks like a smaller version of his famous memorial to Sir Walter Scott that stands in Edinburgh.

The Earls of Feversham lived at **Duncombe Park**, whose extensive grounds sweep up to within a few yards of the Market Place. Most of the original mansion, designed by Vanbrugh and built in 1713, was gutted by a disastrous fire in 1879 and only the north wing remained habitable and that, in its turn, was ruined by a second fire in 1895. The Fevershams lavished a fortune on rebuilding the grand old house, largely to the original design, but the financial burden eventually forced them to lease the house and grounds as a preparatory school for girls. Happily, the Fevershams were able to return to their ancestral home in 1986 and the beautifully restored house and lovely grounds are now open to the public between April and October, Sundays to Thursdays.

Before they were ennobled, the Feversham's family name was Duncombe and it was Sir Thomas Duncombe, a wealthy London goldsmith, who established the family seat here when he bought **Helmsley Castle** (English Heritage) and its estate in 1687. Founded in the early 1100s and severely damaged during the Civil War, the castle was in a dilapidated state but its previous owner, the Duke of Buckingham, had continued to live there in some squalor and discomfort. Sir Thomas quickly decided to build his more suitable residence nearby, abandoning the ruins to lovers of the romantic and picturesque. Visitors to the castle can see a special exhibition detailing its history while, at the boundary of the castle, is the Helmsley Walled Garden, a glorious Victorian garden that originally dates back to 1756 and incorporates an organic kitchen garden, bold borders, glass houses and over 150 varieties of clematis climbing up the imposing walls.

Just to the west of Helmsley and standing among wooded hills beside the River Rye, rise the indescribably beautiful remains of **Rievaulx Abbey** (English Heritage), which has been described as the most exquisite monastic site in Europe: Turner was enchanted by this idyllic landscape and Dorothy Wordsworth spellbound. Founded in 1131, Rievaulx was the first Cistercian abbey in Yorkshire and, with some 700 people – monks, lay brothers, servants – eventually living within its walls, it also became one of the largest.

Looking down on the extensive remains of the abbey is **Rievaulx Terrace** (National Trust), a

Rievaulx Abbey

breathtaking example of landscape gardening completed in 1758.

HUTTON-LE-HOLE

Long regarded as one of Yorkshire's prettiest villages, Hutton-le-Hole has a character all of its own. Facing the village green and standing on one of Hutton's oldest sites, is the **Ryedale Folk Museum**, an imaginative celebration of 4,000 years of life in North Yorkshire from prehistoric times to the present day. Among the historic buildings to be seen at this large open-air museum are a complete Elizabethan Manor House rescued from nearby Harome and reconstructed here; a medieval crofter's cottage with a thatched, hipped roof, peat fire and garth; and an old village Shop and Post Office fitted out as it would have looked just after Elizabeth II's Coronation in 1953.

Anyone interested in unusual churches should make the short trip from Hutton-le-Hole to **St Mary's Church, Lastingham**, about three miles to the east. The building of a monastery here in the 7th century was recorded by no less an authority than the Venerable Bede, who visited Lastingham not long after it was completed. That monastery was rebuilt in 1078 with a massively impressive crypt that is still in place – a claustrophobic space with heavy Norman arches rising from squat round pillars. The church above is equally atmospheric, lit only by a small window at one end.

Malton has been the historic centre of Ryedale ever since the Romans came and, in fact, there are three Maltons, the Roman, the old and the new, which can all be found in separate places. The Romans built a large fort and called it 'Derventio' after the river Derwent beside which it stood and, for many years, archaeologists were puzzled by the large scale of the fort. However, the mystery was solved in 1970 when a building dedication was uncovered that revealed that the fort housed a cavalry regiment, the Ala Picentiana, and the extra space was needed to accommodate their horses.

In the centre of Old Malton stands a beautiful fragment of **St Mary's Priory** that incorporates a particularly fine Norman doorway. The priory was built in around 1155 by the only monastic order in Christendom to have originated entirely in England – the Gilbertines. The River Derwent has always been vitally important to the town and it rises in the moors near Scarborough and then runs inland through the Vale of Pickering, bringing with it an essential element for what was once a major industry in Malton – brewing. In the 19th century, there were nine breweries here but, now, only the Malton Brewery Company survives, operating in a converted stable block behind the Crown Hotel in Wheelgate.

The Malton of today is a traditional agricultural town that is renowned for its livestock, street and farmers' markets. Many relics from the Roman excavation site, showing the sophisticated life-style of the Roman centurions and civilians, can be seen in the **Malton Museum** where there are also items from the Iron Age settlement that preceded the Roman garrison.

A mile or so north of Old Malton is **Eden Camp**, a modern history theme museum that is dedicated to re-creating the dramatic experiences of ordinary people living through World War II. Right next door is **Eden Farm Insight,** a working farm with a fascinating collection of old farm machinery and implements, lots of animals, a blacksmith's and a wheelwright's shop, as well as a choice of farm walks, all clearly signposted and with useful information boards. The farm also offers a café, gift shop and a picnic and play area.

To the southwest of Malton stands **Castle Howard**. Vanbrugh's first commission as an architect, and a resounding success, this glorious palace is filled with equally superb collections of furniture, paintings and china but most people will remember it as Brideshead in the 1980s television adaptation of the Evelyn Waugh novel, *Brideshead Revisited.*

NUNNINGTON

This delightful old agricultural village is home to **Nunnington Hall** (National Trust), which lies just to the east beside the banks of the River Rye and has a picturesque packhorse bridge within its grounds. A manor house dating back to the late 17th century, the house has a magnificent panelled hall, fine tapestries and china and the famous Carlisle collection of miniature rooms that are exquisitely furnished in different period styles – all to one eighth scale. Nunnington Hall is also famous for its haunted room. Outside in the grounds is a walled garden with delightful mixed borders, spring flowering meadows and orchards of traditional Ryedale fruit varieties.

PICKERING

This busy little town developed around an important crossroads where the Malton to Whitby and the Thirsk to Scarborough roads intersect. It is also the largest of the four market towns in Ryedale and is, quite possibly, the oldest as it claims to date from 270BC when the market is said to have been founded by a King of the Brigantes called Peredurus. In an attempt to dominate the local area, William the Conqueror ordered the construction of a motte and later, in the 12th century, the once splendid **Pickering Castle** (English Heritage) and a royal hunting lodge were erected on the site. Though now ruined, the castle and lodge still offer visitors, through the exhibitions, an insight into lives at both the castle and within the royal forest some 800 years ago.

Another building worthy of the visit is the parish **Church of St Peter and St Paul** as it contains some remarkable 15th

Pickering Castle

southern terminus of the North York Moors Railway, the most popular heritage railway in Britain; from here visitors can take a nostalgic steam journey through 18 miles of stunning scenery to the northern terminus at Grosmont. **Pickering Station** itself has recently been restored to its 1937 condition, with the help of a Heritage Lottery Fund, and, of particular interest, are the original fixtures and fittings that have been installed in the Booking and Parcel Office.

century murals. During the glum days of Puritanism, these lively paintings were denounced as idolatrous and plastered over and they stayed forgotten for some 200 years before being rediscovered when the church was being restored in 1851. Due to the town being situated at the heart of the fertile Vale of Pickering, it is not surprising that its early reputation was based on farming and, in the case of Pickering, it was the breeding and rearing of pigs and horses. Vast quantities of pork were transported across the moors to Whitby, salted and used as shipboard rations while the famous Cleveland Bay horses, with their jet-black manes and tails, were extensively bred in the area and in Eskdale, a little further north, they still are.

Housed in a gracious Regency mansion is the **Beck Isle Museum**, whose numerous display areas are crammed full of a wonderful assortment of curious, mysterious and commonplace items from the last 200 years or so. Pickering is the

ROBIN HOOD'S BAY

Artists never tire of painting this 'Clovelly of the North', a picturesque huddle of red-roofed houses clinging to the steep face of the cliff. Bay Town, as locals call the village, was a thriving fishing port throughout the 18th and 19th centuries but by 1920 there were only two fishing families left in Bay Town, mainly because the harbour was so dilapidated, and the industry died out. Today, small boats are once again harvesting the prolific crab grounds that lie along this stretch of the coast. Shipwrecks off the shore of Bay Town were once frequent, with many a mighty vessel tossed on to its reefs by North Sea storms. On one memorable occasion in the winter of 1881, a large brig, *The*

Robin Hoods Bay

Visitor, was driven on to the rocks. The seas were too rough for the lifeboat at Whitby to be launched there so it was dragged eight miles through the snow and let down the cliffside by ropes and six men were rescued. The same wild seas threatened the village itself, every storm eroding a little more of the chalk cliff to which it clings but, fortunately, Robin Hood's Bay is now protected by a sturdy sea wall. **The Old Coastguard Station**, which dates from the 19th century, is being restored by the National Trust in partnership with the North York Moors National Park Authority. Also in the village is the **Robin Hoods Bay and Flyingdales Museum**, a small, volunteer-run museum that concentrates on local history, farming, maritime history and the seashore.

SALTBURN-BY-THE SEA

A charming seaside resort set on a high cliff above a long sandy beach. To transport visitors from the town to the promenade and pier below, an ingenious water-balanced **Tramway** was constructed and is still in use as the oldest of its kind in Britain. The history of the town, including its time as a busy centre of the smuggling trade, is told in the **Saltburn Smugglers Heritage Centre**.

SCARBOROUGH

With its two splendid bays and dramatic clifftop castle, Scarborough was targeted by the early railway tycoons as the natural candidate for Yorkshire's first seaside resort. The railway arrived in 1846, followed by the construction of luxury hotels, elegant promenades and spacious gardens, all of which confirmed the town's claim to the title 'Queen of Watering Places'. High society and people like the eccentric Earls of Londesborough, established palatial summer residences here and an excellent train service brought countless thousands of 'excursionists' from the industrial cities of Yorkshire's West Riding.

Even before the advent of the railway, Scarborough had been well known to a select few. They travelled to what was then a remote little town to sample the spring water discovered by Mrs Tomyzin Farrer in 1626 and popularised in a book published by Dr Wittie who named the site Scarborough Spaw. Anne Brontë came here in the hope that the spa

Scarborough Bay

Museum, which includes among its exhibits a genuine ducking stool for witches as well as numerous displays on the history and local history of the area. Also worth visiting is the **Wood End Museum** on The Crescent, which was once the home of the eccentric Sitwell family. There is always something new to see at the **Scarborough Art Gallery**, whose exhibitions feature paintings of the town and also works by local artists. The three pyramids of the **Scarborough Sea Life Centre** are home to thousands of fascinating sea creatures including orphaned, sickly or injured seal pups; **Atlantis** is a heated outdoor waterpark with two of the world's largest waterslides; Kinderland is a unique landscaped park full of traditional play structures and activities for children; and Millennium takes visitors on an adventure through the last 1,000 turbulent years of the country's history.

town's invigorating air would improve her health, a hope that was not fulfilled. She died at the age of 29 and her grave lies in St Mary's churchyard at the foot of the castle.

Scarborough Castle (English Heritage) was built in the 12th century on the site of a 4th century Roman fort and signal station and its gaunt remains stand high on Castle Rock Headland, which lies between and dominates the town's two sweeping bays. Along with its two sandy beaches, this long-established resort moves with the times in offering a vast choice of family entertainment. There is **Peasholm Park**, with its glorious gardens and events, including the unique sea battle in miniature on the lake, while there are the intellectual attractions of the town's theatre and museums. **The Stephen Joseph Theatre** is well known for staging the premiere performances of comedies written by its resident director, Alan Ayckbourn, the world's most performed living playwright. On Vernon Road is the country's finest Georgian museum, the **Rotunda**

STAINTONDALE

This small coastal village is home to two very different animal centres. At the **Staintondale Shire Horse Farm** visitors can enjoy a 'hands-on' experience with these noble creatures, watch a video of the horses working and follow a scenic route around the area. Cart rides are also usually available and there is also a café, souvenir shop, picnic area and a play area with a variety of small farm animals to entertain the children including eight

Shetland ponies. At nearby **Wellington Lodge Llamas** treks on llama-back are on offer, ranging from a three or four hour journey to a whole day's outing.

STAITHES

Visitors to this much-photographed fishing port leave their cars at the park in the modern village at the top of the cliff and then walk down the steep road to the old wharf and the old stone chapels and the rather austere houses that testify to the days when Staithes was a stronghold of Methodism. The little port is proud of its associations with Captain James Cook, who came here, not as a famous mariner, but as a 17-year-old assistant in Mr William Sanderson's haberdashery shop. However, James did not stay here long and he left in 1746 to begin his naval apprenticeship in Whitby. The **Captain Cook and Staithes Heritage Centre**, which includes a life size street scene from 1745 along with Sanderson's shop, has over 200 books dating from 1773 of Cook's life and his famous voyages. Also here are 62 of Webber's original engravings, which were made during the great seafarer's third voyage of discovery, and a scale model of his ship *Endeavour*.

Staithes is still a working port with one of the few fleets in England still catching crabs and lobsters and, moored in the harbour and along the river, are the fishermen's distinctive boats. Known as cobles, they have an ancestry that goes back to Viking times. Nearby is a small sandy beach, popular with families

(and artists), and a rocky shoreline extending north and south pitted with thousands of rock pools hiding starfish and anemones. The rocks here are rich in fossils and also ingots of 'fools gold', which is actually iron pyrites and virtually worthless.

THORNTON-LE-DALE

As long ago as 1907, a *Yorkshire Post* poll of its readers acclaimed Thornton-le-Dale as the most beautiful village in Yorkshire and, despite very stiff competition for this title, most visitors find themselves in agreement. Such is the village's charms that the North York Moors National Park actually creates a special loop in its boundary to include this picture postcard village.

WHITBY

Whitby has several claims to fame – it was Captain James Cook's home port and it was, according to Bram Stoker's famous novel, the place where Count Dracula, in the form of a wolf, loped ashore from a crewless ship that had drifted into the harbour – but its greatest claim is as being one of the earliest and most important centres of Christianity in England. High on the cliff that towers above the picturesque old fishing town stand the imposing and romantic ruins of **Whitby Abbey** (English Heritage) where in AD664 many of the most eminent prelates of the Christian Church were summoned to attend the Synod of Whitby. They were charged with settling

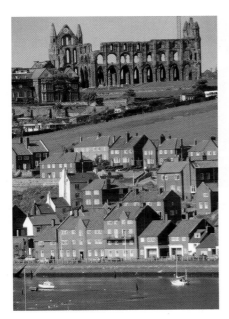

Whitby Abbey

from the same period and the huge ear trumpets for a rector's deaf wife were put in place about 50 years later.

Bram Stoker began writing his famous novel, *Dracula*, in 1895 while staying on the coast of Scotland but he had previously visited Whitby and it is his detailed, happy descriptions of the abbey ruins, St Mary's churchyard and other places in the town that make his story all the more sinister.

The old port of Whitby developed on the slim shelf of land that runs along the east bank of the River Esk, an intricate muddle of narrow, cobbled streets and shoulder-width alleys. Grape Lane is typical, a cramped little street where ancient houses lean wearily against each other. Young James Cook lived here during his apprenticeship and he lodged at the handsome house in the lane that was owned by his master, the Quaker shipowner, Captain John Walker. The house where Cook and the other apprentices studied and slept when not aboard Walker's coal ships sailing between Newcastle and London is now the **Captain Cook Memorial Museum**. As well as celebrating the years that Cook spent in Whitby, along with his later achievements, the museum also features other displays on life in the navy during the 18th century. The town's other museum, the **Whitby Museum**, is a true treasure trove of Whitby's past.

Between 1753 and 1833, Whitby was the capital of the whaling industry, bringing home 2,761 whales in 80 years. The whaling industry is now of course

once and for all a festering dispute that had riven Christendom for generations: the precise date on which Easter should be celebrated. The complicated formula they devised to solve this problem is still in use. Today's visitors can climb the 199 steps up to the haunting abbey ruins and, from here, there are commanding views over the town and beyond. Not surprisingly, the beauty of the dramatic ruins has also inspired many writers, painters and engravers.

Just a short walk from the abbey is **St Mary's Church**, a unique building "not unlike a house outside and very much like a ship inside." Indeed, the interior, with its clutter of box-pews, iron pillars and long galleries, was reputedly fashioned by Whitby seamen during the course of the 18th century. The three-decker pulpit is long dead, but fortunately the town's fishing industry is not, as many of Whitby's restaurants bear witness – they are famous for their seafood menus. The **Whitby Archives Heritage Centre**, which is open all year, holds an exhibition of local photographs and along with its local history research facilities also has a shop and heritage gallery. The **Museum of Victorian Whitby** has a re-creation of a 19th century lane in the town complete with interiors and shop windows along with miniature rooms and settings.

Whitby Harbour

One of Whitby's unique attractions is **The Sutcliffe Gallery,** in Flowergate, which celebrates the great photographer Frank Meadow Sutcliffe who was born in Whitby in 1853. His studies of local people, places and events powerfully evoke the Whitby of late-Victorian and Edwardian times in photographs that are both beautifully composed and technically immaculate. A popular souvenir of the town is jet, a lustrous black stone that enjoyed an enormous vogue in Victorian times as, after the death of Prince Albert, jewellery in jet was the only ornament the Queen would allow herself to wear. The Court and the middle classes naturally followed her example and for several decades Whitby prospered greatly from the trade in jet. By 1914, workable deposits of the stone were virtually exhausted and a new generation shunned its gloomy association with death. Recent years have seen a revival of interest in the glossy stone and several shops have extensive displays of jet ornaments and jewellery. The original **Victorian Jet Works**, established in 1867, are open daily and visitors can see the craftsmen at work as well as purchase jet from a wide range of interesting and contemporary jewellery designs.

THE ANVIL INN

MAIN STREET, SAWDON, NR SCARBOROUGH,
NORTH YORKSHIRE YO13 9DY
TEL: 01723 859896

Directions: From junction 49 of the A1, take the A168 north to the A170. Take this east towards Pickering. Sawdon is a couple of miles north off the A170 Scarborough-Pickering Road, reached by turning off the A170 at Brompton.

The Anvil Inn is an outstanding pub with great food, drink and accommodation. The buildings date back to the 1700s, and as the name suggests, it was once home to the village smithy, and the forge remains on the premises.

Owned and run by Ant and Ros Eastwood since April of 2003, in a very short time they have made the inn a place to visit for both locals and visitors thanks to their culinary skills, hospitality and fine array of well-kept ales.

There's always a minimum of five real ales on tap. Regulars include Black Sheep pand Charles Welles Bombardier, together with changing guest ales bringing the total up to seven to choose from at the height of the season. There's also a keg bitter, two draught lagers, a draught cider and a draught stout, along with a good range of wines, spirits and soft drinks.

Meals are available at lunch Tuesday to Sunday and at dinner Tuesday to Saturday. The menus boast a range of tempting dishes including specialities such as crispy duck, stuffed pork fillets, vegetarian cannelloni, seafood quennells, beef stroganoff and more, expertly prepared and presented. The no-smoking restaurant seats 32. Booking is required on Friday, Saturday and Sunday.

Here at this superb inn are four lovely guest bedrooms – twins on the ground floor, and doubles upstairs – all en suite, cosy and comfortable. The tariff includes a hearty breakfast.

- Mon-Sat 11.00-23.00; Sun 12.00-22.30
- Tues-Sat and Bank Hols 12.00-14.30 and 19.00-21.30; Sun 12.00-14.30
- Visa, Mastercard, Switch, Delta, Eurocard, Solo
- 4 rooms en suite
- Off-road parking, beer garden, patio area
- Scarborough 6 miles, Pickering 8 miles, Filey 10 miles, Malton 12 miles, North Yorks Moors National Park 15 miles

THE BLACKSMITHS COUNTRY INN

HARTOFT END, ROSEDALE ABBEY, PICKERING,
NORTH YORKSHIRE YO18 8EN
TEL: 01751 417331 FAX: 01751 417167

Directions: From Pickering take the A170 towards Kirkbymoorside; half a mile past Aislaby, turn right at Wrelton, sign for Cropton, Hartoft, Rosedale Abbey. Rosedale Abbey is 2½ miles past Cropton down a dip, up a slope.

Built round a farmhouse with origins in the 16th century, **The Blacksmiths Country Inn** has immense charm and is run with warm friendliness by resident owners Philip and Ann Wheatcroft. Its first advantage is the setting, high on a ridge overlooking moorland and forest at the heart of the North Yorkshire Moors National Park. Behind the handsome façade – the stones of the original farmhouse came from the ruins of Rosedale Abbey – the past and the present combine happily and the recent extension (the Millennium Wing) demonstrates the care and attention to detail evident throughout this

outstanding hotel. There are 19 bedrooms, each one furnished and equipped to the highest standards, and all with full en suite facilities. Fourteen standard rooms, six with balconies, are situated on the first floor, while on the ground floor are four superb superior rooms with French doors opening on to stunning views of Cropton Forest. All the rooms are non-smoking.

Hospitality is the keyword here, and guests will find instant relaxation in the warm, inviting bars and lounges. In the two restaurants the professional chefs prepare the best of traditional Yorkshire and modern European cuisine, and more informal bar meals are available lunchtime and evenings. The Blacksmiths Country Inn is without doubt one of the best places to eat or stay, and a perfect base for exploring the area.

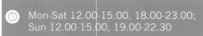

- 🕐 Mon-Sat 12.00-15.00, 18.00-23.00; Sun 12.00-15.00, 19.00-22.30
- 🍴 Mon-Sun 12.00-14.00, 18.00-21.00
- 💷 Visa, Mastercard, Switch, Delta, Eurocard, Solo
- 🛏 19 rooms en suite
- 🅿 Car park
- @ e-mail: office@blacksmithsinn-rosedale.co.uk
  website: www.blacksmithsinn-rosedale.co.uk
- ❓ Pickering 7 miles, Cropton Brewery Visitor Centre 2½ miles, Goathland (Mallyan Spout waterfall) 8 miles

65 HIGH STREET, LOFTUS, SALTBURN BY THE SEA,
CLEVELAND TS13 4HG
TEL: 01287 640612

Directions: Loftus is found on the A169 southeast of Middlesborough.

All are offered a warm welcome at **The Britannia**. Located on the border with North Yorkshire, near the coast and not far from Whitby and Staithes, it earns a place in this guide due to its proximity to that county and its great food, drink and hospitality. Run by Cheryl Welford, who has been landlady here since May of 2002, this amiable pub is well worth seeking out. Cheryl's a bubbly and welcoming host with a great sense of humour and a warm smile for all her guests. Together with her hardworking and friendly staff, she offers a high standard of service to all comers.

The pub is a Grade II listed building dating back to the 1800s, constructed of sandstone. Resembling a family home more closely than a pub, it is cosy and welcoming inside and out. Spacious, clean and homely, the décor and

furnishings are traditional and comfortable.

Set back on the main High Street of the village, in a pretty sloping row of terraced cottages, it is popular with locals and visitors alike. A good selection of real ales, keg bitters, lagers, cider, stout, wines, spirits and soft drinks awaits guests here. Food is served every day at lunchtime, with the chef creating a tempting range of delicious traditional bar snacks and meals.

Entertainments available at this convivial pub include live music on Saturday evenings, and a disco Sunday nights. Football fans will be happy to know that live matches are screened here. The village is within easy distance of many sights and attractions, including Whitby, North Yorks Moors National Park and Rosedale Abbey.

- Mon-Sat 11.00-23.00; Sun 12.00-22.30
- Mon-Sun 12.00-14.00
- Beer garden, car parking, dogs welcome
- Live music Saturdays; disco Sundays
- Whitby 12 miles, Staithes 4 miles, Castleton 7 miles, Goathland 12 miles

THE FEVERSHAM ARMS INN

CHURCH HOUSES, FARNDALE, KIRKBYMOORSIDE,
NORTH YORKSHIRE YO62 7LF
TEL: 01751 433206

Directions: From Pickering take the A170 for 14 miles to Kirkbymoorside, turning off the A170 and continuing north to Church Houses

Surrounded by picturesque and unspoilt countryside, **The Feversham Arms** is in the heart of the North Yorkshire Moors Daffodil Valley. A delightful stopping-place for anyone exploring the area, this charming rural retreat is owned and personally run by Frances Debenham, who has been here for over 17 years and has made this one of the most popular inns in the area. The 200-year-old premises are cosy and characterful and offer a spacious interior and a large beer garden. With its exposed beamwork, stone walls and other original features, it is stylish and tasteful as well as traditional.

Black Sheep and Tetleys are always on tap here, and occasionally a guest ale, together with a good selection of lagers, wines, spirits, cider, stout and soft drinks.

Award-winning home-cooked bar meals, daily specials and a la carte are available here every day at lunch and dinner. They feature an excellent choice of home-cooked dishes such as steak and kidney pie and other favourites, cooked to perfection by Frances herself. The pub is renowned for its delicious Sunday lunch. Children are welcome, and parties can be catered for.

The three en suite family-sized guest bedrooms are truly lovely, with homely furnishings and tasteful décor, guaranteed to make you feel welcome. In addition there's a beautiful self-catering cottage which sleeps four and is available for weekly breaks in season and breaks of three nights or more at other times.

- 🕐 Mon-Sat 11.00-15.00, 17.00-23.00; Sun 12.00-15.00, 19.00-22.30. Closed Mondays in winter.
- 🍴 Summer: Mon-Sun 11.30-14.30, 18.00-21.15; Winter: Tues-Sun 12.00-14.00, 18.00-21.00
- £ Visa, Mastercard, Switch, Delta, Eurocard, Solo
- 🛏 3 en suite guest bedrooms
- Ⓟ Beer garden, off-road parking
- @ fevershamfarndale@hotmail.com www.fevershamarmsinn.co.uk
- ❓ Helmsley 11 miles, Kirkbymoorside 10 miles, Pickering 14 miles, walking, birdwatching, fishing, mountain biking

THE FYLINGDALES INN

THORPE LANE, FYLINGTHORPE, WHITBY,
NORTH YORKSHIRE YO22 4TH
TEL: 01947 880433

Directions: From Whitby take the B1447 for five miles southeast to Fylingthorpe

Standing at the heart of the quiet little village of Fylingthorpe less than a mile from Robin Hood's Bay, **The Fylingdales Inn** has thrived under the management of Terry and Rita Milson, who took over here in late 1998. Before that, Rita had worked at the inn for some 15 years. They and their friendly, attentive staff offer all their guests great service.

Built in 1905 as a private house, Fylingdales became an inn in 1955 and nowadays offers top-quality food, drink, accommodation and hospitality. Meals are available every day all year round, with five or more special main courses each day including tempting dishes such as Whitby cod, seafood platter, salmon,

steak and ale pie, beef lasagne, roast vegetable moussaka, garlic chicken and more, all expertly prepared and presented to order. Meals can be enjoyed in the bars or in the lovely, spacious conservatory (no smoking). Children are welcome.

At least four real ales – John Smiths Cask, Theakstons Black Bull, Charles Welles Bombardier plus a changing guest ale – are always on tap, and in summer there's also the treat of Theakstons Olde Peraviat as well, together with a good range of lagers, spirits, cider, stout, wines and soft drinks. Other attractions at this traditional country pub include the unusual circular pool table. Outside there's a very attractive beer garden with a safe children's play area. And for guests who'd like to prolong their stay, there are three guest bedrooms, all comfortably and tastefully furnished and decorated with all the home comforts.

Winter: Mon-Sat 11.00-15.00, 17.00-23.00; Sun 12.00-15.00, 19.00-22.30. Summer: Mon-Sat 11.00-23.00; Sun 12.00-22.30

Mon-Sun 12.00-14.00, 18.00-21.00

Visa, Mastercard, Switch, Delta, Eurocard, Solo

3 guest bedrooms (2 en suite, 1 with private bath)

Off-road parking, large beer garden and children's play area

Live music Saturdays from 22.00

Whitby 5 miles, Robin Hood's Bay 1 mile,

THE HARE & HOUNDS

HIGH HAWSKER,WHITBY,NORTH YORKSHIRE YO22 4LH
TEL: 01947 880453

> **Directions:** Four miles south of Whitby just off the A171 Whitby · Scarborough road.

Set midway between Robin Hood's Bay and Whitby, just a short drive from the coast, the handsome village of High Hawsker is home to **The Hare & Hounds**, a distinguished and distinctive inn dating back to the 1800s.

Inside and out, this fine inn has real style. Welcoming, comfortable and attractive, it is a relaxed and pleasant place to enjoy the great food, drink and hospitality on hand.

Jeff and Diane, a local couple, became tenants here in April of 2003. Already, in a very short time, they have put the premises on the map thanks to the quality of the food, drink and service. They and their friendly, attentive staff ensure that every guest here feels most welcome.

Four real ales are on tap – Camerons

Strongarm, Camerons Creamy, Marstons Pedigree and a changing guest ale – complemented by a good choice of lagers, cider, stout, wines, spirits and soft drinks.

Excellent food is served at lunch every day and at dinner Monday to Saturday. This place is justly popular for its food, so booking is advised at all times. Guests choose off the menu or specials board from a changing selection of quality dishes made with care and expertise using only the freshest ingredients, from local suppliers wherever possible. The no-smoking restaurant seats 22.

Accommodation is available all year round in a completely refurbished self-catering cottage adjacent to the inn. Sleeping up to four people, it is tastefully furnished and decorated, comfortable and cosy – a real home from home. Also, between March and September there are two caravans, each sleeping four.

- 🕐 Mon-Fri 12.00-15.00, 18.00-23.00; Sat 12.00-23.00; Sun 12.00-22.30
- 🍴 Mon-Sun 12.00-14.30; Mon-Sat 18.00-20.30
- £ Visa, Mastercard, Switch, Delta, Access, Eurocard, Solo
- 🛏 Self-catering cottage and caravans
- Ⓟ Beer garden, off-road parking, children's games room
- ❓ Whitby 4 miles, Robin Hood's Bay 4 miles, Scarborough 17 miles

THE HUNTSMAN INN

22 MAIN ROAD, AISLABY, NR WHITBY, NORTH YORKSHIRE YO21 1SW
TEL: 01947 810637

Directions: Take the A171 1 mile out of Whitby, then turn left onto the minor road signposted Aislaby.

The Huntsman in Aislaby is a neat, well-kept little pub that started life as a coaching inn over 180 years ago. It stands on the edge of the Moors above the valley of the River Esk, but is only a couple of miles from Whitby and the sea, thus offering easy access to all the varied delights of this lovely part of the world.

The congenial host, Barry Crowther, puts a great emphasis on food, and folk in the know travel for miles to tuck into plates of cod and haddock fresh from the boats at Whitby. Quality is also to the fore in the meat dishes, for which the main ingredients are supplied by a first-class local butcher. Homemade steak pie and chilli are specialities of the house. Occasionally there are food-themed evenings – please ring for details. Booking is required Friday, Saturday and Sunday evenings and Sunday lunchtime. Children are welcome. To drink, there are three real ales – Timothy Taylor Landlord, Black Sheep and John Smiths – together with a good complement of lagers, cider, stout, wines and spirits.

The pub's convenient location naturally attracts overnight guests, for whom two en suite guest bedrooms – a twin and a family room with full amenities and facilities – provide warm, comfortable accommodation all year.

Local attractions include Grosmont, where the car can be temporarily swapped for the delights of a ride behind a steam engine on the gloriously scenic North Yorkshire Moors Railway; Goathland – known as 'Aidensfield' in the TV series *Heartbeat*, and whose railway station features in the *Harry Potter* films, and the Moors Visitor Centre at Danby.

- Mon-Sat 12.00-15.00, 19.00-23.00; Sun 12.00-22.30
- Mon-Sat 12.00-14.00, 19.00-21.00; Sun 12.00-15.00, 18.30-20.00
- 2 rooms en suite
- Car park, front terrace
- Darts, pub games, quiz night (alternate Tuesdays), occasional food themed evenings
- Whitby 2 miles, Grosmont 5 miles, Danby 9 miles

THE PLOUGH

180 COACH ROAD, SLEIGHTS, WHITBY,
NORTH YORKSHIRE YO22 5EN
TEL: 01947 810412

Directions: From Whitby take the A171 west and then the A169 south to reach Sleights.

The Plough is a large and handsome former coaching inn. Spacious, traditional and welcoming, this excellent inn offers great food, drink and accommodation. The interior is rustic and comfortable, with a real homely feel and relaxed atmosphere. Well-decorated and furnished throughout, the walls are adorned with a host of bygone memorabilia.

Very much family run, it is run by Tony and Carole Ward since 1996, and before that it was in the hands of Carole's parents Colin and Pat for 12 years. Assisted by Tony and Carole's son Gregg and daughter Rachel, this quality inn provides excellent service and friendly hospitality.

Featuring in *The Good Beer Guide*, there are four real ales are tap at this superb Free House – John Smiths, Theakstons Black Bull, Marstons Pedigree and a changing guest ale – together with a good complement of lagers, cider, stout, wines, spirits and soft drinks. Morning coffee is also served.

The inn is justly popular for its delicious food, and booking is advised particularly for Friday, Saturday and Sunday. Guests choose from the menu, specials or vegetarian specials board from a range of tempting home-cooked dishes, expertly prepared and presented and using the freshest local ingredients. Carole is a superb cook and delights in creating traditional and more innovative fare for her guests. Children welcome.

Accommodation is available in the form of three very comfortable guest bedrooms (two twins and a double). The tariff includes a hearty breakfast. An ideal base from which to explore.

- Mon-Sat 11.00-15.00, 17.00-23.00; Sun 12.00-15.00, 19.00-22.30. Summer: Mon-Sat 11.00-23.00; Sun 12.00-22.30
- Mon-Sun 12.00-14.15, 19.00-21.00 (18.00-21.00 in summer)
- Visa, Mastercard, Switch, Delta,
- 3 rooms en suite
- Beer garden, patio area, car park
- Live music Mon; quiz night Tues
- Goathland 3 miles, Whitby 5 miles, Robin Hood's Bay 8 miles, Rosedale Abbey 10 miles

THE QUEENS HEAD PUBLIC HOUSE, CANTONESE RESTAURANT & TAKEAWAY

HIGH STREET, AMOTHERBY, NR MALTON,
NORTH YORKSHIRE YO17 6TL
TEL: 01653 693630

Directions: From the A64 at Malton take the B1257 for three miles to the village of Amotherby

The Queens Head, located in the quiet village of Amotherby, appears at first to be a traditional country inn. Dating back to 1860, the property has undergone a complete refurbishment, thoughtfully and tastefully done and is now both a Free House and a Cantonese restaurant and takeaway. The concept was the brainchild of owners Jon and Mandy Woollen, who bought the place in April 2001 and are clearly onto a winner. They and their helpful, friendly staff offer high-quality service, food, drink and hospitality. Visitors can enjoy a fine pint, with two real ales always available. Tetleys is a permanent feature along with a local brew from the Malton brewery.

The elegant no-smoking restaurant can seat up to 50 diners, and here guests can sample one of the best Chinese meals available in the area. The menu offers a superb choice of traditional favourites. On Wednesday and Thursday evenings, special seafood dishes are added to the menu, which is also available for takeaway. The restaurant is open every evening except Christmas Day and Boxing Day. Bookings are essential on Friday and Saturday nights and meals can also be taken in the bar area. Children are welcome and have their own play area to the rear of the pub. There's also a new conservatory under construction to increase seating for the restaurant, together with a toilet area with disabled facilities.

- Mon-Sun 17.00-23.00
- Bar meals and snacks. A la carte
- Visa, Mastercard, Switch, Delta, Eurocard, Solo
- Off-road parking
- qhmotherby@aol.com
- Malton 3 miles, Castle Howard 4 miles, York 15 miles

THE SEVEN STARS

MARKET PLACE, GUISBOROUGH, NORTH YORKSHIRE TS14 6BN
TEL: 01947 603937

Directions: Guisborough is on the A171, some 10 miles southeast of Middlesborough.

Set on an imposing corner site, **The Seven Stars** is one of the first sights that greets visitors to the busy town of Guisborough, just over the North Yorkshire border and close to the conurbation of Middlesborough. This thriving little town is packed with busy shops and pubs. All are welcome here, and the clientele boasts local office-workers, builders, families and more, along with a growing list of visitors to this part of the county.

Built in 1837, this fine pub is a substantial establishment with a smart cream exterior, offering a welcoming face to the world. Inside guests will find a spacious, uncluttered open-plan interior which reflects the taste of the young couple who now own it. Phillip and Gina Nash have been here since early in 2003, and they and their friendly, dedicated staff offer a high standard of service and hospitality. The environment created for customers by the décor and furnishings is relaxed and welcoming.

Open for every session Monday to Thursday, and all day Friday to Sunday, the choice of drinks here is broad and interesting, with a good range of first-class real ales, bitters and lagers together with cider, stout, wines, spirits and soft drinks. There's a full menu of home-cooked food served at lunchtime every day. Freshness is the byword here, as all ingredients are locally sourced wherever possible and combined to create some delicious traditional snacks and meals. Home-prepared to order, they are well worth sampling.

Local sights and attractions in the area include, apart from Guisborough itself, Middlesborough, places along the coast including Whitby, and the North Yorks Moors National Park with its centres at Goathland and Pickering among others.

Mon-Thur 12.00-15.00, 19.00-23.00; Fri-Sat 11.00-23.00; Sun 12.00-22.30

Mon-Sun 11.30-14.30

Middlesborough 8 miles, Redcar 6 miles, Whitby 15 miles, North York Moors National Park 4 miles

THE TAP & SPILE

NEW QUAY ROAD, WHITBY, NORTH YORKSHIRE YO21 1DH
TEL: 01947 603937

Directions: 18 miles north of Pickering on the A169. The Tap & Spile is opposite the Quay and across from the railway station

Built as a cellar pub at the end of the end of the 19th century, **The Tap & Spile** was rebuilt much as it looks today in 1937. It enjoys a delightful setting among the little shops and restaurants on the New Quay side of the town, and attracts a regular and loyal clientele with its pleasant atmosphere and convivial surroundings. The present owners, Peter and Sheree Fleming, have a wealth of pub management experience and took over the tenancy of this pub in 2000, although they had been working here as managers since 1994. They and their staff engender a happy feeling at the pub, where evening entertainment features music for all tastes four nights a week.

The Tap & Spile (two terms relating

to a beer barrel) is well known for its selection of cask ales – with between four and eight available, together with one real cider and a good selection of lagers, stout, spirits, wines and soft drinks - and is also a popular choice for a meal – a quick snack for those in a hurry or a leisurely two or three courses for those with time to relax and enjoy them.

The attractive seaside town of Whitby is known for its jet and its links with early Christianity – the old town is dominated by the ruins of Whitby Abbey high up on a cliff. Captain James Cook's home port, the house where he lodged during his apprenticeship is now the Captain Cook Memorial Museum. There's a Dracula connection, too, for Whitby was the place where, according to Bram Stoker's novel, the Count came ashore, in the form of a wolf.

Mon-Sat 12.00-23.00; Sun 12.00-22.30; winter: Sun 12.00-16.00, 19.00-22.30. Late closing 1st June to 30th September: Fri-Sat midnight, Sun 23.00

Mon-Sat 12.00-19.00; Sun 12.00-16.00

Live music four nights a week; quiz nights Thursdays; Sunday nights Open Folk Session.

Whitby Abbey, Egton Bridge (Gooseberry Show) 7 miles, Goathland (Mallyan Spout) 8 miles, Beck Hole (World Quoits Championship) 7 miles

88	The Ash Tree, Barkston Ash, Tadcaster	100	The Gold Cup Inn, Nether Silton, Thirsk
89	The Black Bull Inn, Boroughbridge	101	The Grey Horse Inn, Elvington, York
90	The Black Dog Inn, Camblesforth, Selby	102	The Hare Inn, Scawton, Thirsk
91	The Black Horse, Tollerton, York	103	The Jolly Miller, Eggborough, Selby
92	The Blacksmiths Arms, Flaxton, York	104	Kings Arms, North Duffield
93	The Blue Bell Country Inn, Alne, York	105	Mother Shipton Inn, Low Bridge
94	The Chequers Inn, Bilton-in-Ainsty, York	106	The Nags Head, Heworth, York
95	The Crooked Billet, Saxton, Tadcaster	107	Queen O'T'owd Thatch, South Milford
96	Cross Keys Inn, Markington, Harrogate	108	The Rockingham Arms, Towton
97	The Crown & Anchor, Sowerby, Thirsk	109	The Royal Oak Inn, Dacre Banks
98	The Durham Ox, Crayke, York	110	The Wellington Heifer, Ainderby Steeple
99	The George Country Inn, Wath, Ripon	111	The White Horse Inn, Upper Poppleton

Please note all cross references refer to page numbers

THE CITY OF YORK AND CENTRAL YORKSHIRE

This region of Yorkshire, between the North York Moors and the East Riding, between West Yorkshire and the Heritage Coast, is dominated by the city of York. The first settlement of any note here was created by the Romans, who named their garrison town Eboracum, and, from then on, York has been an important and influential force not only in Yorkshire but also in the rest of the country.

Allerton Park, Nr Knaresborough

Many of the towns in this area were founded by the Romans and, indeed, both Tadcaster and Malton date back to the days of the Imperial rule. Both, too, have a history of brewing and, although many of the breweries have long since gone, the tradition still continues to this day.

The land in this region is key agricultural land and the vast open expanses have been cultivated for centuries. The economy of much of the area has been reliant on farming and, although now not as labour

PLACES OF INTEREST

Beningbrough 71	Selby 79
Boroughbridge 71	Sion Hill 80
Bramham 71	Skelton 80
Camblesforth 71	Spofforth 81
Coxwold 72	Studeley
Elvington 73	Roger 81
Harrogate 73	Sutton-under-
Kilburn 75	Whitestonecliffe
Knaresborough 75	82
Northallerton 76	Tadcaster 82
North Stainley 77	Thirsk 83
Osmotherley 77	Wetherby 83
Riccall 77	York 84
Ripon 77	

intensive as it once was, this remains a major industry here. Throughout this area the skyline is dotted with the spires and towers of churches that were built in those relatively prosperous times but there are two other features of the landscape that are of particular interest.

The two towns of Harrogate and Knaresborough dominate

The Shambles, York

the lower section of Nidderdale, while further north lies Ripon, a cathedral city since Victorian times. Though the city endeavoured to cash in on the Victorian fashion for 'taking the waters', it did not have its own healing springs and so water had to be pumped in from Aldfield, near Fountains Abbey; many Edwardian spa buildings remain, along with some fine art nouveau features and their surrounding gardens. Ripon, also, is home to one of the country's most beautiful racecourses, and throughout the summer season there are race meetings here on what is known as Yorkshire's Garden Racecourse. Nearby, at Thirsk, is another of the county's delightful racecourses' although the town is best known as having been the home of the real life James Herriot, Alf Wight.

Although ancient monuments litter this area such as the Devil's Arrows near Boroughbridge and many of the settlements have Roman roots, it is the magnificent ruin of Fountains Abbey for which this region is best known. Set beside the River Skell, this was one of the wealthiest Cistercian houses in the country in medieval times and, today, the remains are Yorkshire's only World Heritage Site. However, there are other places of interest to see close by including the fine stately home of Newby Hall, the Northern Horticultural Society's Harlow Carr Botanical Gardens and the breweries at Masham.

BENINGBROUGH

On the banks of the River Ouse, at the edge of the great Forest of Galtres, this ancient settlement is the location of the fine **Beningbrough Hall** (National Trust). With one of the most impressive baroque interiors in the country, the hall is the perfect backdrop for the collection of portraits on display from the National Portrait Gallery, and there is also a Victorian laundry and potting shed to explore.

BOROUGHBRIDGE

This attractive and historic town was once on a main thoroughfare used by both the Celts and the Romans. The bridge over the River Ure, from which the village takes its name, was built in 1562 and formed part of an important road link between Edinburgh and London. Busy throughout the coaching days with traffic passing from the West Riding of Yorkshire to the North, Boroughbridge has now returned to its former unassuming role of a small wayside town now bypassed by the A1(M) that takes most of the 21st century traffic from its streets.

The great **Devil's Arrows**, three massive Bronze Age monoliths, stand like guardians close to the new road and form Yorkshire's most famous ancient monument, which is thought to date from about 2000 BC. The monoliths, the tallest of which is 30 feet high, stand in a line running north to south and are fashioned from millstone grit that has been seriously fluted by weathering. A local legend, however, attributes the great stones to the Devil suggesting that they were, actually, crossbow bolts that he fired at nearby **Aldborough** that was, at the time, a Christian settlement. A quiet little backwater today, at the time of the Romans, Aldborough was a thriving town known as 'Isurium Brigantum', the capital of the Celtic tribe of the Brigantes. The **Aldborough Roman Museum** houses relics of the town's past, and nearby are some of the original walls and tesselated pavements of the ancient settlement.

BRAMHAM

Bramham Park, to the southwest of the village, is one of Yorkshire's most exquisite country houses, with several features that make it particularly special. The house itself dates from the Queen Anne era and was built by Robert Benson, Lord Bingley, between 1698 and 1710, in the superbly proportioned elegant and restrained classical style that is typical of that era. However, the final effect is more French than English as the gardens were modelled on Louis XIV's Versailles, with ornamental canals and ponds, beech groves, statues, long avenues and a superb arboretum with a collection of rare and unusual trees. The interior contains elegant furniture and paintings by artists such as Kneller and Sir Joshua Reynolds.

CAMBLESFORTH

Just to the south of this village is **Carlton Towers**, a stately home that

Carlton Towers, Camblesforth

should on no account be missed. This extraordinary building, "something between the Houses of Parliament and St Pancras Station," was created in the 1870s by two young English eccentrics, Henry, 9th Lord Beaumont, and Edward Welby Pugin, son of the eminent Victorian architect. Together, they transformed the original traditional Jacobean house into an exuberant mock-medieval fantasy in stone, complete with turrets, towers, gargoyles and heraldic shields. The richly-decorated High Victorian interior, designed in the manner of medieval banqueting halls, contains a minstrels' gallery and a vast Venetian-style drawing room. Carlton Towers is now the Yorkshire home of the Duke of Norfolk and is open to the public during the summer months.

COXWOLD

One of the area's most picturesque villages, Coxwold is set in a narrow valley on the edge of the Hambledon

Hills and its main street is lined with well-tended grassy banks and attractive stone cottages. At the western end of the village stands the 500-year-old **Shandy Hall,** the home of Laurence Sterne, Coxwold's vicar in the 1760s and the author of *Tristram Shandy*, a wonderfully bizarre novel that opened a vein of English surreal comedy leading directly to The Goons and the Monty Python team. The architecture of the hall, which is Tudor in origin, includes some appropriately eccentric features – strangely-shaped balustrades on the wooden staircases, a Heath Robinson type of contraption in the bedroom powder-closet by which Sterne could draw up pails of water for his ablutions and a tiny, eye-shaped window in the huge chimney stack opening from the study to the right of the entrance. A more conventional attraction here is the priceless collection of Sterne's books and manuscripts.

Just to the south of Coxwold is **Newburgh Priory,** which was founded in 1145 as an Augustinian monastery but, since 1538 after the Dissolution, it has been the home of the Fauconberg family. Now a mainly Georgian country house, the priory is noted for its fine interiors and its beautiful water garden. Another ancient ecclesiastical building, **Byland Abbey** (English Heritage), now in ruins

Byland Abbey

displays and exhibitions throughout the year, a historic military vehicle collection to explore and homecooked food served in the museum's famous NAAFI restaurant.

HARROGATE

Well recognised as one of England's most attractive towns and a frequent winner of 'Britain in Bloom', Harrogate features acres of gardens that offer a vast array of colour throughout the year, open spaces and broad tree-lined boulevards. However, until the 17th century Harrogate – or 'Haregate' as it was then called – was nothing more than just a collection of cottages close to the thriving market town of Knaresborough. One day, while out walking his dog, William Slingsby, of Bilton Hall near Knaresborough, discovered a spring bubbling up out of the rock and, having tasted the water, Slingsby found it to be similar to that he had drunk at the fashionable wells of Spa, in Belgium. Expert opinion was sought and, in 1596, Dr Timothy Bright confirmed the spring to be a chalybeate well and the waters to have medicinal powers – curing a wide variety of illnesses and ailments, from gout to vertigo. Slingsby's well became known as **Tewit Well**, after the local name for pewits, and it can still be seen today covered by a dome on pillars. Other wells were soon found in the area: St

set in tranquil green meadows, can be found just to the northeast of Coxwold. The ruined west front of the abbey, with only the lower arch of its great rose window still in place, gives a vivid impression of how glorious this building once was and visitors can also see the largest collection of medieval floor tiles, still in the their original settings, here.

ELVINGTON

During World War II, RAF Elvington was the largest Bomber Command station and it was from here that British, Canadian and French crews flew on missions to Europe. Today, the former airfield is now the **Yorkshire Air Museum**, a living museum to the allied air forces who served in Yorkshire throughout the war. Housed in authentic buildings, numerous exhibits trace the history of aviation, and visitors can also gain a unique insight into just what life was like for a lone air gunner in his turret or hear the sounds of a wartime bomber station. There are various flying

John's Well in 1631 and the **Old Sulphur Well** that went on to become the most famous of Harrogate's springs. Though this particular spring had been known locally for years it was not until 1656 that this sulphurous smelling well, nicknamed the 'Stinking Spaw', began to attract attention.

Royal Baths Assembly Rooms

During the mid 17th century bathing in the heated sulphurous waters became fashionable as well as a cure for various ailments and lodging houses were built around the sulphur well in Low Harrogate; inns and hotels followed when the stagecoaches and later the railways arrived. In 1842 the Old Sulphur Well was enclosed in the splendid Royal Pump Room and this major water place for spa visitors has been painstakingly restored to illustrate all aspects of Harrogate's history. Now the **Royal Pump Room Museum**, it has a number of interesting displays and exhibitions that include stories of watery miracles, Russian royalty and even disappearing crime writers. The sulphur water, the strongest in Europe, still rises beneath the building and can still be sampled. The **Royal Baths Assembly Rooms** that in their heyday were full of rich visitors sampling the waters have been restored to house the Turkish Baths where visitors can enjoy a sauna and

solarium, and they are open to the public daily. Housed in the oldest of the town's surviving spa buildings and originally built in 1806, the **Mercer Art Gallery** is home to a superb collection of fine art along with the Kent Bequest – an archaeological collection that includes finds from both ancient Greece and Egypt.

Though its status as a spa town has declined, Harrogate is still a fashionable place, a sought after conference location, home of the annual Northern Antiques Fair and a town with much to offer the visitor.

Another attractive aspect of the town is **The Stray** that is unique to Harrogate and virtually encircles the town centre. These 200 acres of open space are protected by ancient laws to ensure that the residents of, and visitors to, the town always have access for sports, events and walking.

Just to the west of the town lie **Harlow Carr Botanical Gardens** that were established in 1948 by the Northern

Horticultural Society and now cover some 68 acres. The gardens feature all manner of plants in a wide variety of landscapes, including herb, scented, rock, bulk and woodland gardens, which allow members of the public to see how they perform in the unsympathetic conditions of northern England. The society, as well as having their study centre here, has also opened a fascinating **Museum of Gardening**.

KILBURN

Kilburn was the home of one of the most famous of modern Yorkshire craftsmen, Robert Thompson – the Mouseman of Kilburn. Robert's father was a carpenter and he apprenticed his son to an engineer; however, at the age of 20, inspired by seeing the medieval wood carvings in Ripon Cathedral, Robert returned to Kilburn and begged his father to train him as a carpenter. An early commission from Ampleforth Abbey to carve a cross settled his destiny and from then, until his death in 1955, Robert's beautifully crafted ecclesiastical and domestic furniture was in constant demand. His work can be seen in more than 700 churches, including Westminster Abbey and York Minster. Each piece bears his 'signature' – a tiny carved mouse placed in some inconspicuous corner of the work. According to a family story, Robert adopted this symbol when one of his assistants happened to use the phrase 'as poor as a church mouse'. Robert Thompson's two grandsons have

continued his work and their grandfather's former home is now both a memorial to his genius and a showroom for their own creations.

Just north of the village is one of the area's most famous features, the **White Horse** that was inspired by the prehistoric White Horse hill-carving at Uffingham in Berkshire. John Hodgson, Kilburn's village schoolmaster, enthused his pupils and villagers into creating this splendid folly in 1857. At some 314 feet long and 228 feet high, the figure is visible from as far away as Harrogate and Otley.

KNARESBOROUGH

This ancient town of pantiled cottages and Georgian houses is precariously balanced on a hillside by the River Nidd while a stately railway viaduct, 90 feet high and 338 feet long and completed in 1851, spans the gorge. There are many unusual and attractive features in the town, among them a maze of steep-stepped narrow streets leading down to the river. The town is dominated by the ruins of **Knaresborough Castle** that was built high on a crag overlooking the River Nidd by Serlo de Burgh, who had fought alongside William the Conqueror at Hastings. Throughout the Middle Ages, the castle was a favourite with royalty and the court and it was to Knaresborough that the murderers of Thomas à Becket fled in 1170, while Queen Philippa, wife of Edward III, also enjoyed staying at Knaresborough and she and her family spent many summers

River Nidd, Knaresborough

here. Along with touring this once royal fortification, with its dungeon and mysterious underground sallyport, visitors to Knaresborough can find out more about the town's history at the **Old Courthouse Museum**.

The nearby Bebra Gardens are named after Knaresborough's twin town in Germany and its attractive flower beds are complemented by luxurious lawns and a paddling pool. In the High Street, visitors should keep an eye out for **Ye Oldest Chymists' Shoppe** in England that dates back to 1720. For the last century and more, it has been owned by the Pickles family who manufacture some 40 lotions, ointments and creams. Knaresborough is probably best known for **Mother Shipton's Cave**, the birthplace of the famous prophetess, and for its **Petrifying Well** that provides a constant source of curiosity to the visitor. The effects that the well's lime-rich water has on objects are truly amazing and an array of paraphernalia,

from old boots to bunches of grapes, are on view – seemingly turned to stone. Both the cave and the well can be found in the Mother Shipton Estate, part of the Ancient Forest of Knaresborough, which offers visitors beautiful walks beside the River Nidd in grounds that were classically landscaped in the 18th century.

Also on the banks of the River Nidd is the famous **St Robert's Cave**, an ancient hermitage, and close by is the **House in the Rock** that was hewn out of the solid rockface by Thomas Hill, an eccentric weaver, between 1770 and 1786.

NORTHALLERTON

The county town of North Yorkshire, Northallerton has a broad High Street of almost half a mile long that is typical of the county's market towns. In the stagecoach era, the town was an important stop on the route from Newcastle to London and several old coaching inns still stand along the High Street. The most ancient is **The Old Fleece**, a favoured drinking haunt of Charles Dickens during his several visits to Northallerton that remains a truly Dickensian place with great oak beams and a charming olde worlde atmosphere.

Northallerton has many old buildings of interest, including an ancient

Grammar School, a grand medieval church, a 15th century almshouse and, of more recent provenance, a majestic County Hall built in 1906 and designed by the famous Yorkshire architect Walter Brierley.

NORTH STAINLEY

The monks of Fountains Abbey knew North Stainley and **Slenningford Grange** is thought to have been one of their many properties; a fishpond dating from medieval times can still be seen here.

Just to the south of the village lies the **Lightwater Valley Theme Park** set in 175 acres of scenic grounds that provides thrills and spills for all the family. The site also contains retail and factory shops, a garden centre, a restaurant and a coffee shop.

OSMOTHERLEY

Long distance walkers will be familiar with this attractive moorland village since it is the western starting point for the **Lyke Wake Walk**, which winds for more than 40 miles over the North York Moors to Ravenscar on the coast. At the centre of the village is a heavily carved cross and, next to it, a low stone table that was probably once a market stall and also served John Wesley as a pulpit.

About a mile northeast of the village lies **Mount Grace Priory**.

RICCALL

This ancient village is listed in the *Domesday Book* although its church does not feature as it was built shortly after the great survey. The south doorway of the church dates back to about 1160 and its fine details have been well preserved by a porch added in the 15th century. However, the village's great moment in history came just prior to the Norman invasion when, in 1066, King Harold Hardrada of Norway and Earl Tostig sailed this far up the River Ouse with some 300 ships. They had come to claim Northumbria from Tostig's half-brother King Harold of England but they were comprehensively defeated at the Battle of Stamford Bridge.

Riccall is a popular place with walkers as from here there are footpaths, southwards, along the River Ouse to Selby and, northwards, towards Bishopthorpe along the trackbed of the now dismantled York to Selby railway. This latter path is part of the 150-mile long **Trans Pennine Trail** linking the west coast at Liverpool with Hull on the east coast.

Just to the east of the village, the Yorkshire Wildlife Trust maintains the **Skipwith Common Nature Reserve**, some 500 acres of lowland heath that is one of the last such areas remaining in the north of England. Regarded as of national importance, the principal interest here is the variety of insect and birdlife, but the reserve also contains a number of ancient burial sites.

RIPON

This attractive cathedral city on the banks of the Rivers Ure, Skell, and Laver

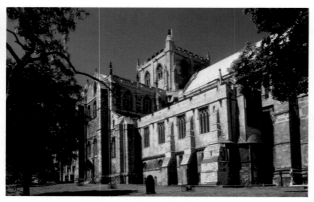

Cathedral of St Peter and St Wilfrid

dates from the 7th century when Alfrich, King of Northumbria granted an area of land surrounding a new monastery to the Church. Later that century, in 672, St Wilfrid built one of England's first stone churches on the high ground between the three rivers and brought in plasterers, stonemasons and glaziers from France and Italy to undertake the work. At the time of the demise of the Northern Kingdom in the mid 10th century, the monastery and church were destroyed, though the Saxon crypt survives to this day. By the time of the Norman Conquest, Ripon was a prosperous agricultural settlement under ecclesiastical rule and it was at this time that a second St Wilfrid's Church, instigated by the first Norman Archbishop of York, Thomas of Bayeux, was erected on the site of the Saxon building.

The magnificent **Cathedral of St Peter and St Wilfrid** now stands on this site, begun in the mid-12th century by Archbishop Roger of York and later

extensively added to. Often referred to as the 'Cathedral of the Dales', the building, though one of the tallest cathedrals in England, is also the smallest. Discovered in 1976 close to the cathedral, the **Ripon Jewel** is the only surviving trace of the magnificence that was characteristic of the cathedral's early history. A small gold roundel inlaid with gemstones, the jewel's design suggests that it was made to embellish a relic casket or cross ordered by St Wilfrid.

Throughout the Middle Ages, the town prospered: its market charter had been granted by King Alfred in the 9th century and, at one time, Ripon produced more woollen cloth than Halifax and Leeds. As well as having three rivers, Ripon also has a canal, which was the most northerly point of England's canal system. The final stretch of the **Ripon Canal** and its Canal Basin have recently been restored and re-opened. The Industrial Revolution largely by-passed Ripon and in the early 20th century the town flourished, though briefly, as a spa. Although it had no spring of its own, it did make a bid to become a fashionable spa resort and the sulphur mineral water was pumped from Aldfield near Fountains Abbey. However, the scheme failed but the **Spa**

Baths building, opened in 1905 by the Princess of Battenberg, is a reminder of those times and now houses the city's swimming pool. It is a fine example of art nouveau architecture and the surrounding Spa Gardens are still a pleasant place for a walk.

The House of Correction, built in 1686, which served as the local prison between 1816 and 1878 and then became the police station until the late 1950s is now home to the **Ripon Prison and Police Museum**, which depicts the history of the police force and gives visitors a real insight into punishments and the lives of prisoners in Victorian times. Almost as unfortunate as those prisoners were the inmates of the local workhouse and **Ripon Workhouse Museum** is one of the city's newer attractions. The restored vagrants' wards of 1877 provide a chilling insight into the treatment of paupers in Yorkshire workhouses and the displays include a 'Victorian Hard Times Gallery'. These museums are open daily from Easter to October.

Ripon Racecourse dates back to 1713 although racing has been held in the town since 1664 and the present course was opened in 1900. Meetings are held here between April and August and the course, known as Yorkshire's Garden Racecourse, is widely regarded as one of the most beautiful in the country.

SELBY

In 1069 a young monk named Benedict, from Auxerre in France, had a vision and, although the exact nature of the vision is unknown, he was inspired to set sail for York and, as his ship was sailing up the River Ouse near Selby, three swans flew in formation across its bows. (Three swans, incidentally, still form part of the town's coat of arms). Interpreting this as a sign of the Holy Trinity, Benedict promptly went ashore and set up a preaching cross under a great oak called the Stirhac. The small religious community he established beside the river went from strength to strength, acquiring many grants of land and, in 1100, it was given permission to build a monastery. Over the course of the next 120 years, the great **Selby Abbey** slowly took shape, the massively heavy Norman style of the earlier building gradually modulating into the much more delicate Early English style, and all of the abbey was built using a lovely cream-coloured stone.

However, over the centuries this sublime church has suffered more than most. During the Civil War it was severely damaged by Cromwell's troops who destroyed many of its statues and smashed much of its stained glass. Then, in 1690, the central tower collapsed and, for years afterwards, the abbey was neglected and, by the middle of the 18th century, a wall had been built across the chancel so that the nave could be used as a warehouse. That wall was removed during a major restoration in the 19th century but, in 1906, there was another calamity when a disastrous fire swept through the abbey. Visiting this serene and peaceful church today it is difficult to believe that it has endured so many misfortunes and yet remains so beautiful. Throughout all the abbey's misfortunes one particular feature has, however, survived intact – the famous Washington Window that depicts the coat of arms of John de Washington, Prior of the Abbey around 1415 and a direct ancestor of George Washington. Prominently displayed in this heraldic device is the stars and stripes motif later adapted for the national flag of the United States.

Away from the abbey church that dominates the town, Selby is an important market centre for the rich agricultural plains of the Vale of York that surround the town. Devotees of railway history will want to pay their respects to Selby's old railway station that was built at the incredibly early date of 1834 and is the oldest surviving station in Britain.

SION HILL

Celebrated as the 'last of the great country houses', **Sion Hill Hall,** with its light, airy and well-proportioned rooms, all facing south, is typical of the work of the celebrated Yorkshire architect, Walter Brierley. Dubbed the 'Lutyens of the North', Brierley completed the building in 1913 for Percy Stancliffe and his wife Ethel, the wealthy daughter of a whisky distiller. Although the rooms have remained unaltered since they were built their contents certainly have changed. In 1962, the Sion Hill Hall was bought by Herbert Mawer, a compulsive but highly

discerning collector of antiques and during the 20 years he lived here, Herbert continued to add to what was already, probably the best collection of Georgian, Victorian and Edwardian artefacts in the north of England. Furniture, paintings, porcelain, clocks (all working) and ephemera crowd the richly furnished rooms and make Sion Hill a delight to visit. A recent addition to the many sumptuous displays is a charming exhibition of dolls from the early 1900s.

In the hall's Victorian walled garden is another major visitor attraction – the **Birds of Prey and Animal Centre** where, in this beautiful English garden, visitors can see eagles, hawks, kites, falcons and owls fly freely during the regularly held demonstrations. There are over 80 birds here from 34 different species and the centre brings to life the skill and art of falconry.

SKELTON

This charming little village has some unusual cottages, dating from 1540, which were built from small handmade bricks with pantiled roofs.

Hidden away just to the south of the village is one of the area's finest stately homes, **Newby Hall**. Designed and built by Robert Adam in the 18th century, much of this superb Georgian house is open to the public and classical statuary, superb tapestries and fine Chippendale furniture are among the items on display.

It is, though, the award-winning **Newby Hall Gardens** that draw most people to the house. The famous double herbaceous borders form the main point of attraction, and also here are formal compartmental gardens, a wonderful Woodland Discovery Walk, a miniature railway, plenty of children's attractions, a shop and a restaurant.

SPOFFORTH

Situated on the tiny River Crimple, this ancient village is home to the stirring ruins of **Spofforth Castle** (English Heritage) that was originally built in the 16th century by the powerful Percy family. Replacing a manor house that had repeatedly been laid to waste, the castle was destroyed during the Civil War. Among the many events that took place here is said to have been the birth of Harry Hotspur.

Just southeast of the village is the splendid Palladian mansion, **Stockeld Park**, which was built between 1758 and 1763 by Paine. Containing some excellent furniture and a fine picture collection, the house is surrounded by extensive parkland that offers garden walks. The house is privately owned and is open only by appointment.

STUDELEY ROGER

This small hamlet, in the valley of the River Skell, is home to **Fountains Abbey**, the only World Heritage Site in Yorkshire and certainly its greatest ecclesiastical ruin. The abbey was one of the wealthiest Cistercian houses in the country and its remains are the most complete of any Cistercian abbey in Britain. Founded in 1132, with the help of Archbishop Thurstan of York, the first buildings housed just 13 monks of the order and, over the centuries its size increased, even spreading across the River Skell itself. The abbey reached its peak in the 15th century with the grandiose designs of Abbot Marmaduke Huby, whose beautiful tower still stands as a reminder of just how rich and powerful Fountains became.

In 1579, Sir Stephen Proctor pulled down some outbuildings, in order to construct **Fountains Hall**, a magnificent Elizabethan mansion that still stands in the abbey's grounds and part of which is open to the public.

Fountains Abbey

Close to the abbey and also in the care of the National Trust are the magnificent **Studley Royal Gardens** that were created in the early 18th century before they were merged with nearby ruins in 1768.

SUTTON-UNDER-WHITESTONECLIFFE

Boasting one of the longest place names in England, Sutton is more famous for the precipitous cliff that towers above it from the east – **Sutton Bank**. From the top of the bank there is one of the grandest landscape views in England, which looks out across the vast expanse of the Vale of York to the Pennine Hills far away to the west.

There is a National Park Information Centre at the summit of Sutton Bank and a well-marked Nature Trail leads steeply down to, and around, **Lake Gormire,** an Ice Age lake trapped here by a landslip. The lake is one of Yorkshire's only two natural lakes, the other being Semer Water in Wensleydale.

Sutton Bank used to be a graveyard for caravans because of its steep (1 in 3) climb and sharp bends. On one July Saturday in 1977, some 30 vehicles broke down on the ascent and five breakdown vehicles spent all day retrieving them. Caravans are now, not surprisingly, banned from this route. Though the bank may be a challenge to cars its sheer-sided cliffs create powerful thermals making this a favoured spot for gliders and bright-winged hang-gliders.

TADCASTER

The lovely magnesian limestone used in so many of Yorkshire's fine churches came from the quarries established here in Roman times and their name for Tadcaster was simply 'Calcaria', meaning limestone. By 1341, however brewing had become the town's major industry, using water from River Wharfe, and three major breweries are still based in Tadcaster: John Smiths, whose bitter is the best selling ale in Britain, Samuel Smiths, established in 1758 and the oldest in Yorkshire, and the Tower Brewery, owned by Bass Charringtons. The distinctive brewery buildings dominate the town's skyline and provide the basis of its prosperity. Guided tours of the breweries are available by prior booking.

Also worth visiting is **The Ark**, the oldest building in Tadcaster that dates back to the 1490s. During its long history, The Ark has served as a meeting place, a post office, an inn, a butcher's shop and a museum and it now houses the Town Council offices and is open to the public during office hours. Tadcaster also offers some attractive riverside walks, one of which takes walkers across the **Virgin Viaduct** over the River Wharfe. Built in 1849 by the great railway entrepreneur George Hudson, the viaduct was intended to be part of a direct line from Leeds to York but, before the tracks were laid, Hudson was convicted of fraud on a stupendous scale and this route was never completed.

A few miles southwest of Tadcaster lies **Hazelwood Castle,** which is now owned by Carmelite Friars who use it as a retreat and conference centre. It was built in lovely white limestone from a quarry at Thevesdale – the same quarry that provided the stone for York Minster and King's College Chapel, Cambridge. The well-maintained gardens and nature trail are open to the public while guided tours of the castle, with its superb Great Hall and 13th century chapel, are by prior arrangement only.

THIRSK

Thirsk has become famous as the home of veterinary surgeon Alf Wight, author of *All Creatures Great and Small,* who is perhaps better known as James Herriot. In his immensely popular books, Thirsk is clearly recognisable as 'Darrowby' and, in 1999, **The World of James Herriot**, housed in the actual 'Skeldale House' of the television series was opened. Visitors can take a trip back in time to the 1940s, explore the life and times of the world's most famous country vet and learn more about Alf Wight. There is the chance to see the old Austin car used in the series and also the opportunity to take part in a TV production. The attraction is open daily, all year round.

Just across the road from this famous surgery is the birthplace of another son of Thirsk. The building is now the town's **Museum** and tourist office and a plaque outside records that Thomas Lord was born here in 1755 and, some 30 years

later, he was to create the famous cricket ground in Marylebone that still bears his name. This pleasant small town of mellow brick houses has a sprawling Market Place and a magnificent 15th century St Mary's Church that is generally regarded as the finest parish church in North Yorkshire. It was here that the real life 'James Herriot' married his wife, Helen. Cod Beck, a tributary of the River Swale, wanders through the town, providing some delightful and well-signposted riverside walks.

On the edge of town, the **Trees to Treske Visitor Centre** is an imaginative exhibition exploring how trees grow, the character of different woods and examples of the cabinet maker's craft. Nearby is **Thirsk Racecourse**, known to devotees of the turf as the 'Country Racecourse'. There are around 12 race meetings each year, all well attended by visitors keen to experience this intrinsic feature of Yorkshire life. Travelling through the areas between the Yorkshire Dales and the North York Moors, visitors are constantly reminded of the great tradition of horse breeding and training for which the county is famous. The tradition runs deep: even the long flat straight stretch of main railway line between York and Darlington is known as the 'racecourse'.

WETHERBY

Due to its position on the Great North Road, this historic market town has also been a staging post and it lies halfway between London and Edinburgh. A bridge here across the River Wharfe was first mentioned in 1233 and, over the years, this has been widened considerably. From the footpath that passes under the bridge, walkers can see evidence of the building work that was undertaken in both the 18th and the 19th centuries. Apart from its shops, galleries, old pubs and cafés, Wetherby also has a popular National Hunt racecourse.

YORK

As Duke of York, George VI once said, "the history of York is the history of England", and though this is a bold claim it is also well justified. For almost 2, 000 years the city has been at the centre of great

York Minster

events and, better than any other city in England, it has preserved the evidence of its glorious past. With one of the grandest cityscapes in the country, York is dominated by the largest medieval gothic cathedral north of the Alps and **York Minster** can be seen from just about anywhere in the city (it is illegal to build a higher structure). A sublime expression of medieval faith, the cathedral was begun in 1220 and the work was on such a scale that it was not

completed until two and a half centuries later. Its stained glass windows – there are more than 100 of them – cast a celestial light over the many treasures within. A guided tour of the Great Tower gives fantastic views across the city while a visit to the crypt reveals some of the relics from the Roman fortress that stood here nearly 2, 000 years ago.

The Minster actually stands on the site of an even older building, the headquarters of the Roman legions and the Imperial troops arrived here in AD71 when the governor, Quintus Petilius Cerealis, chose this strategic position, beside the Rivers Ouse and Foss, as his base for a campaign against the tribe of the Brigantes. The settlement was named 'Eboracum' and it was from this garrison that Hadrian directed the construction of his great wall and, later, General Constantine was proclaimed Emperor here. The legions finally left the city around AD410 but the evidence of their three and a half centuries of occupation is manifest all around York in buildings like the **Multangular Tower,** in rich artefacts treasured in the city's museums and even in a pub: at the **Roman Bath Inn** are the remains of steam baths used by the garrison residents. The Multangular Tower is a neighbour of the **Yorkshire Museum** where visitors can take a journey back through time and discover the history and treasures of York and Yorkshire from Roman times, through the Saxon and Viking eras, to the days of the Middle Ages. Here, too, are the majestic ruins of **St Mary's Abbey**, a monastic house that was once one of the most powerful and influential in the north of England.

Little is known of York during the Dark Ages but by the 8th century the city had been colonised by the Anglo-Saxons, who named it 'Eoferwic', and it was already an important Christian and academic centre. The Vikings put an end to this settled period in the city's history when they invaded in the 9th century and changed the name once again, this

time to 'Jorvik'. The story of York during those years of Danish rule is imaginatively told in the many displays at the **Jorvik Centre**. Using technology from the 21st century, the centre transports visitors back to the Viking age when Jorvik was the trading hub of the Viking world. the items as they would have appeared in the Viking age.

The only remaining part of York Castle, which was built by William the Conqueror, is **Clifford's Tower**, a proud symbol of the might of the medieval kings. Opposite the tower is the **York Castle Museum**, a marvellous place that details the everyday life of the people of Britain over the past 400 years. The city was once one of the country's three main centres of memorial brass manufacture along with London and Norwich and, close to the Minster, brasses were engraved by hand in medieval workshops ready for distribution to the north of England and the Midlands. For an insight into this craft a visit to the **Jorvik Brass Rubbing Centre** is a must.

The network of medieval streets around the Minster is another of the city's major delights and the narrow lanes are criss-crossed by even narrower footpaths – ginnels, snickets or snickelways – that have survived as public rights of way despite being built over, above and around. The most famous of these ancient streets is **The Shambles**, whose name comes from 'Fleshammels', the street of butchers and slaughterhouses. The houses here were deliberately built close together to keep the street out of direct sunlight and thus protect the carcasses that were hung outside the buildings on hooks. Many of the hooks can still be seen in place.

Located in the very heart of the city is the elegant **Treasurer's House** (National Trust), which was originally the home of the Treasurers of York Minster. Restored to its former splendour by Yorkshire industrialist Frank Green in the late 19th and early 20th centuries, this glorious house has important collections of furniture, glass and china from the 16th to the 20th centuries, an impressive medieval hall and a delightful garden in the shadow of the Minster.

The 19th century saw York take on a new role as the hub of the railway system in the north. At the heart of this transformation was the charismatic entrepreneur George Hudson, founder of what became the Great Northern Railway and part visionary, part crook. His wheeler-dealing eventually led to his disgrace but even then the citizens of York twice elected him as Lord Mayor and he still has a pub named after him. It was thanks to Hudson that York's magnificent railway station, with its great curving roof of glass, was built, and it remains a tourist attraction in its own right. Nearby, in Leeman Street, is the

King William College, York

National Railway Museum, the largest of its kind in the world. This fascinating museum covers some 200 years of railway history, from Stephenson's *Rocket* to the Channel Tunnel. Among the thousands of exhibits demonstrating the technical and social impact of the 'Iron Horse' are Gresley's record-breaking locomotive, *Mallard,* Queen Victoria's royal carriage and displays demonstrating the workings of the railway system. There is also an extensive library and reading room (booking advised) and the 'Brief Encounter' restaurant is themed on the classic movie.

Another aspect of railway history is on view at the **York Model Railway**, next to the station, which has almost one third of a mile of track and up to 14 trains, from modern Intercity to freight trains and even the Orient Express, running at any one time. Machinery of a very different kind is on display at the **Museum of Automata**, which explores the world of man-made objects that imitate the movement of both humans and other living creatures. In a beautifully restored church close to the Shambles is the **Archaeological Research Centre**, an award-winning hands-on exploration of archaeology for visitors of all ages. Along with meeting practising archaeologists, who are happy to demonstrate how to sort and identify genuine finds or to try out ancient crafts, visitors also have the chance, through a series of interactive computer displays, to learn how modern technology helps to provide an interpretation of the past.

Along with the numerous museums, galleries and places of interest that this city has to offer visitors there is one, very popular, attraction that is well worth seeking out. The **Original Ghostwalk of York**, which starts from the King's Arms pub on Ouse Bridge each evening, provides an entertaining and unusual insight into the more macabre aspects of York's long history.

THE ASH TREE

LONDON ROAD, BARKSTON ASH, TADCASTER,
NORTH YORKSHIRE LS24 9PP
TEL: 01937 557247 FAX: 01937 558182

Directions: From Tadcaster take the A162 south to reach Barkston Ash, which is located adjacent to the A162.

The Ash Tree in Barkston Ash is a public house with a long and distinguished pedigree. Associated closely with the Battle of Towton, its exterior is absolutely gorgeous, covered in creeping ivy.

Inside the pub there's plenty of bygone memorabilia, including a vast array of mugs and jugs to be found hanging from the exposed beams. The restaurant is very eye-catching. Charming, cosy and friendly, The Ash Tree feels more like a home than an inn.

This Free House boasts at least four real ales – John Smiths Cask, Theakstons Best, Theakstons Cool Cask and Theakstons Olde Peculiar. Other keg ales are also on hand, together with a good range of stouts, cider, wines, spirits and soft drinks.

Very much a family-run inn, this outstanding place is personally run by Christine Martin along with her son Richard and daughter Jayne. An outstanding place to eat, it is well known locally and much further afield, and is always busy. Meals are served at lunch and dinner every day, with a large range of choices of tempting dishes available. Booking is essential on Friday and Saturday evenings and Sunday lunchtime. Children are welcome.

The outstanding beer garden to the rear is another bonus. It boasts a pristine, well-kept lawn, climbers and thoughtful, colourful planting. It also features a private area that is fenced off and includes a pond with Koi carp.

- Mon-Sat 11.00-15.00, 17.00-23.00; Sun 12.00-15.00, 19.00-22.30
- Mon-Fri 11.30-14.00, 18.00-21.30; Sat-Sun 12.00-14.00, 18.30-21.30
- All major
- Off-road parking, beer garden
- occasional food themed evenings – please ring for details
- e-mail: goodfood@ashtreeinn.co.uk website: www.ashtreeinn.co.uk
- Tadcaster 5 miles, Sherburn in Elmet 5 miles, Selby 8 miles, York 10 miles, Leeds 10 miles

THE BLACK BULL INN

6 ST JAMES SQUARE, BOROUGHBRIDGE,
NORTH YORKSHIRE YO51 9AR
TEL: 01423 322413 FAX: 01423 323915

> **Directions:** From junction 48 of the A1/M1, Boroughbridge is just off the B6265.
> The Black Bull Inn is located in the heart of the village.

The Black Bull Inn is a picture-postcard pub – reminiscent of Dickens' Old Curiosity Shop in size and shape – is an historic premises that dates back to 1262. This ancient coaching inn is located along what was once the Thirsk-to-Harrogate coaching route.

Inside, the old stands alongside the new – lots of traditional features remain, complemented by the up-to-date decor and furnishings. There's an old-fashioned snug and a delightful, intimate restaurant. Intricate exposed beamwork and exposed brick uprights add to the cosiness and comfort of this excellent inn.

Three real ales are served here – Black Sheep, John Smiths and a changing guest

ale – along with a choice of draught keg bitters, lagers, cider, stout, wines, spirits and soft drinks.

The superb restaurant is renowned for its cuisine. It seats 48 and is no-smoking; booking is advised on Saturday nights. The professional chefs prepare an impressive range of delicious dishes including steaks and grills, fresh fish dishes, pork loin, duck breast, pan-fried chicken, lamb cutlets, vegetarian meals and more. The mouth-watering desserts are also well worth leaving room for. Children are very welcome.

This fine inn also offers six quality en suite guest bedrooms (four doubles and two singles), available all year round.

Owners Anthony and Jillian Burgess have been in the trade for some 15 years, and have personally run this excellent inn since 1999. Their experience shows in the service and hospitality they offer all their guests.

- 🕐 Mon-Sat 11.00-23.00; Sun 12.00-22.30
- 🍴 Mon-Sat 12.00-14.00; Sun 12.00-14.30; Mon-Thur and Sun 18.00-21.00; Fri-Sat 18.00-21.30
- £ Visa, Mastercard, Switch, Delta, Eurocard, Solo
- Ⓟ Car park
- 🛏 6 en suite guest bedrooms
- ❓ Fountains Abbey 3 miles, Studley Royal Gardens 3 miles, Ripon 6 miles, Harrogate 10 miles, Thirsk 12 miles

THE BLACK DOG INN

SELBY ROAD, CAMBLESFORTH, SELBY, NORTH YORKSHIRE YO8 8HX
TEL: 01757 618247

Directions: 4 miles south of Selby on the A1041

A late 19th-century inn by the road that runs south from Selby to Snaith, the tenants of **The Black Dog Inn** are Gary and Tracy Dolman, here since May of 2002. A local Yorkshire couple, this is their first venture into the business and they have made it a real success. Hard-working and enthusiastic, they recognise the virtues of good service and value for money. Behind its neat, handsome frontage, the interior is equally well cared for, with the look of a well-furnished home. Traditional and very comfortable, it makes for a relaxing place to enjoy a fine drink or meal.

There are four real ales available – Greene King IPA, Abbot, Tetleys and a guest ale – along with a good range of lagers, cider, wines, spirits and soft drinks. Food is served at lunch and dinner every day. Tracy is a superb cook,

creating a range of tempting dishes. The menu changes frequently, and there's also a specials board. Homemade dishes include delicious pies and lasagne; other favourites include steaks, chicken korma, cumberland sausage, prawn salad and a good range of vegetarian dishes, all expertly prepared and presented. The spacious dining room and no-smoking conservatory are pleasant and very comfortable. Children are welcome.

Close to The Black Dog is an unusual attraction worth visiting: Carlton Towers was created in the 1870s by two young English eccentrics, Henry, 9th Lord Beaumont, and Edward Welby Pugin, son of the famous architect. Together they transformed a traditional Jacobean house into a mock medieval fantasy with turrets, towers, gargoyles and heraldic shields. The High Victorian interior, is modelled on medieval banqueting halls and contains a minstrels' gallery and a vast Venetian-style drawing room.

- Mon-Fri 11.00-15.00, 17.00-23.00; Sat 11.00-23.00; Sun 12.00-22.30
- Daily 12.00-14.30, 18.00-21.30
- Visa, Mastercard, Switch, Delta, Amex, Eurocard, Solo
- Off-road parking, beer garden, adjacent campsite
- Folk club second Wednesday of the month; steak night Thurs and Sunday
- Selby 4 miles, Drax 2 miles, York 20 miles

THE BLACK HORSE

NEWTON ROAD, TOLLERTON, YORK, NORTH YORKSHIRE YO61 1QT
TEL: 01347 838280

> **Directions:** From junction 47 of the M1, take the A59 east to the A19. Tollerton is west of the A19, north of York and south of Easingwold.

Dating back to the late 18th century, **The Black Horse** is a charming and distinctive hostelry that once had stables to the rear and the village smithy next door. Always known as The Black Horse throughout its 200-year-plus history, it has been a hub of the village and a draw for locals and visitors alike for its great food and drink and warm hospitality.

The exterior is handsome, as this imposing brick building has a multitude of casement windows, and commands from its corner location a prime spot. Inside, new tenants Ray, Jo and Phil have undertaken refurbishment to make the back bar a traditional room combining original features with modern comforts. The lounge is also welcoming and comfortable, and the front room houses an intimate restaurant.

Ray is a chef by profession, and it shows in the delicious range of dishes available at lunch and dinner every day.

Guests choose off the printed menu or from the specials board. Specialities include steaks and traditional English dishes with an innovative twist. Meals can be taken in the bar, lounge or no-smoking restaurant. Booking is required on Friday and Saturday evenings and for Sunday lunch. Real ales at this fine pub include John Smiths and a changing guest ale, together with a good selection of draught keg bitters, lagers, cider, stout, wines, spirits and soft drinks.

Ray, Jo and Phil have maintained the pub's reputation for quality, and they and their welcoming, conscientious staff ensure that every guest enjoys the best in hospitality and service.

- 🕐 Mon-Fri 11.00-15.00, 17.00-23.00; Sat 11.00-23.00; Sun 12.00-22.30
- 🍴 Mon-Sun 12.00-14.30, 18.00-21.00
- 💷 All major
- 🅿 Off-road parking
- 🎵 Quiz every other Tuesday from 9 p.m.; food themed evenings – please ring for details
- ❓ York 5 miles, Easingwold 6 miles, Harrogate 14 miles.

THE BLACKSMITHS ARMS

FLAXTON, YORK, NORTH YORKSHIRE YO60 7RJ
TEL: 01904 468210

Directions: 8 miles northeast of York off the A64

Located about halfway between York and the grandeur of Castle Howard, the picturesque village of Flaxton is best known for its outstanding pub, **The Blacksmiths Arms**. This distinguished hostelry has been at the heart of village life for more than 250 years, a pedigree borne

witness to by the characterful old beams and real open fires. Owned since 1995 by Jeff and Alison Jordan, the inn serves quality food Tuesday to Sunday evening and at Sunday lunchtime (booking required Friday and Saturday evenings and Sunday lunch). There's a separate non-smoking restaurant room or you can enjoy your meal in either of the bars. The menu and specials board feature a variety of tempting dishes – the speciality here is the Flaxton Flipper. Alison does all the cooking, whipping up a range of traditional and creative

favourites to suit every palate. Hearty and wholesome, the dishes make use of the freshest local ingredients cooked and prepared to order.

The well-kept ales on offer at this convivial Free House include Timothy Taylor Landlord, John Smiths and Black Sheep, together with a good range of draught keg bitter, lagers, cider, stout, wines, spirits and soft drinks.

Flaxton is a peaceful place to choose as a base for exploring the area, and the Blacksmiths has two self-catering cottages available from March to the end of October. They have been ingeniously converted from former barn buildings, and each sleeps up to four people. Comfortable and cosy, they are available on a weekly basis or for shorter breaks out of season. If not occupied by self-catering guests, the Jordans will happily let them on a bed & breakfast basis.

Mon-Sat 17.00-23.00; Sun 12.00-15.00, 19.00-22.30

Tues-Sun 19.00-21.30; Sun 12.00-15.00

12 double rooms en suite

Off-road parking

York 8 miles, Castle Howard 7 miles, Malton 10 miles

MAIN STREET, ALNE, YORK, NORTH YORKSHIRE YO61 1RR
TEL: 01347 838331

Directions: 11 miles northwest of York off the A19

It's well worth making the short detour from the A19 to this secluded and attractive little village set beside the River Kyle in order to sample the food, drink and relaxing atmosphere to be found at **The Blue Bell Inn**. Run by Michael and Annette Anson, this former farmhouse is a hostelry maintaining the best traditions of English country pubs. Cheerful and welcoming inside and out, there are well-kept gardens to the front and rear, and an air of warm hospitality throughout. Lots of style and class are in evidence in the handsome lounge, bar and restaurant.

Here guests will find a choice of at least three real ales (John Smiths, Black Sheep and Timothy Taylor Landlord) and a good selection of wines, and lagers, cider, stout, spirits and soft drinks – something, in fact, to quench every thirst.

The comprehensive menu offers a range of all the traditional favourites along with some delicious fish dishes. Tempting delights such as roast duckling, fillet steak, loin of pork, spring lamb, venison and haddock, monkfish, salmon and sea bass are just a sample of what's on offer. Annette, who is in charge of the kitchen, has worked hard to maintain a fine reputation for fresh, delicious food, and she has succeeded in making this a destination pub for great meals. Lunch or dinner can be enjoyed either in the Stable Restaurant with its low-beamed ceiling or in the cosy lounge with open fires. Food is available at lunchtimes Thursday to Sunday and Bank Holiday Mondays and in the evenings Monday to Saturday.

During the lifetime of this edition this fine inn will be offering accommodation that will be located no more than 200 yards away. Please ring for details.

- Thurs-Sun 12.00-15.00; Mon-Sat 18.00-23.00
- Thurs-Sun 12.00-14.00; Mon-Sat 18.00-21.00
- Visa, Mastercard, Switch, Delta, Eurocard, Solo
- Gardens, off-road parking
- www.bluebellalne.co.uk
- York 11 miles, Harrogate 12 miles, Castle Howard 14 miles

THE CHEQUERS INN

BILTON-IN-AINSTY, YORK, NORTH YORKSHIRE YO26 7NN
TEL: 01423 359066 FAX: 01423 358096

> **Directions:** From Wetherby take the B1224, turning right after about 5 miles onto a minor road signposted Chequers Inn. Follow this road to the end; the inn will be on your right.

The Chequers Inn, a pub of real character in a pretty little village a few miles out of Wetherby, is run by Selina and Eric Orme and their staff. Selina is a local woman and she and Eric have run this charming inn since July of 2002. Spotlessly kept and retaining much of the charm of its 19th-century coaching days, the inn offers a warm, relaxed ambience and excellent home cooking. The professional chef cooks everything to order using the freshest ingredients, locally sourced wherever possible. Booking is required Friday to Sunday. The attractive no-smoking restaurant seats 65 people. Children welcome. Bar snacks are also available.

There are three real ales on tap – John

Smiths, Tetleys and a changing guest ale – as well as a good selection of lagers, cider, stout, wines, spirits and soft drinks.

The inn is a very pleasant place to spend an hour or two but with the delights of the countryside all around and the major centres of Wetherby and York an easy drive away, the Chequers is also a good place for an overnight stay. There are three letting rooms – a family room, double and a single – which are comfortable and cosy.

The next village along the York road is Long Marston, where in 1644 the Battle of Marston Moor was fought. The night before the battle, Oliver Cromwell and his battle chiefs stayed at Long Marston Hall. South of Bilton is the village of Healaugh, where the 12th-century Church of St Helen and St John bears a bullet-shaped scar - reputedly made by a Cromwellian trooper on his way to the battle .

🕐	Tues-Sat and Bank Hols 12.00-14.30; Mon-Sat 18.00-23.00; Sun 12.00-15.00, 19.00-22.30
🍴	Tues-Sun 12.00-14.00; Mon-Sat 18.30-21.00
£	Visa, Mastercard, Switch, Delta, Amex, Access, Eurocard, Solo
🛏	3 en suite rooms
Ⓟ	Off-road parking, beer garden
🎵	Quiz night Weds
?	Marston Moor 2 miles, Wetherby 5 miles, York 10 miles, Tadcaster 10 miles

THE CROOKED BILLET

WAKEFIELD ROAD, SAXTON, TADCASTER,
NORTH YORKSHIRE LS24 9QN
TEL/FAX: 01937 557389

Directions: From Tadcaster take the A162 south and then the B1217 west towards Aberford to reach Saxton. The Crooked Billet is located about two miles further on from Saxton on the B1217.

The Crooked Billet is just over 100 years old, built on the site of an earlier public house. Brickbuilt and impressive, it takes up a good piece of land and includes a conservatory area at one end. Numerous hanging baskets and window boxes give it a real picture-postcard look. The pub is located close to the site of the Battle of Towton, and legend has it that the Earl of Warwick stayed here at the time of the battle.

Tastefully furnished and decorated throughout, features include the real fire with stone surround and photographs of the Crooked Billet and Saxton in days gone by. Plates, knick-knacks, brass ornaments and other homely individual touches enhance the appeal of this traditional pub. The conservatory doubles as a spacious dining area and there is an attractive patio area to the rear.

The real ale here is John Smiths Cask. Other beverages to choose from include a range of lagers, cider, stout, spirits, wines and soft drinks. Recommended for its food, this fine pub serves meals at lunch and dinner every day. Booking is advised Saturday night and Sunday lunchtime. The restaurant seats 60, with a no-smoking area and guests can choose from the menu or the specials board. A good variety of dishes are available and includes giant Yorkshire puddings with different fillings. Children are welcome.

Leaseholders Melanie and David, here since November of 2002, have made a real success of this, their first venture into the trade.

- 🕐 Mon-Fri 12.00-15.00, 18.00-23.00; Sat 12.00-23.00; Sun 12.00-22.30
- 🍴 Mon-Fri 12.00-14.00, 18.30-21.00; Sat 12.00-21.30; Sun 12.00-20.00
- £ Visa, Mastercard, Switch, Delta, Eurocard, Solo
- Ⓟ Off-road parking, rear patio area
- @ crookedbillet@ukonline.co.uk
- ❓ Tadcaster 4 miles, Wetherby 8 miles, Selby 9 miles, York 10 miles, Leeds 12 miles

CROSS KEYS INN

HIGH STREET, MARKINGTON, NR HARROGATE,
NORTH YORKSHIRE HG3 3NR
TEL: 01765 677555

The City of York & Central Yorkshire

Directions: From Harrogate take the A61 north through Killinghall and Ripley.
Five miles after Ripley turn left onto the minor road signposted Markington.

Cross Keys Inn is a well-established roadside hostelry in the middle of the attractive village of Markington. Spacious and handsome, it is well worth seeking out for the great food, drink and hospitality on offer here.

Owner Marie Denton, ably assisted by her sister Victoria, has been here since October of 2002. Her first improvement was to have the front area of the inn completely refurbished, to incorporate traditional features such as the exposed beamwork, reinstating the flagstone floors and updating the décor and furnishings to offer guests the very best in comfort and quality. The ambience is always friendly, relaxed and welcoming here. The well-tended beer garden is just the place to enjoy a pleasant drink or meal on fine days.

The two real ales – Black Sheep and

Tetleys - are accompanied by a good range of draught keg bitters, lagers, cider, stout, wines, spirits and soft drinks.

Marie does all the cooking, creating traditional favourites and more innovative dishes, all using the freshest ingredients, locally sourced whenever possible. Guests choose off the menu or specials board. Steaks are the speciality here, but there are also very good variation of other dishes, including vegetarian. Booking is required for Friday evenings. Children welcome.

The area around Markington is particularly well endowed with castles and grand ecclesiastical buildings: the magnificent Cathedral of St Peter and St Wilfrid at Ripon, the imposing ruins of Knaresborough Castle, Ripley Castle set in a lovely Capability Brown landscape, Robert Adam's Newby Hall at Skelton, and the evocative ruins of Fountains Abbey.

🕐 Mon-Sat 12.00-15.00, 18.00-23.00;
Sun 12.00-15.00, 19.00-22.30

🍴 Mon-Sun 12.00-14.00; Mon-Weds
and Fri-Sun 19.00-21.00

🅿 Beer garden, off-road parking

🎵 Occasional karaoke, discos, quiz
and pool nights – please ring for
details

❓ Harrogate 8 miles, Ripon 6 miles

THE CROWN & ANCHOR

138 FRONT STREET, SOWERBY, THIRSK, NORTH YORKSHIRE YO7 1JN
TEL: 01845 522448

> **Directions:** 1 mile south of the centre of Thirsk off the B1448

Situated in the heart of this lovely village which boasts Georgian houses, an old packhorse bridge, the lovely Millgate Gardens and attractive footpaths that lead across fields and alongside a quiet stream, **The Crown & Anchor** was built in the mid-19th century on the site of an earlier public house known as The Flying Horse. The handsome brickbuilt exterior presents an impressive face to the world, while inside, the tasteful décor and furnishings enhance the inn's welcoming ambience. Cosy and clean, it makes a wonderfully relaxing place to enjoy a great meal or drink.

The two real ales at this fine pub are John Smiths Cask and a changing guest ale, which along with a good range of lagers, cider, stout, wines, spirits and soft drinks means there's something to wet every whistle.

Food is available every day, from opening time until closing, and guests choose from a menu that includes bar snacks and pizza dishes. The pizzas are home-prepared and delicious, and can be enjoyed at the inn or as take-aways. Children are welcome.

Tenants Sue and Mark share the cooking, and bring enthusiasm and an understanding of the importance of quality and service to running this fine inn. A local couple, this is their first venture into this type of business, though Sue worked here for two years before they took over as tenants back in 2001. Friendly and helpful, they and their capable staff offer warm hospitality to all their guests, and have built up an enviable reputation for the pub.

- 🕐 Mon-Sat 11.00-23.00; Sun 12.00-22.30
- 🍴 Daily, all day
- 🅿 Beer garden, off-road parking, children's play area
- 🎵 Live entertainment Friday and Saturday from 9 p.m. – please ring for details
- @ markandsuesbar@hotmail.com
- ❓ Thirsk 1 mile, Sion Hill 5 miles, Sutton Bank 5 miles, Ripon 10 miles, Northallerton 10 miles, Rievaulx Abbey 12 miles

The City of York & Central Yorkshire

THE DURHAM OX

WESTWAY, CRAYKE, YORK, NORTH YORKSHIRE YO61 4TE
TEL: 01347 821506 FAX: 01347 823326

Directions: From York take the A19 to Easingwold. In Easingwold main street, turn right through the marketplace and straight up the hill to Crayke. Or take the B1363 and turn left at Stillington, then the first right to Crayke..

The Durham Ox in Crayke is a delightful, convivial inn offering great food, drink, accommodation and hospitality. Three hundred years old and situated on the hill of 'Grand Old Duke of York' fame, the inn is located in a marvellous village with redbrick houses and 15th century church and castle. Two huge open fires in ancient stone fireplaces, flagstone floors, oak panelling and antique furnishings enhance the wonderfully atmospheric setting for relaxation and enjoying top-quality, freshly prepared dishes using the pick of

the local produce. The superb menu is complemented by Early Bird specials and Fish and Chip dinners. Booking advised at all times at this justly popular eatery.

Four real ales on tap – John Smiths Cask, Theakstons Black Bull and two changing guest ales – are complemented by a good choice of lagers, cider, stout, wines, spirits and soft drinks.

The accommodation is luxurious, within cottages at the rear of the premises. Suites comprise two large bedrooms (double or twin), Jacuzzi bath, lounge and galley kitchen, suitable for four guests; junior suites feature double rooms, suitable for two. 'The General's Quarters', with a double room, adjacent twin bedroom and bath, is ideal for families and located within the inn itself. Pampering touches include the wrought-iron beds, fresh fruit, chocolates and a library of tapes for the video TV. See the inn's website for more details.

🕐 Mon-Sat 11.00-15.00, 17.00-23.00; Sun 12.00-15.00, 19.00-22.30

🍽 Mon-Sun 12.00-14.30; Mon-Fri 18.00-21.30, Sat 18.00-22.00, Sun 18.00-20.30

£ Visa, Mastercard, Switch, Delta, Amex, Diners, Access, Eurocard, Solo

🛏 Cottages – see main text

Ⓟ Patio area, shop selling local produce

🎵 Live music Thurs and Sun evenings

@ enquiries@thedurhamox.com www.thedurhamox.com

❓ Easingwold 4 miles, Sutton Park 6 miles, Newburgh Priory 8 miles, Castle Howard 7 miles, York 12 miles, golf, shooting, riding, walking

MAIN STREET, WATH, RIPON, NORTH YORKSHIRE HG4 5EN
TEL: 01765 6400202 FAX: 01765 640632

Directions: From Ripon take the A61; after about 1 mile turn left on to minor road signposted Wath, or turn left 1 mile further along and reach Wath through Melmerby. Also can be reached east off the A6108, turning at West Tanfield.

The eye-catching exterior of **The George Country Inn** in the heart of the village of Wath is a welcoming sight. A hub of village life, this attractive inn, dating back to the 18th century, has picnic tables and tubs of flowers outside while inside, the bar area is cosy and comfortable, with stone fireplaces, exposed beams, leather armchairs and all the character of a traditional village pub.

There are two real ales to savour – Tetley and Black Sheep – as well as a good range of draught keg bitters, lagers, cider, stout, wines, spirits and soft drinks.

The décor changes as you step into the restaurant area, home of the Thai House at Wath, where all is decorated and furnished as befits the Far East. Here in this truly international Thai restaurant, where authentic Thai cuisine runs alongside quality English dishes, the excellent chefs prepare a range of delicacies that have earned high praise from local and national food critics. The extensive menu includes beef, chicken, seafood and vegetarian dishes, all expertly prepared to order with the freshest ingredients. Booking is required at weekends.

The inn also boasts six excellent en suite guest bedrooms, all spacious and comfortable, and the tariff includes a hearty breakfast. Special weekend breaks are available. The George Country Inn is run by Stuart and A Marr, who have a wealth of experience in the trade and take pride in making all their guests feel most welcome. They and their courteous, attentive staff provide excellent service and hospitality.

- Weds-Mon 12.00-15.00; Mon-Sat 17.00-23.00; Sun 17.00-22.30
- Weds-Mon 12.00-14.30 and 19.00-22.30
- All major except for Diners
- Six rooms en suite
- Off-road parking, beer garden
- georgecountryinn.wath@btopenworld.com
- Norton Conyers 1 mile, Ripon 3 miles, North Stainley 2 miles, Lightwater Theme Park 2 miles

THE GOLD CUP INN

NETHER SILTON, NR THIRSK, NORTH YORKSHIRE YO7 2JZ
TEL: 01609 883416 FAX: 01609 883692

Directions: 3½ miles off the A1, north of Thirsk

Named after the famous horse race that ran for many years during the 18th and 19th century, **The Gold Cup Inn** occupies a picture-postcard setting across from the village green in the charming Nether Silton. One of the most sought-after villages to live in in North Yorkshire, this beautiful place is also handy for many of the area's most favoured sights and attractions, including Rievaulx Abbey and Terrace, Thirsk itself, Northallerton, Ripon, Sowerby and beyond. The inn is particularly popular with walkers as well as locals and visitors from near and far. The quality interior is superbly decorated and furnished, and boasts a cosy and intimate

restaurant as well as the traditional bar and lounge areas. Two real ales – John Smiths Cask plus a changing guest ale – are complemented by a range of draught keg bitters, lagers, cider, stout, wines, spirits and soft drinks.

After many years in the corporate entertainment business, owner Ronnie Bennett took over at the inn in December of 2002. He and his dedicated staff offer the highest standard of quality and service. Friendly and welcoming, they offer all their guests genuine hospitality. The top-of-the-range cuisine is available Wednesday to Saturday evenings and for lunch Friday to Sunday. Ronnie does all the cooking, and his speciality is charcoal-grilled steaks, made from meat supplied by the very good local butcher. The menu and specials board include a good selection to tempt every palate. The restaurant area is no-smoking and children are welcome.

- 🕐 Mon-Thurs 17.00-23.00; Fri-Sat 11.00-15.00, 17.00-23.00; Sun and Bank Hols 12.00-15.00, 19.00-22.30
- 🍴 Fri-Sat 12.00-14.00; Weds-Sat 18.00-21.00; Sun 12.00-16.00
- £ Visa, Mastercard, Switch, Delta, Eurocard, Solo
- 🅿 Off-road parking
- 🎵 Quiz night Weds from 9 p.m.; monthly themed food evenings on a Monday – please ring for details/to book
- ❓ Thirsk 4 miles, Sowerby 5 miles, Northallerton 8 miles, Ripon 12 miles, Rievaulx Abbey and Terrace 15 miles

MAIN STREET, ELVINGTON, YORK, NORTH YORKSHIRE YO41 4AG
TEL: 01904 608335 FAX: 01904 607961

> **Directions:** From junction 47 of the M1, take the A59 towards York and the A64, then the B1228. Elvington is on the B1228 some six miles southeast of York

The Grey Horse Inn is a picture-postcard village inn, opposite the village green and dating back to the late 18th century. Whitewashed and pristine, with picnic tables, hanging baskets and window boxes adorning the frontage, this fine inn is equally charming inside, where a wealth of wood, subtle lighting and cosy seating enhances the welcoming ambience. The lounge area has plush leather sofas, while upstairs is the bright and stylish Hayloft Restaurant with its warm yellow walls adorned with watercolours, pale wood furniture, and intimate atmosphere. There's lots of bygone memorabilia on display such as old photographs of village life. Owner

Bob Sykes collects antique clocks, and there are many on display to admire throughout the inn.

CAMRA (York Branch) Country Pub of the Year in 2000, there are five real ales on tap here at this excellent Free House – John Smiths, Timothy Taylor Landlord, Black Sheep and two changing guest ales. Guests can also choose from a good range of lagers, cider, stout, wines, spirits and soft drinks.

Excellent food is available from the menu or specials board, with a range of tempting dishes which are complemented by the delicious starters and sweets. All dishes are expertly prepared and presented by the inn's team of professional chefs. Booking is required at weekends. Two en suite guest rooms – a double and a family room – are available all year round and offer superb accommodation with full facilities.

- 🕐 Mon-Fri 12.00-14.30, 17.30-23.00; Sat 12.00-23.00; Sun 12.00-22.30
- 🍴 Mon-Sat 12.00-14.00, 18.00-21.00; Sun 12.00-15.00, 18.00-21.00
- £ Visa, Mastercard, Switch, Delta, Eurocard, Solo
- P Off-road parking
- 🛏 2 guest rooms en suite
- ♫ Quiz night Thursdays from around 9 p.m.
- @ thegreyhorsepub@hotmail.com
- ? York 6 miles, Selby 10 miles, Market Weighton 12 miles, Beverley 23 miles

THE HARE INN

SCAWTON, THIRSK, NORTH YORKSHIRE YO7 2HG
TEL: 01845 597289 FAX: 01845 597158

Directions: 1 mile off the A170 Thirsk-to-Helmsley Road, close to Sutton Bank

One of the prettiest inns you'll come across, **The Hare Inn** in Scawton occupies a very scenic, secluded location. The premises date back to the 12th century and are mentioned in the Domesday Book. Built of the same local stone as nearby Rievaulx Abbey, this superior inn is impressive inside and out. The interior is divided into several cosy, charming rooms with original features such as low beams and flagstone floors adding to the welcoming ambience.

There are three real ales served here – Timothy Taylor Landlord, Black Sheep and a changing guest ale – together with a selection of lagers, cider, stout, wines, spirits and soft drinks. Very popular for its excellent food, the inn employs three qualified professional chefs. Meals are served every day at lunch and dinner, with tempting dishes such as roasted monkfish, char-grilled sirloin steak, Caribbean chicken, oven-roasted duck breast, mushroom tagliatelle and cold poached salmon. The mouth-watering desserts like lemon posset with homemade shortbread, strawberry tart and dark chocolate truffle terrine are also well worth leaving room for. Booking is required every evening and for Sunday lunch. Owners Maggie and Lloyd have a wealth of experience, and they and their capable, friendly staff offer a high standard of service and quality together with warm hospitality.

Excellent accommodation is available in a purpose-built Norwegian-style log cabin, let at a bed and breakfast rate. Breakfast is taken in the inn. Sleeping four, the cabin is comfortably and tastefully decorated and furnished, and makes a relaxing and enjoyable retreat.

- 🕐 Mon-Sat 11.00-15.00, 17.00-23.00; Sun 12.00-15.00, 19.00-22.30. Summer: Mon-Sat 11.00-23.00; Sun 12.00-22.30
- 🍴 Every day 12.00-14.30, 18.30-21.00
- £ Visa, Mastercard, Switch, Delta, Eurocard, Solo
- Ⓟ Off-road parking, beer garden, function room
- @ www.thehareinn.co.uk
- ❓ Rievaulx Abbey 2 miles, Helmsley 4 miles, Thirsk 8 miles, Castle Howard 12 miles, Malton 15 miles, Pickering 15 miles

THE JOLLY MILLER

KELLINGTON LANE, EGGBOROUGH, NR SELBY,
NORTH YORKSHIRE DN14 0LB
TEL: 01977 661348

Directions: From junction 34 of the M62, near Whitley Bridge, it's half a mile to the village of Eggborough.

Just minutes from the M62, **The Jolly Miller** makes a convenient and convivial place to stop off and enjoy a quiet drink, good food and great hospitality. Traditional inside and out, this large and charming inn has a white-washed exterior with hanging baskets and picnic tables on the side patio, while inside there are real fires, lots of local memorabilia, a piano and comfortable seating. Hosts Tracey Meekin and David Clive are a local couple from Selby who have been the tenants here since early in 2003. They've brought with them over 15 years' experience in catering and the licensing trade. Together with their capable, friendly staff, they offer their guests a warm welcome and great service.

A great favourite with locals and visitors alike, the real ale here is Tetley's Cask. Guests can also choose from

draught keg ales such as Carlsberg, Kronenberg, Fosters John Smiths Smooth and Tetley's Smooth, together with cider, stout, wines, spirits and soft drinks. Tracy is also the chef, putting together delicious meals including specialities such as homemade steak-and-kidney and steak-and-ale pies. Guests choose off a menu of tempting favourites on weeknights, while on Sundays there's a choice of three roasts. Children are welcome in the separate dining room, which seats 32.

Handy for sightseeing in the region, with local attractions such as the Aire & Calder Canal, Yorkshire Garden World in West Haddesley, Whitley Bridge and Selby itself, and Pontefract, Castleford and Leeds not much further afield, this inn is a great place to spend a few pleasant hours.

- 🕐 Mon-Fri 16.00-23.00; Sat 11.00-23.00; Sun 12.00-22.30
- 🍴 Mon-Fri 18.00-20.30; Sun (Carvery) 11.30-14.00
- 🅿 Patio area, off-road parking
- 🎵 Quiz night Wednesdays from 9 p.m.
- ❓ Selby 9 miles, Pontefract 7 miles, Hull-Leeds Railway and the Aire & Calder Canal, Yorkshire Garden World 5 miles

KINGS ARMS

MAIN STREET, NORTH DUFFIELD, NORTH YORKSHIRE YO8 5RG
TEL: 01757 288492

Directions: From Selby take the A19 north and then the A163 east.

In a beautiful setting in the heart of this picturesque village, opposite the village green and duck pond, the **Kings Arms** in North Duffield dates back to the late 18th century. Large and impressive, this handsome whitewashed inn has a lovely garden to one side, perfect for enjoying a relaxing drink or meal on fine days. Inside, the walls are painted in subtle period colours, enhancing the original features and complementing the cosy ambience. The décor and furnishings throughout this fine pub are of a high standard of comfort and quality.

Tenants Glenn and Gail have been here since April 2003, bringing with them over 18 years' experience in the licensing trade. Their expertise shows in the warm hospitality and excellent service they and their friendly staff offer all their guests. To drink, there are five real ales available. Regulars are Black Sheep, Greene King Abbot, Timothy Taylor Landlord and John Smiths, and there's a changing guest ale. Thirsty punters can also choose from a good range of lagers, cider, stouts, wines, spirits and soft drinks.

The no-smoking restaurant seats 24. Gail does the cooking, creating a variety of delicious dishes at lunchtime every day and at dinner Monday to Saturday. Specialities include homemade steak pie, mixed grills, and plaice stuffed with prawns and mushrooms. On Sundays, Sunday lunch is added to the normal menu. Guests choose off the menu or specials board. Booking required Friday and Saturday evening. Children are welcome.

There are many local sights and attractions in this lovely part of the county and this fine pub is a relaxing and welcome stopping-off point for anyone sightseeing in the area.

🕐 Mon-Sat 11.00-23.00; Sun 12.00-22.30

🍴 Mon-Sat 12.00-15.00, 18.00-21.00; Sun 12.00-16.00

£ Visa, Mastercard, Switch, Delta, Amex, Eurocard, Solo

🅿 Off-road parking, beer garden

🎵 Quiz night Sundays from 9 p.m.

❓ Selby 5 miles, Sutton upon Derwent 5 miles, Elvington 7 miles, York 10 miles

MOTHER SHIPTON INN

LOW BRIDGE, KNARESBOROUGH, NORTH YORKSHIRE HG5 8HZ
TEL: 01423 862157

> **Directions:** At the main traffic lights in the centre of Knaresborough, turn into Gracious Street. Follow this road for about half a mile, cross the bridge and Mother Shipton Inn is on your right..

Dating back to 1645, the **Mother Shipton Inn** takes its name from the famous local prophetess born in 1488 and said to have had the gift of second sight. Mother Shipton's Cave, a renowned tourist attraction in which she is said to have been born, is now located to the rear of the inn, though for centuries visitors had to pass through the inn and sign the visitors book, which boasts the names of Royal personages such as Queen Anne and other leading lights of English history. The interior is charming and traditional, with lots of bygone memorabilia on display.

Leaseholders Emma and Ross have put this charming place back on the map, having taken over in August 2002, and they and their staff offer all their guests great hospitality. There's always a minimum of five real ales on tap, as well as a selection of lagers, wines, spirits, cider, stout and soft drinks.

Delicious home-made food draws visitors from near and far. The lunchtime menu features soups, sandwiches, jacket potatoes, salads and hot dishes while at dinner the menu offers tempting options like steaks, lasagne (beef or vegetarian), chicken in cider, Barnsley chop and a 'Shiptons Mighty Mixed Grill'. Specials and mouth-watering puddings are listed on blackboards. Booking required on Saturday evenings. Children welcome. There is an excellent family room available, and a separate no-smoking restaurant seating 24. Entertainments include the quiz night on Monday evenings, which includes a free supper.

- 🕐 Winter: Mon-Sat 11.00-15.00, 17.00-23.00; Sun 12.00-15.00, 19.00-22.30. Summer: Mon-Sat 11.00-23.00; Sun 12.00-22.30
- 🍴 Tues-Sat and Bank Hols 11.30-14.30, 18.00-21.00; Sun 12.00-15.00
- £ Visa, Mastercard, Switch, Delta, Access, Eurocard, Solo
- Ⓟ Patio area, family room
- 🎵 Quiz night Mon; barbecue and themed cocktails every other Sat in summer (weather permitting)
- ❓ Knaresborough 1 miles, Harrogate 4 miles, Wetherby 7 miles

THE NAGS HEAD

56 HEWORTH ROAD, HEWORTH, YORK,
NORTH YORKSHIRE YO31 0AD
TEL: 01904 422989 FAX: 01904 413354

Directions: Heworth is just a short drive or walk east from the centre of York, off the A1079

Situated in Heworth, a superb village within the conurbation of York, **The Nags Head** dates back to the early 19th century. Large and impressive, it is bedecked with hanging baskets and window boxes in spring and summer, presenting a welcoming face to all guests.

This convivial pub is popular with locals and visitors alike, not least for its handsome decor and comfortable furnishings. There's lots of bygone memorabilia on display, and plenty of brass ornaments to admire. Cosy and comfortable, there's a warm welcome assured for everyone. The two real ales here are John Smiths Cask and Magnet. Guests can also choose from a range of draught keg lagers, ciders, stout, wines, spirits and soft drinks. Food is served every day at lunch and Monday to Saturday evening. The menu and specials board offer a good and varied choice of dishes, and the Sunday carvery roast is justly popular. The no-smoking conservatory dining area seats 20.

There are five attractive and welcoming guest bedrooms – a family room, a double, two twins and a single - in an adjacent annex, so guests can come and go as they please. The inn is of course ideally situated for anyone exploring York itself, but is also within easy driving distance of Easingwold, Tadcaster, Selby, Harrogate and many picturesque villages in the region.

Leaseholders James Melsom and George Forman have been here since 2001. They and their friendly staff offer a high standard of service and hospitality.

- 🕐 Mon-Sat 11.00-23.00; Sun 12.00-22.30
- 🍴 Mon-Sat 12.00-14.30, 17.30-20.00; Sun 12.00-16.00
- 💷 Visa, Mastercard, Switch, Delta, Access, Eurocard, Solo
- 🛏 5 en suite rooms
- 🅿 Off-road parking
- 🎵 General knowledge quiz Tues; music quiz Thur; Sky sports
- @ www.nagshead.co.uk
- ❓ York 1 mile, Stamford Bridge 5 miles, Easingwold 15 miles, Tadcaster 15 miles, Selby 12 miles

101 HIGH STREET, SOUTH MILFORD, NORTH YORKSHIRE LS25 5AQ
TEL: 01977 682367

Directions: From Pontefract take the A628 towards Knottingley, then take the A0162 to South Milford

The Queen O' T'owd Thatch is a quality public house standing in the centre of the village of South Milford, just off the A162. Gracious and elegant inside and out, the inn is welcoming, with a relaxed ambience that enhances enjoyment of your pint. Dating back in parts to the year 1760, we must of course include a few words about its name: quite simply, it was once the largest thatched property in the village, and though the thatching is gone, the name remains – though is usually affectionately shortened to 'The Thack'. Tenants Janet and Clive have been here since early in 2002. The licensing trade runs through Janet's family, as her brother is the licensee of the nearby Crooked Billet, also featured in this book.

There are three real ales sold here – John Smiths Cask along with two changing guest ales – together with a good choice of lagers, stout, cider, wines,

spirits and soft drinks, to quench any thirst. A full Sunday lunch is the only meal served, (although mid week meals will be available early in 2004), but it's quite the treat, with a choice of at least six main courses, along with starters and desserts. Clive does all the cooking, using the freshest ingredients, locally sourced whenever possible. Booking is advised. The dining area is very cosy and comfortable, painted in warm colours and adorned with features such as an open fire and sideboard that give it the feeling of a traditional country kitchen. There are also picnic tables to the front, in a delightful patio area sheltered by large hedgerows and trees, where guests can enjoy their meal or drink on fine days. Children are welcome.

There's live entertainment on Saturday nights, and this excellent pub is also a good stopping-off place while exploring the area.

- 🕐 Mon-Fri 16.00-23.00; Sat 12.00-23.00; Sun 12.00-22.30
- 🍴 Sun 12.00-16.00
- 🅿 Off-road parking
- 🎵 Live music Sat from 20.30
- ❓ Knottingley 4 miles, Pontefract 5 miles, Castleford 5 miles, Leeds 10 miles

THE ROCKINGHAM ARMS

TOWTON, NR TADCASTER, NORTH YORKSHIRE LS24 9PB
TEL/FAX: 01937 832811

The City of York & Central Yorkshire

Directions: From Tadcaster take the A162 due south for two miles to Towton.

The Rockingham Arms is a distinguished and distinctive traditional pub dating back in parts to 1650 and named after a past Queen's Earl Marshal. Large and spacious, the exterior is adorned with attractive hanging baskets all year round, and its pale yellow paintwork increases its friendly, wholesome appeal.

The décor and furnishings are high in quality and comfort throughout this excellent pub. Bold paintwork above the brickbuilt fireplace and a wealth of ornaments add to the cosy, rustic feel. Equestrian prints and other homely touches combine to convey a relaxed and very pleasant ambience. One unusual feature is the circular, revolving pool table in the bar area. Outside, the beer garden is a real sun-trap.

The pub is run by a lovely couple who have been here since 1984 as tenants, and who have a wealth of local knowledge and are friendly and welcoming to all their guests. They have built up a fine reputation for service, excellent food and ales, and genuine hospitality. The real ale on tap is John Smiths Cask, while there's also a good range of lagers, cider, stout, wines, spirits and soft drinks.

Food is served every day at lunch and dinner. The pub is known not just county-wide, but country-wide for its fish and chips and its sirloin steaks - mouth-watering treats that should not be missed. There are no-smoking areas, and children are welcome. Other delights of the menu include 12-inch pizzas, hot and cold sandwiches, gammon, and more.

- 🕐 Mon-Sat 11.00-15.00, 17.00-23.00; Sun 12.00-22.30
- 🍴 Mon-Sat 12.00-14.00, 18.00-21.00; Sun 12.00-20.00
- Ⓟ Beer garden, off-road parking
- ♫ Sport quiz Fridays from 10 p.m.; general knowledge quiz and 'high/low' card game Sundays from 9.30 p.m.; darts Tuesdays; dominos Thursdays
- @ therockinghamarms@yahoo.co.uk
- ❓ Tadcaster 2 miles, Boston Spa 6 miles, Wetherby 8 miles, York 11 miles, Leeds 13 miles, Harrogate 15 miles

OAK LANE, DACRE BANKS, HARROGATE, NORTH YORKSHIRE HG3 4EN
TEL: 01423 780200 FAX: 01423 781748

> **Directions:** From Harrogate take the A59 west for 6 miles, then turn right onto the B6451 and follow this road for 3 miles

The Royal Oak Inn brings to life all that is best about a traditional coaching inn: the cosy bar has open fires, low timber beams, stone floors and exposed stone walls, while the atmosphere is always relaxed and welcoming. Family owned and run by Steve, his partner Anna and Anna's parents Pete and Pat, they and their friendly staff provide excellent hospitality to guests from far and wide. The four real ales on tap include Yorkshire Dales bitter and Nidderdale best bitter plus two changing guest ales. There's also a good selection of lagers, cider, stout, wines, spirits and soft drinks as well as a collection of malt whiskies and a range of cocktails. The high standards have been recognised by the *Good Beer Guide* and the *Good Pub Guide*. Guests can sit in comfort and read the numerous quotations and old sayings

about food and drink painted on the beams and oak panels, and on a sunny day there's the lovely terrace garden, with superb views.

The inn also boasts a restaurant seating 70, and there's further room in Eric's Pantry (both non-smoking). Guests can also eat outside in two separate areas. Choosing off the printed menu or specials board, all meals are expertly prepared by Jon, the excellent chef. A wide selection of tempting dishes using the freshest locally-sourced seasonal produce is available. Reservations are essential at weekends. Favourites include steak and kidney pie, rabbit pie and Nidderdale trout.

The accommodation comprises two twins and one double room, all well-appointed and comfortable. Rated 4 Diamonds by the ETB, the tariff includes a delicious breakfast. Special deals are available. Children welcome.

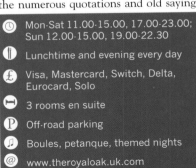

- 🕐 Mon-Sat 11.00-15.00, 17.00-23.00; Sun 12.00-15.00, 19.00-22.30
- 🍴 Lunchtime and evening every day
- £ Visa, Mastercard, Switch, Delta, Eurocard, Solo
- 🛏 3 rooms en suite
- Ⓟ Off-road parking
- ♫ Boules, petanque, themed nights
- @ www.theroyaloak.uk.com
- ❓ Harrogate

THE WELLINGTON HEIFER

AINDERBY STEEPLE, NORTHALLERTON,
NORTH YORKSHIRE DL7 9PU
TEL: 01609 775542 FAX: 01609 761683

Directions: From Northallerton take the A684 southwest towards Bedale to Ainderby Steeple.

Situated in the lovely village of Ainderby Steeple across from the church, **The Wellington Heifer** is a picture-postcard inn with scenic views over open countryside. This former coaching inn dates back to the early 1700s and is full of atmosphere. The interior – bar, no-smoking lounge, and no-smoking restaurant – is handsomely decorated and furnished throughout and features exposed brickwork, open fires and other attractive features, enhancing the inn's welcoming ambience.

After a career in the RAF, leaseholder Bob Hedley retired in 2002 and he and his wife Cath took over here. Chef

Damien has been here since 2000, and prepares excellent meals at lunch and dinner featuring a good selection of delicious dishes. Specialities include Wensleydale chicken and home-made steak and ale pie made with Black Sheep bitter. Booking required on Sundays. Children welcome. Weekday specials are available at lunchtime, featuring two courses for a special price. Other deals include the Senior Citizens special two-course lunches on Monday, Tuesday and Wednesday. Party menus – for groups of more than six – are available all year round.

Three ales are on tap – Tetleys, Black Sheep and a changing guest ale – and are complemented by a good choice of lagers, cider, stout, wines, spirits and soft drinks. All proceeds from the quiz nights – held once a fortnight on Sunday evening – go to the Great North Air Ambulance Charity.

🕐	Mon-Sat 11.00-15.00, 17.00-23.00; Sun 12.00-15.00, 19.00-22.30
🍴	Mon-Sat 11.30-14.00, 18.00-21.00; Sun 12.00-14.00, 18.00-21.00
£	Visa, Mastercard, Switch, Delta, Access, Eurocard, Solo
Ⓟ	Off-road parking
🛏	2 en suite rooms
🎵	Quiz once a fortnight, Sun – see main text for details
@	catelou@fsmail.net Z:\Hotel\hotels\wellingtonheifer.html
❓	Northallerton 2 miles, Catterick Racecourse 13 miles, golfing, fishing, horse-riding

THE WHITE HORSE INN

THE GREEN, UPPER POPPLETON, YORK,
NORTH YORKSHIRE YO26 6DF
TEL: 01904 606921

> **Directions:** Upper Poppleton is found close to where the A1237 (the York ring road) meets the A59..

The White Horse Inn is a superb pub overlooking the village green in the picturesque village of Upper Poppleton. A public house has been recorded on this site for hundreds of years, though the present building dates from 1903. Leaseholders Greg and Julie Watson have been here since 1999, serving up excellent drink and food, and, together with their dedicated and hardworking staff, offering warm and genuine hospitality to all their guests.

The exterior presents a welcoming and impressive sight and has recently been given a facelift including a stylish patio area, beer garden and well-equipped secure children's play area. Inside, all is cosy and comfortable. The long polished wood bar, brick fireplace and attractive seating all add to the ambience.

The two real ales here are John Smiths and Bass, while there's also a good selection of draught keg bitters, lagers, cider, stout, spirits, wines and soft drinks. Food is served every lunchtime and evening except Sunday. Booking advised on Friday and Saturday evenings. Children welcome. Guests can dine throughout the inn, but the 24 seat conservatory is no-smoking. Guests choose off the menu or specials board from a range of delicious freshly prepared meals cooked to order. The Sunday roast is justly popular.

As befits a pub at the heart of village life, this convivial inn supports local groups such as The Poppleton Players and Poppleton United Football Club.

- ⏰ Mon-Fri 11.30-23.00; Sat 11.00-23.00; Sun 12.00-22.30
- 🍴 Mon-Sat 12.00-14.00, Sun 12.00-14.30; Mon-Wed 19.00-21.00, Thur-Sat 18.00-21.00
- £ Visa, Mastercard, Switch, Delta, Eurocard, Solo
- Ⓟ Beer garden, patio area, children's play area, parking
- ♪ Quiz night Mondays; occasional musical evenings – please ring for details
- @ whitehorseinn@tesco.net
- ? York 4 miles, Tadcaster 10 miles, Harrogate 20 miles

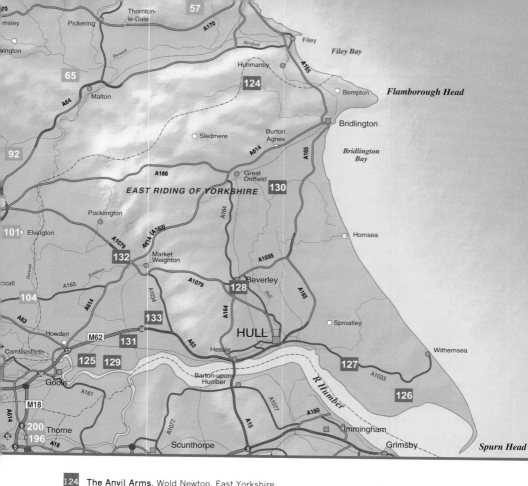

124 **The Anvil Arms**, Wold Newton, East Yorkshire

125 **The Bricklayers Arms & Stables Restaurant**, Laxton, East Yorkshire

126 **The Burns Head Inn**, Patrington Haven , East Yorkshire

127 **The Crooked Billet**, Ryehill, East Yorkshire

128 **The Foresters Arms**, Beverley, East Yorkshire

129 **The Hope & Anchor**, Blacktoft, East Yorkshire

130 **The Plough Inn**, Foston-on-the-Wolds, Driffield, East Yorkshire

131 **The Railway Hotel**, Gilberdyke, Brough, East Yorkshire

132 **The Ship Inn**, Shiptonthorpe, East Yorkshire

133 **The White Hart Inn**, North Cave, Brough, East Yorkshire

Please note all cross references refer to page numbers

THE EAST RIDING AND NORTH HUMBERSIDE

The East Riding of Yorkshire tends to be overlooked by many visitors: it has none of the spectacular moorland and dale scenery of the North York Moors or the Yorkshire Dales, appears to lack the sophistication of Harrogate, Leeds and the county's other major

The Humber Bridge

towns and cities and, perhaps, more importantly, it is not on route to anywhere else. However, those who overlook East Yorkshire will find that they are missing out on discovering charming agricultural villages, a rich history and architectural gems such as Beverley Minster.

To the south and east of Beverley lies the old Land of Holderness whose name comes from Viking times: a 'hold' was a man of high rank in the Danelaw and 'ness' has stayed in the language and means promontory. This area is quite different from any other in Yorkshire and its flat, wide plain has been fighting an incessant, and losing battle, with the North Sea that forms its eastern border. Gradually, the coastline is being eroded away and the southern tip, Spurn Head, is constantly being rearranged by the winter storms. However, this promontory protects the entrance to the River Humber that has, for centuries, been a major route inland. Here, on the northern banks lies the great port of Hull, more formally known as Kingston-upon-Hull, which first realised its potential when Edward I purchased land here from the monasteries to create a supply depot during his journey north to hammer the Scots. Still a major port, today, Hull is best known for the impressive Humber Bridge that lies just upstream; it was also the birthplace of the slavery abolitionist William Wilberforce.

BEMPTON

At 400 feet high, **Bempton Cliffs** mark the northernmost tip of the great belt of chalk that runs diagonally across England from the Isle of Wight to Flamborough Head. The sheer cliffs at Bempton provide an ideal nesting place for huge colonies of fulmars, guillemots, kittiwakes, razorbills, puffins and Britain's largest seabird, the gannet. In Victorian times, a popular holiday sport was to shoot the birds from boats while, above them, crowds gathered to watch gangs of 'climmers' make a hair-raising descent by rope down the cliffs to gather the birds' eggs. The climmers also massacred kittiwakes in their thousands as kittiwake feathers were highly prized as accessories for hats and for stuffing mattresses. The first Bird Protection Act of 1869 was specifically designed to protect the kittiwakes at Bempton: although a ban on collecting eggs here did not come into force until 1954. Bempton Cliffs are now an RSPB bird sanctuary, a refuge during the April to August breeding season for more than 200,000 seabirds making this the largest colony in Britain.

Bempton Cliffs RSPB Bird Sanctuary

BEVERLEY

An attractive market town, Beverley was once the capital of Yorkshire's East Riding and it still retains its strong trading links with busy general and cattle markets. With a long history that dates

Beverley Minster

was established in the early 12th century, is also richly endowed with fine carvings, many of them brightly coloured, and striking sculptures. Lewis Carroll visited St Mary's when he stayed with friends in the town and was very taken with a stone carving of a rabbit – the inspiration, it is believed, for the March Hare in *Alice in Wonderland*.

back to before the Norman invasion, the town was, in the Middle Ages, one of the country's most prosperous and, today, it is a delightful architectural blend of past and present. The town's horizon is dominated by two key buildings: the medieval St Mary's Church and its majestic Minster whose twin towers soar over the old town. Founded in around 705, the **Beverley Minster** of today dates from 1220, as the previous building was destroyed by a great fire in 1188, and it took over 200 years to complete. As a result, the Minster provides a textbook demonstration of the evolving architectural styles of those decades. Among its many treasures are the superb wood carvings from the Ripon school and a 1,000 year old fridstool, or sanctuary seat, carved from a single block of stone. Unlike the plain-cut fridstool, the stone canopy of the 14th century Percy Shrine is elaborately decorated with carvings, and the Minster also contains a wealth of wood carvings.

Built with the backing of the town's musical guilds, **St Mary's Church**, which

The wide market square in the heart of the town is graced by an elegant Market Cross, a circular pillared building that bears the arms of Queen Anne in whose reign it was built at the expense of the town's two Members of Parliament. At that time, of course, parliamentary elections were flagrantly corrupt but at Beverley the tradition continued longer than in most places and, in 1868, the author Anthony Trollope stood as a candidate here, but was defeated in what was widely acknowledged as a breathtakingly fraudulent election.

The **Guildhall**, nearby, was built in 1762 and is still used as a courtroom and this impressive room has an ornate plasterwork ceiling on which there is an imposing Royal Coat of Arms and also the familiar figure of Justice holding a pair of scales although, unusually, she is not wearing a blindfold. When an 18th century town clerk was asked the reason for this departure from tradition, he replied, "In Beverley, Justice is not blind."

Beverley can boast three separate museums and galleries: the Beverley Art Gallery contains an impressive collection of local works including those by Frederick Elwell RA; the **East Yorkshire Regimental Museum** has six rooms of exhibits chronicling the area's long association with the regiment; and the **Museum of Army Transport** offers visitors a fascinating insight into the history of military transport from the days of the Boer War to the staff car that Field Marshal Montgomery used in France and Germany during World War II.

On the edge of the town is open pasture, Beverley Westwood, which provides a wonderful green belt of land and here, too, can be found **Beverley Racecourse**, where meetings have been taking place since the late 17th century.

The Sands, Bridlington

BRIDLINGTON

Situated at the northern tip of the crescent of hills that form the Wolds, Bridlington, with its 10-mile stretch of sandy beach, award-winning promenades and historic harbour, is certainly one of the country's best loved seaside resorts. Here, there is a mixture of traditional entertainment, such as the funfair, amusement arcades and donkey rides and more modern family attractions like **Leisure World**, an indoor waterpark with wave pool, water slides and tropical rain storm. In the old town, originally known as Burlington, lies **Bridlington Priory**, which was once one of the wealthiest houses in England but was ruthlessly pillage during the Reformation. Externally it is somewhat unprepossessing but, inside, the majestic 13th century nave is unforgettably impressive. Little remains of the priory today except for Bayle Gate, the gatehouse, which survived Henry VIII's dissolution and still stands proudly in the heart of Bridlington's old town. Today, it is home to the **Bayle Museum**, where the long history of the town and its people is brought vividly to life with the help of evocative old paintings, photographs and artefacts.

The seaside resort area of Bridlington was once known as Bridlington Quay and the harbour here is, undoubtedly, the centre of attraction. Pleasure boats steam in and out of the difficult harbour mouth taking visitors to see the splendour of Flamborough Head during the summer while, to the south, are the town's best sandy beaches. Situated in a dramatic cliff top position, on the northern outskirts of Bridlington, is **Sewerby Hall**, a monumental mansion that was built between 1714 and 1720. Set in 50 acres of garden and parkland (where there is also a small zoo), the house was first opened to the public in 1936 by Amy Johnson, the dashing, Yorkshire-born aviatrix who had captured the public imagination by her daring solo flights to South Africa and Australia. The hall is now home to various collections including some fascinating memorabilia of Amy's pioneering feats along with displays of motor vehicles, archaeological finds and some remarkable paintings among which is perhaps the most famous portrait of Queen Henrietta Maria, wife of Charles I. The hall is also the home of the **Museum of East Yorkshire**, which features a photographic gallery and a display of regional history along with a varied programme of regional contemporary arts and crafts.

Close by is **Bondville Miniature Village**, one of the finest model villages in the country and where there are more than 1,000 hand-made and painted characters, over 200 individual and unique villages, and carefully crafted scenes of everyday life, all set in a beautifully landscaped site.

BURTON AGNES

The overwhelming attraction in this unspoilt village is the sublime Eliza-bethan mansion, Burton Agnes Hall, but visitors should not ignore **Burton Agnes Manor House** (English Heritage) that is a rare example of a Norman house: a building of great historical importance but burdened with a grimly functional architecture.

Built between 1598 and 1610, **Burton Agnes Hall** is much more appealing and is particularly famous for its splendid Jacobean gatehouse, wondrously decorated ceilings and overmantels carved in oak, plaster and alabaster. Still lived in by the descendants of Sir Henry Griffith, who had the hall built, it is also home to a valuable collection of paintings and furniture. The equally impressive grounds include a yew topiary, a maze and an old walled garden filled with roses, clematis, herbs and other unusual plants.

FLAMBOROUGH HEAD

Here sea and land are locked in an unremitting battle as the huge waves of the North Sea roll in and slowly but remorselessly wash away the chalk cliffs and the shoreline. Paradoxically, the outcome of this elemental conflict is to produce one of the most picturesque locations on the Yorkshire coast and one that is much visited and much photographed. Victorian travel writers loved Flamborough and not just because of its dramatic scenery but also because of the people who believed in many strange superstitions: no boat would ever set sail on a Sunday, wool could not be wound in lamplight, anyone who mentioned a hare

Flamborough Head

or pig while baiting the fishing lines was inviting doom and no fisherman would leave harbour unless he was wearing a navy-blue jersey, knitted by his wife in a cable, diamond mesh peculiar to the village and one that is still worn today. This fishing connection is renewed here every year, on the second Sunday in October, by a service dedicated to the Harvest of the Sea, when the area's seafarers gather together in a church decorated with crab pots and fishing nets.

Flamborough Head's first, and England's oldest surviving **Lighthouse** was built in 1674 and its beacon was a basket of burning coal. An octagonal chalk tower, it stands on the landward side of the present lighthouse that was con-

structed in 1806 and originally signalled with four white flashes. Developments over the years have included a fog horn, in 1859, and in more recent years, a signal of radio bleeps. Until it was automated in 1995, Flamborough Head was the last manned lighthouse on the east coast.

Just to the north of Flamborough is **Danes Dyke**, a huge rampart four miles long designed to cut off the headland from hostile invaders.

GOOLE

Despite being some 50 miles from the sea, Goole lies at the hub of a waterways network that includes the River Ouse, the River Don (known here as the Dutch River), the River Aire and the Aire and Calder Navigation. Life here is still centred on the docks, locks and canal basins that were built in the early 19th century and, now filled with hundreds of private leisure craft, the docks are still dominated by the distinctive 'Salt and Pepper' water towers. The **Waterways Museum and Adventure Centre,** located on the dockside, tells the story of Goole's development as a canal terminus and port through a series of interactive exhibits and walk-in displays. In the town centre the **Goole Museum and Art Gallery** provides more information on the port and the town.

Further down the River Humber is the **Blacktoft Sands RSPB Reserve** where the lagoons and reedbeds are home to many rare breeding birds including marsh harriers and avocets.

From the **Humber Bridge Country Park** there are superb views of the massive bridge and across the Humber Estuary. A haven for birds, this park is one of their most important feeding grounds on the east coast. The Humber Bridge lies at the southern end of the 79-mile Wolds Way National Trail, a long distance footpath that follows the crescent of the Yorkshire Wolds.

It is here that the River Humber narrows and where the Romans maintained a ferry, the Transitus Maximus, a vital link in the route between Lincoln and York. The ferry remained in operation for almost 2,000 years until it was replaced, in 1981, by the Humber Bridge whose mighty pylons soar more than 800 feet above the village. The great bridge dwarfs Cliff Mill, built in 1810 to mill the local chalk and, although it remained wind-driven, a gas engine was installed in 1925.

HORNSEA

There was a settlement of sorts here before the Norman invasion but, today, it is best known as a seaside town with an excellent sandy beach, a promenade and plenty of amusements and attractions for all the family. The excellent **Hornsea Folk Museum** occupies a Grade II listed former farmhouse and is well worth a visit.

Another popular attraction here is **Hornsea Pottery**, an extensive complex that includes the famous pottery where visitors can watch craftsmen at work and buy their wares. Those looking for peace and tranquillity among all the bustle of this busy seaside town should make for **Hornsea Mere**, where there is an RSPB reserve centred on this large freshwater lake.

HOWDEN

Although not as grand as Yorkshire's other minsters, **Howden Minster**, which was built in the late 13th and early 14th centuries, is a beautiful building despite the chancel and the chapter house having fallen into ruin after the Dissolution. It is one of the largest parish churches in East Yorkshire, and from the top of its soaring 135 foot tower there are wonderful views of the surrounding countryside.

The town itself is a pleasing jumble of narrow, flagged and setted streets with a picturesque stone and brick Market Hall in the market place. The celebrated aircraft designer Barnes Wallis knew Howden well: he lived here while working on the R100 airship that was built at Hedon airfield nearby. It made its maiden flight in 1929 and successfully crossed the Atlantic. Another famous Howden resident was Neville Shute, an aeronautical engineer who also worked on the R100, although he is, perhaps, best known as the author of such stirring novels as A Town Like Alice. At the nearby Breighton Aerodrome is the **Real Aeroplane Museum**, which illustrates the history of flight through the work of Yorkshire aviation pioneers.

About four miles northwest of Howden are the striking remains of **Wressle Castle** that was built in 1380 for Sir Henry Percy and is the only surviving example of a medieval fortified house in East Yorkshire.

HULL

Hull's history as an important port goes back to 1293 when Edward I, travelling north on his way to hammer the Scots, stopped off here and immediately recognised the potential of the muddy junction where the River Hull flows into the Humber. The king bought the land from the monks of Meaux Abbey (at the usual royal discount) and the settlement, henceforth, was known as "Kinges town upon Hull". The port grew steadily through the centuries and, at one time, had the largest fishing fleet of any port in the country with more than 300 trawlers on its register. The primitive facilities were greatly improved by the construction of a state-of-the-art dock in 1778 but, now superseded, that dock has been converted into the handsome **Queen's Gardens**, one of the many attractive open spaces created by this flower-conscious city. The addition to waymarked walks, such as the Maritime Heritage Trail and the **Fish Pavement Trail**, help visitors to make the most of the city's dramatic waterfront.

After a terrible battering during World War II, Hull has risen phoenix-like from the ashes and is,

today, the fastest growing port in England. The port area extends for seven miles along the River Humber with several miles of quays servicing a constant flow of commercial traffic arriving from, or departing for, every quarter of the globe. Every day, a succession of vehicle ferries link the city to the European gateways of Zeebrugge and Rotterdam.

Among a remarkable collection of historic houses, art galleries and museum, perhaps the most evocative is the **Wilberforce House Museum** in the old High Street. It was in this building, in 1759, that William Wilberforce was born and, later, it was from here that he and his father lavished thousands of pounds in bribes to get William elected as Hull's Member of Parliament. There was nothing unusual about that kind of corruption at the time, but William then redeemed himself by his resolute opposition to slavery. His campaign took more than 30 years and William was already on

Hull Marina

his deathbed before a reluctant Parliament finally outlawed the despicable trade. The museum presents a shaming history of the slave trade along with the more uplifting story of Wilberforce's efforts to eliminate it forever.

As a boy, Wilberforce attended the Old Grammar School, which was built in 1583, and this lovely building is now home to **Hands on History**, a museum of Victorian social history that also tells the story of Hull and its citizens. Also concerned with displaying images of life in Hull is **Streetlife, Hull's Museum of Transport**, which looks at 200 years of transport from penny farthing bicycles and carriages to the motor car and trams. However, the town's most unusual museum has to be the **Spurn Lighthouse**, which was once stationed on active duty off Spurn Point but that is now moored in the town's marina. Visitors can explore the 75 year old vessel with the help of its knowledgeable crew. More of Hull's maritime history is explained at the **Maritime Museum**, housed in the impressive former Town Docks Office while, in the former corn exchange, is the **Hull and East Riding Museum**. Anyone looking for more cultural pursuits should visit the **Ferens Art Gallery** that houses a sumptuous collection of paintings and sculpture that ranges from European Old Masters to challenging contemporary art and includes works by Canalletto and Hockney.

It is the **Humber Bridge**, five miles to the west, which people associate most with Hull. The longest single-span suspension bridge in the world, it was opened in 1981 and it is so long that, due to the curvature of the Earth, the two towers appear to lean away from each other although they are perfectly vertical.

POCKLINGTON

Set amidst rich agricultural land, Pocklington is a lively market town with an unusual layout of twisting alleys running off the market place. Its splendid, mainly 15th century church certainly justifies its title as the Cathedral of the Wolds (although strictly speaking Pocklington is just outside the Wolds). William Wilberforce, the famous slave law reformer, went to the old grammar school here and, a more dubious claim to fame, is that the last burning of a witch in England took place in Pocklington.

Although the market has been in existence since the 13th century, it was the building, in 1815, of a canal linking the town to the River Ouse, and later the arrival of the railway, which set the seal on the town's prosperity.

The people of Pocklington have good reason to be grateful to Major Percy Marlborough Stewart who, on his death in 1962, bequeathed **Burnby Hall and Gardens** to the town. A godson of the Duke of Marlborough and a expert huntsman, Stewart travelled the world no fewer than seven times before settling at the hall and, along with enjoying the glorious gardens that had been created under his direction, he also put his energies into amassing what is now the

National Collection of Hardy Water Lilies. The gardens, which are open daily from March to September, provide a glorious haven of beauty and tranquillity and, along with the two lakes, there is a secret garden, a walled Victorian garden and natural woodland.

SLEDMERE

This village is home to **Sledmere House**, a noble Georgian mansion built by the Sykes family in the 1750s. Inside, there is fine furniture by Chippendale and Sheraton and superb decorated plasterwork by Joseph Rose, while the Turkish Room – inspired by the Sultan's salon in Istanbul's Valideh Mosque – is a dazzling example of oriental opulence.

The Sykes family founded the famous Sledmere Stud and the 2nd Sir Tatton Sykes spent nearly two million pounds on building and restoring churches in the area. In 1911, Sledmere House itself was ravaged by fire and, when a servant rushed in to tell Sir Tatton, then 85 years old, the news, he insisted on finishing his lunch. An armchair was set out on the lawn for him so that he could complete his meal in safety while his servants laboured to rescue the house's many treasures. After the fire, Sledmere was quickly restored and the Sykes family is still in residence. Along with the splendid interiors, another great feature of the house is its glorious Capability Brown landscaped parkland that contains a beautiful old rose garden and a recently laid out knot garden. The house is open from Easter to September,

but not on Saturdays or non Bank Holiday Mondays and the house's famous pipe organ is played for visitors on Wednesdays, Fridays and Sundays.

Across the road from Sledmere House are two remarkable, elaborately detailed, monuments: the **Eleanor Cross**, modelled on those set up by Edward I in memory of his Queen, was erected by Sir Tatton Sykes in 1900 while the **Waggoners Memorial**, designed by Sir Mark Sykes, commemorates the 1,000-strong company of men he raised from the Wolds during World War I. Their knowledge of horses was invaluable in their role as members of the Army Service Corps and the finely-carved monument is made up of panels depicting the Waggoners' varied duties during the war.

SPROATLEY

Just to the north of the village lies **Burton Constable Hall,** which is named after Sir John Constable who, in 1570, built this stately mansion that incorporates parts of an even older house dating back to the reign of King Stephen in the 1100s. The hall was again remodelled, on Jacobean lines, in the 18th century and contains some fine work by Chippendale, Adam and James Wyatt. In the famous Long Gallery hangs a remarkable collection of paintings, among them Holbein's portraits of Sir Thomas Cranmer and Sir Thomas More and Zucchero's Mary, Queen of Scots. The extensive parklands were designed by Capability Brown, apparently inspired by the gardens at Versailles. Perhaps it was this connection that motivated the Constable family to suggest loaning the hall to Louis XVIII of France during his years of exile after the French Revolution. Also in the grounds of the hall are collections of agricultural machinery, horse-drawn carriages and 18th century scientific apparatus.

The descendants of the Constable family still bear the title Lords of Holderness and along with it the rights to any flotsam and jetsam washed ashore on the Holderness peninsula. Many years ago, when the late Brigadier Chichester Constable was congratulated on enjoying such a privilege, he retorted, "I also have to pay for burying, or otherwise disposing of, any whale grounded on the Holderness shore – and it costs me about £20 a time!" The huge bones of one such whale are still on show in the grounds of the hall.

Lighthouse Museum

WITHERNSEA

This small and traditional resort has a long, sandy beach as well as plenty of entertainment for all the family and also a busy market that is open several days a week. The most striking feature of the town is its old lighthouse from the 127 foot tower of which there are some marvellous views. Decommissioned in 1976, the building is now the **Lighthouse Museum** covering both the history of the Royal National Lifeboat Institution and the actress Kay Kendall. Born in Withernsea and later achieving fame on the London stage as a sophisticated comedienne, Kay Kendall is best remembered for her role in *Genevieve*. Her grandfather helped to build the lighthouse in 1892 and he was the last coxswain of the deep-sea lifeboat.

To the south of the resort stretches a desolate spit of flat windswept dunes, Spurn Point, which lead to Spurn Head, the narrow hook of ever-shifting sands that curls around the mouth of the Humber estuary. One of the oldest places in Britain, during World War I there was a fort at the Head with a railway supply line but now all that can be seen is the lighthouse on the very tip of the point although around it are underground fortifications. Much of this fascinating land formation is now the **Spurn National Nature Reserve** and it is a fascinating place that is home to thousands of migrating birds.

THE ANVIL ARMS

BRIDLINGTON ROAD, WOLD NEWTON, EAST YORKSHIRE YO25 3YL
TEL: 01262 470279

> **Directions:** 2 miles east of the B1269 just before the village of Foxholes when travelling north

Set in the very picturesque village of Wold Newton, **The Anvil Arms** is housed in a Grade II listed building dating back some 300 years, and reputedly haunted. Formerly cottages with a smithy attached, the pub's long, impressive exterior has been completely refurbished with taste and an eye for retaining the inn's traditional charm and appearance. Inside, traditional features such as exposed beamwork, open fires and tasteful, comfortable seating mix well with more modern features to provide excellent comfort and attractive furnishings and décor.

Sheila Dave and their youngest daughter Cara have been here since October of 2002. Together with their business partner Jarvis, they have made their first venture into the licensing trade quite the success, with a growing reputation among locals and visitors alike for great food, drink and hospitality. They and their welcoming, efficient staff make sure that all their guests have a relaxing and pleasant time while at the pub.

The restaurant area is elegant, intimate and gracious. It seats 24 and is no-smoking. Dinner is served here Friday and Saturday evening, and Sunday lunchtime. Homemade dishes are just one speciality here. Booking is required for Sunday lunch. Sheila does all the cooking and is renowned for her delicious pies, grills, steaks and other traditional favourites.

There are two real ales at this Free House – John Smiths Cask and a weekly changing guest ales – together with a good range of draught keg bitters, lagers, cider, stout, wines, spirits and soft drinks.

🕐 Mon-Sat 11.00-15.00, 17.00-23.00; Sun 12.00-15.00, 19.00-22.30

🍴 Bar meals Mon-Tues 12.00-14.00 and 19.00-21.00; Thurs OAP lunches 12.30-14.00, bar snacks 19.00-21.00; Fri-Sat bar snacks 12.00-14.00, restaurant 19.00-21.00; Sunday lunch 12.30-15.00

💷 Visa, Mastercard, Switch, Delta, Amex, Diners, Eurocard, Solo

🅿 Off-road parking

🎵 Please ring for details

❓ Filey 10 miles, Driffield 8 miles, Bridlington 12 miles

THE BRICKLAYERS ARMS AND STABLES RESTAURANT

FRONT STREET, LAXTON, EAST YORKSHIRE DN14 7TS
TEL: 01430 430111

Directions: Laxton is found on an un-named/un-numbered road off either the A614 via Howden or the B1230 via Gilberdyke

The Bricklayers Arms is a picturesque public house in a pretty and tranquil village. Well worth seeking out, the premises were once part of the Salt Marsh Estate, and started life in the early 19th century selling only bottled beers. Since that time this range has expanded so that now there are two real ales – John Smiths Cask and a changing guest ale – together with Beamish Red, Becks, Fosters, Guinness and Strongbow to choose from on draught, and a good selection of wines, spirits and soft drinks.

Experienced owners Terry and Nancy Whitehead have been in the licensing trade for 16 years. They've owned and personally run the Bricklayers Arms since 1992, and have built up a well-earned reputation for great ales, food and hospitality. They and their friendly, helpful staff ensure that every guest enjoys a relaxing and comfortable ambience along with the superb drink on offer.

Attractive and tasteful, the interior boasts good furnishings and décor, very olde worlde with traditional features such as exposed beams, cosy corners and a large brickbuilt fireplace.

In the elegant **Stables Restaurant**, diners can enjoy a tempting evening meal Friday and Saturday nights from 7 until 10, and a delicious Sunday menu that changes weekly and is served from midday until 3.30. Good, wholesome homecooked food is the rule here, and guests choose from an a la carte menu and bar menu. The restaurant seats 35 and children are welcome.

- Mon-Fri 19.00-23.00; Sat 11.00-23.00; Sun 12.00-22.30
- Fri-Sat 19.00-22.00 and Sun 12.00-15.30
- Off-road parking, beer garden
- Goole 2 miles, Beverley 15 miles

THE BURNS HEAD INN

PATRINGTON HAVEN, EAST YORKSHIRE HU12 0QJ
TEL: 01964 630530

Directions: From Hull, take the A1033 15 miles east to Patrington, then follow the Patrington Haven sign

The Burns Head Inn is an eye-catching public house, set in a charmingly peaceful rural spot, not far from the coast. Parts of the premises date back to the 1760s and were once cottages, a small farm and an alehouse. Large and whitewashed, it presents a pleasant face to the world. The interior is tasteful and attractive, spacious and airy, with the supremely comfortable furnishings and lovely décor adding to the relaxed ambience.

Owners Marlene and Dennis Wicks have run this Free House since 1988, and have been in the licensing trade for nearly 30 years. Dennis is well known in these parts for his culinary skills, and fresh food is definitely a highlight of any visit to the pub. English and Indian dishes are the fare here, with tempting delights such as beef madras, vegetable balti, kashmiri lamb and more. The bar menu features steaks, fish, chicken, lamb and vegetarian dishes, while the children's menu has all the choices favoured by youngsters. All dishes are freshly prepared and cooked to order, and make use of the freshest locally-sourced ingredients. Served Tuesday to Sunday at lunchtime, and Monday to Sunday evenings, guests can eat in the bar, lounge or separate restaurant (which seats 32), or outside in the lovely garden, which is well-tended and includes a feature pond with fish and ducks. Part of the restaurant is no-smoking.

This convivial pub hosts live music on Friday nights and a lively quiz on Tuesdays. Marlene, Dennis and their friendly, capable staff offer all their guests a warm welcome.

- 🕐 Mon 19.00-23.00; Tues-Thurs 11.00-15.00, 17.00-23.00; Fri-Sat 11.00-23.00; Sun 12.00-22.30
- 🍴 Tues-Sun 12.00-14.00; Mon-Sun 18.00-21.00
- Ⓟ Beer garden, off-road parking
- 🎵 Quiz night Tuesdays; live music Fridays from 9 p.m.
- @ burnshead02@aol.com
- ❓ Patrington Haven Leisure Park 200 yards, Withernsea 4 miles, Grimsby 8 miles, Hull 15 miles, Beverley 22 miles

THE CROOKED BILLET

PITT LANE, RYEHILL, EAST YORKSHIRE HU12 9NN
TEL/FAX: 01964 622303

> **Directions:** 9 miles east of Hull off the A1033

The tiny village of Ryehill is set back from the main Hull to Withernsea road, just east of the larger village of Thorngumbald. The main reason for seeking out Ryehill is to call in at the delightful pub known as **The Crooked Billet**, a traditional country inn in all the best senses of the term, where hospitality has been dispensed since the late 1600s. Convivial and welcoming, this charming inn boasts a friendly staff offering excellent service. Ancient beams, real fires, lots of local memorabilia and flagstone or quarry-tiled floors all add to the appeal and warm ambience.

Originally known as The Royal Oak, the pub's name was changed in 1880 to The Crooked Billet, referring to the rough-hewn walking stick or staff made from a tree branch and used widely by poorer people as both a walking aid and a defensive weapon. Tenants John and

Sylvia Pizer took over here in 1997 and have made the inn a welcoming and popular place. Clare offers an extensive regular menu supplemented by five daily specials. Food is available Wednesday to Friday lunchtime, Monday to Saturday evening and all day Sunday. Booking is advised on Friday and Saturday nights. Homemade dishes are justly popular here, especially the delicious homemade steak pie. Sunday lunch features Sunday roasts plus a vegetarian choice plus other choices. Children are welcome.

Carol the barmaid helps John and Sylvia serve up the well-kept three real ales, all from the Burtonwood Brewery: Burtonwood Bitter, Top Hat and a brewery guest ale. There's also Carling, Kronenberg, Strongbow, Guinness and Burtonwood Dark Mild, together with a good range of wines, spirits and soft drinks.

- Mon-Sat 11.00-23.00; Sun 12.00-22.30
- Weds-Fri 12.00-14.30; Mon-Sat 17.00-21.00; Sun 12.00-20.00
- Off-road parking
- Quiz night Wednesday
- Withernsea 9 miles, Hull 9 miles, Beverley 12 miles, Hornsea 13 miles

THE FORESTERS ARMS

3 BECKSIDE NORTH, BEVERLEY, EAST YORKSHIRE HU17 0PR
TEL: 01482 867943 FAX: 01482 869549

Directions: Beckside North is located off the B1230 through Beverley

The Foresters Arms was built in 1939 to replace a pub that stood on the same site. A full refurbishment to the exterior has left its handsome original features while tastefully updating this large and impressive inn. The interior is attractive and welcoming, with a long, well-stocked bar, comfortable lounge area with plenty of cosy nooks, and separate dining area.

Local man John Marson and his wife Susan have been leaseholders at The Foresters Arms since 1995. John is a butcher by trade, and still runs the local butcher shop, so you can be assured that all the meat on the menu is the very freshest and choicest available. Guests choose off the menu and specials board from a variety of delicious dishes such as

steaks, chicken in a Stilton sauce, seafood platter, vegetarian choices and more. The Sunday roast is served at lunch and in the evening as well, in addition to the main menu. There's also a choice of mouth-watering puddings worth leaving room for.

There are two or three real ales on tap, with Ridings Bitter and Cameron Cream always featured along with a guest ale. Other brews available include Mansfield Smooth, Marstons Pedigree, Mansfield Dark, Fosters, Carlsberg, Stella Artois, Woodpecker, Strongbow, Scrumpy Jack and regular and extra cold Guinness, together with a good selection of wines, spirits and soft drinks.

Entertainment at this convivial pub includes the musical stylings of Enid, pianist here for 46 years. Accompanied by her able drummer and a compere, Enid entertains guests with her free and easy sing-along session.

- 🕐 Mon 19.00-23.00; Tues-Sat 11.00-23.00; Sun 12.00-22.30
- 🍴 Tues-Sun and Bank Hols 12.00-14.00, 16.30-19.00
- £ Visa, Mastercard, Switch, Delta, Eurocard, Solo
- Ⓟ Off-road parking
- ♪ Karaoke Fridays from 20.30; Music Saturdays from 20.30; live music some Thursdays – ring for details
- @ john@foresters.karoo.co.uk www.forestersarmsbeverley.co.uk
- ❓ Beverley, Hull 7 miles, Hornsea/the coast 12 miles

THE HOPE & ANCHOR

MAIN STREET, BLACKTOFT, EAST YORKSHIRE DN14 7YW
TEL/FAX: 01430 440441

> **Directions:** From Goole, take the B1228 to the junction with the A63, then the B1230; turn right at Gilberdyke onto the minor road to Blacktoft. From Hull, take the A63 to the junction with the M62 then the B1230 to Gilberdyke, then the minor road on your left to Blacktoft.

Standing adjacent to the River Ouse close to where it meets the River Trent, **The Hope & Anchor** is well off the beaten track and well worth a visit as it has a great deal to offer. Quaint and cosy behind its smart white exterior, the interior boasts a wealth of wood beams, pannelling and extremely comfortable seating, as well as an impressive brickbuilt fire and a warm ambience. This fine Free House has been owned and run by Eddie and Liz Payne since 1999, and they have made it a big success.

Meals are served at lunch Wednesday to Sunday and at dinner Tuesday to Sunday. Booking is required Friday to Sunday here, where Liz is the cook and creates specialities including homemade steak pie and fresh fish, as well as a range of other delicious dishes. Everything is fresh, and as far as possible, is sourced locally. Sunday lunch is always a big occasion. The no-smoking dining area seats 18; guests can also dine in the bar, lounge and outside in the garden that features a children's playground and a small caravan park. The views from the garden are quite superb. The four real ales served here are John Smiths, Theakstons and two changing guest ales. Also available is keg Boddingtons, John Smiths Smooth, Fosters, Guinness, Strongbow, Kronenberg and Woodpecker, together with a good range of wines, spirits and soft drinks.

- 🕐 Mon-Tues 16.00-23.00; Weds-Sat and Bank Hols 11.00-23.00; Sun 12.00-22.30
- 🍴 Weds-Sat 12.00-14.00; Tues-Sat 18.00-21.00; Sun 12.00-15.00, 17.00-19.30
- 💷 Visa, Mastercard, Switch, Delta, Eurocard, Solo
- 🅿 Off-road parking, beer garden
- 🎵 Happy Hour every night from 17.00-18.30
- @ hopeandanchor@btconnect.com
- ❓ Goole 8 miles, Hull 12 miles. On the Pennine Trail Route

THE PLOUGH INN

FOSTON-ON-THE-WOLDS, DRIFFIELD, EAST YORKSHIRE YO25 8BJ
TEL: 01262 488303 FAX: 01262 481303

Directions: From Bridlington, take the A165 for 7 miles south to Beeford and turn off following the signs to Foston-on-the-Wolds

The Plough Inn is the place to seek out in Foston-on-the-Wolds for great food, drink and hospitality. As you might expect of a hostelry which dates back to the early 1700s, The Plough has bags of character – low beams, lots of exposed brickwork, real fires, a vintage bread oven and a fascinating collection of local memorabilia. This Free House is owned and run by Gordon and Jeannette Staples, who after many years working abroad have ventured into the licensing trade. They have enhanced the inn's reputation for good food and well-kept ales which include three real ales in summer and two in winter. John Smiths

and Black Sheep are always here, together with a guest ale. Also on tap are John Smiths Smooth, Strongbow, Stella Artois, Fosters, Guinness and a selection of wines, spirits and soft drinks.

Jeannette and the inn's chef cook up tempting delights at lunch and dinner Tuesday to Sunday and all day Bank Holiday weekends. Guests choose off the menu or specials list from a good range of dishes including steaks, homemade steak-and-ale pie, lasagne, mixed grill, vegetarian and seafood dishes and salads. Booking is required at weekends. The no-smoking restaurant seats 40, but guests can also dine in the bar areas or in the attractive beer garden. Children are welcome. On-site there's also a small caravan site for up to five caravans, with electric hook-ups and soft and hard standing spaces. Caravanners are welcome to use the facilities at the inn during opening hours.

- 🕐 Mon 19.00-23.00 Tues-Fri 12.00-14.30, 19.00-23.00; Sat 12.00-15.00, 19.00-23.00 Sun 12.00-15.00, 19.00-22.00 All day Bank Hol weekends.

- 🍴 Tues-Sun 12.00-14.00 and 19.00-21.00 All day Bank Hol weekends

- £ Visa, Mastercard, Switch, Delta, Eurocard, Solo

- Ⓟ Off-road parking, beer garden

- 🎵 Occasional themed food evenings – ring for details

- @ theploughinn.foston@btinternet.com www.theploughinn.cjb.net

- ❓ Cruckley Animal Farm 1 mile, Driffield 6 miles, Bridlington 8 miles, Beverley 10 miles, Filey 15 miles

THE RAILWAY HOTEL

STATION ROAD, GILBERDYKE, BROUGH, EAST YORKSHIRE HU15 2ST
TEL: 01430 440302

> **Directions:** From junction 38 of the M62, take the B1248 until you see the sign for Gilberdyke and the railway station; the hotel is on Station Road on your right.

Between Selby and Hull the railway track runs straight for 18 miles – the longest such stretch in Britain. Gilberdyke Station stands at almost exactly the halfway point along this line, and just across the road from the station is **The Railway Hotel**, which has been providing hospitality to travellers since 1869. Run by Alan and Natalie Lambert, a friendly couple who have been in the hotel trade for many years, this impressive inn is handsome inside and out. The charming interior boasts traditional features and modern comforts, with the bar and lounge being both cosy and welcoming. The attractive no-smoking restaurant seats 24. Outside, the lovely beer garden is spacious, with

tall trees offering privacy and paved and gravelled paths making access easy.

Food is available at lunchtime Tuesdays to Sundays, and the inn serves evening meals Monday to Saturday. Booking is advised on Sundays for the delicious carvery, when there are at least four different roasts and seasonal vegetables to choose from. Both Alan and Natalie cook, creating a range of traditional favourites to order.

Tetleys is the real ale here, along with a changing choice of guest ales and a good complement of lagers, stout, cider, wines, spirits and soft drinks.

The accommodation is superb, with two twin rooms, one double and one family room, all en suite. Comfortable and with a pleasant décor and good furnishings, these rooms are welcoming, and the tariff includes a hearty breakfast.

- Mon 16.00-23.00; Tues-Sat 11.00-23.00; Sun 12.00-22.30
- Mon 17.00-19.00; Tues-Sat 12.00-14.00, 17.00-19.00; Sun 12.00-16.00
- 4 rooms en suite
- Beer garden, off-road parking
- Live entertainment Friday and Saturday night; pop and general knowledge quiz Thursday night
- lambert@railwayhotel.fsnet.co.uk
- South Cave 6 miles, Goole 8 miles, Market Weighton 10 miles

THE SHIP INN

30 YORK ROAD, SHIPTONTHORPE, EAST YORKSHIRE YO43 3PG
TEL: 01430 872006

> **Directions:** Shiptonthorpe is on the A1079, close to its junction with the A614

For a true taste of Yorkshire hospitality, a visit to **The Ship Inn** is strongly recommended. Hosts Tricia and Ed Brindley bought this fine 150-year-old inn in 2003. The inn had been completely refurbished a few years back, when new wooden floors were laid down and the walls were lined with half-panelling. Handsome, spacious and airy, this welcoming pub has a really friendly ambience and a cosiness enhanced by the wealth of brass ornaments and implements, comfortable seating and tasteful décor.

Real ale-lovers will feel right at home with the inn's four to five real ales on offer – John Smiths, Tetley, Tetley Mild and changing guest ales – plus there's

drink for those who prefer lagers, cider, stout, wines, spirits or soft drinks. Ably assisted by right-hand woman Trudy, Tricia cooks up a range of delicious dishes, hearty and filling, and reasonably priced, served in the bar, lounge or in the separate no-smoking dining room. The comprehensive menu and daily specials include a broad selection of traditional and more innovative meals at lunch and dinner-time.

Live entertainment at this convivial pub is on hand every Thursday evening from about 9 p.m. The excellent accommodation comprises 11 handsome and high-quality guest bedrooms, one of which is on the ground floor and has been specially adapted for guests with disabilities. Available all year round, all the rooms are either doubles or twins, and all are en suite. The tariff includes a hearty breakfast to set you up for a day's sightseeing.

- 🕐 Mon-Fri 11.00-15.00, 17.00-23.00; Sat 11.00-23.00; Sun 12.00-15.00, 19.00-22.30
- 🍴 Mon, Weds-Fri 12.00-14.00, 17.00-21.00
- 💷 All major
- 🛏 11 rooms en suite
- 🅿 Off-road parking; private parking for residents
- 🎵 Live entertainment Thursday evening; occasional quiz nights
- @ shipinn@telinco.co.uk·
- ❓ York 15 miles, Beverley 12 miles, Malton 20 miles, coast 25 miles

THE WHITE HART INN

20 WESTGATE, NORTH CAVE, BROUGH, EAST YORKSHIRE HU15 2NJ
TEL: 01430 422432

Directions: From the M62 junction 38 take the B1230 for about 2 miles. From Beverley take the B1230, crossing the A1034, for about 8 miles.

Fiona and Davie have been at **The White Hart Inn** since 2002 and their experience and winning personalities have assured their success. This late 19th-century inn presents a big, bold face to the world, and inside there's a choice between the superbly furnished lounge-dining room and the lovely little public bar

with its intimate lighting and cosy alcoves. A professional chef for over 30 years, Davie creates superb dishes including his justly popular homemade pasta dishes, soups, lasagne, steak pie and more. Everything on the menu is freshly made and most of it is locally sourced, offering a variety of good, wholesome dishes with daily specials adding to the

written menu. On Sundays there's a traditional roast plus a smaller select menu which includes a vegetarian dish. Booking is required Saturday evening and Sunday lunchtime, and also for the monthly gourmet evenings, when Davie really pulls out all the stops.

Ridings Cask is the permanent real ale here, together with a changing guest ale and a full range of draught lagers, ciders and stouts, wines, spirits and soft drinks.

With the M62 close by, the pub is well placed for easy access to the west, but here are also plenty of attractions and places of interest in the vicinity. The village of South Cave, only a couple of miles away, is officially a town with its own town hall in the marketplace. The name is said to be a corruption of South (and thereby North) Cove, since the southern end of the parish is set around a backwater of the Humber.

- 🕐 Mon-Thur 11.00-15.00, 17.00-23.00; Fri-Sat 11.00-23.00; Sun 12.00-22.30
- 🍽 Mon-Sat 12.00-14.00 and 17.00-20.00; Sun 12.00-19.00
- 💷 Visa, Mastercard, Switch, Delta, Eurocard, Solo
- 🅿 Off-road parking
- 🎵 Live entertainment Wednesdays from 9 p.m.; gourmet evenings monthly on a Friday night – booking required
- ❓ South Cave 2 miles, Beverley 8 miles

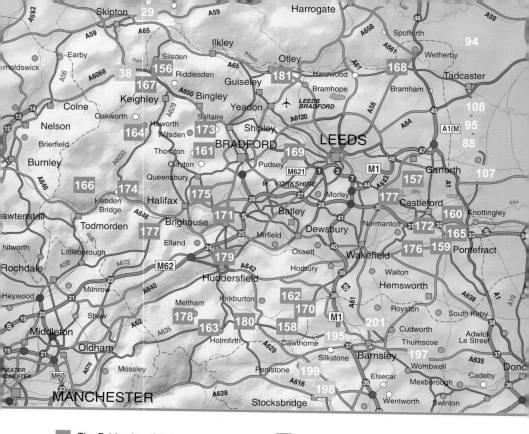

Please note all cross references refer to page numbers

WEST YORKSHIRE

The county of West Yorkshire, while having the scenery of the Pennines, is still dominated by the effects of the Industrial Revolution that turned this region into one of the world's great wool manufacturing areas. The land had been farmed, mainly with sheep, since the Middle Ages and, in order to supplement their wages, the cottagers took to hand loom weaving in a room of their home. However, the advances in technology, beginning in the 18th century, replaced the single man powered looms with water powered machinery that was housed in the large mill buildings in the valley bottom and close to the source of power – the fast flowing streams and rivers coming down from the surroundings hills and moors.

Wadsworth Moor

During the 19th century there was an explosion of building and the quiet riverside villages grew into towns and the South Pennine textile boom was in full flow. At first the conditions in the mills were grim as, indeed, were the living conditions for the mill workers but, with the reduction in the hours of the working day, people were able to take the opportunity to discover, and in some cases rediscover, the beauty of the surrounding moorland. Not all the villages were completely taken over by the mills and, in many, the old stone built weavers cottages, with their deep windows to let in light for the worker within, survive.

Although the Yorkshire woollen textile industry is now almost a thing of the past the heritage of those prosperous days can be seen in almost any town or village of the region. Many of the long redundant mills are now being put to other uses while places such as Bradford, Leeds, Huddersfield and Wakefield are finding new industries to take the place of the old.

There are several grand stately homes in the area, such as Temple Newsam near Leeds, East Riddlesden Hall near Bradford and Harewood House, but the foremost residence that most people make a pilgrimage to in West Yorkshire is The Parsonage at Howarth. It was here that the Brontë family moved to in 1820 and, surrounded by the wild Pennine landscape, the three sisters, Charlotte, Anne and Emily, became inspired by their surroundings and wrote some of the most moving novels in the English language. Now a museum dedicated to the tragic sisters, this fine Georgian house is a starting point for a 40-mile footpath that takes in many of the places that feature in the Brontë novels.

BATLEY

This typical industrial town, in the Pennine moorland, is home to the **Bagshaw Museum**, which is housed inside a strangely Gothic residence in Wilton Park. The museum was founded by the Bagshaw family and much of the contents were gathered by them on their travels including items brought back from Alaska by Violet Bagshaw in her 100th year! From ancient Egypt to Asia and the Americas, there are all manner of exhibits and they, along with the exotic interior of this Victorian house, make a visit here particularly memorable. In the park itself there are nature trails and also the **Butterfly Conservation Centre**, which houses a rich assortment of butterflies, many of which are becoming close to extinction in the wild. Elsewhere in the town the Batley Art Gallery plays host to a changing programme of exhibitions that, in particular, feature local artists, while, in the historic Alexandra Mill is the **Skopos Motor Museum**. The collection of cars on display here ranges from a Benz Motor Wagon of 1885 to a Ferrari F40.

Bradford Theatre

BRADFORD

Ever since the 16th century, Bradford has been associated with the wool and textile industries and in the 19th century, the area where the wealthy wool merchants' settled and erected their opulent buildings became known as Little Germany. For an insight into the city's industrial heritage there is the **Bradford Industrial Museum and Horses at Work**, which is housed in an original worsted spinning mill complex built in 1875. Here, life in Bradford in late-Victorian era is faithfully re-created and the museum offers horse-bus and tram rides, a Shire Horse centre, the chance to dress up in Victorian clothing, a reconstructed mill owner's house and the workingmen's back to back cottages. The complex also includes a café, shop and picnic area and the museum is open all year from Tuesdays to Sundays and Bank Holiday Mondays.

Architecturally, the most striking building in Bradford must be **Lister's Mill**, whose huge ornate chimney dominates the city skyline and it is claimed that the chimney is wide enough at the top to drive a horse and cart round. The mill fell silent some years ago though its exterior has been cleaned

up and there are plans to use it to house a museum to the industry that brought the city its wealth – wool. A rather quirkier sign of the city's former riches is **Undercliffe Cemetery** where the wool barons were buried, each in a more opulent Gothic mausoleum than the last. It is easy to spend an hour here admiring the Victorian funereal art on show with the cityscape laid out below. The fact that the city has a **Cathedral** is an indication of its importance and the first evidence of Christian worship on this site is provided by the remains of a Saxon preaching cross. Today, the cathedral contains many items of interest, including beautiful stained glass windows, some of which were designed by William Morris, carvings and statuary. Bradford was awarded city status in 1897.

However, Bradford does not only look back to its past but also to the future and it is home to the very popular **National Museum of Photography, Film and Television** that houses IMAX, one of the largest cinema screens in the world.

Of related interest is the **Colour Museum**, Britain's only museum of colour, where the concept of colour, how it is perceived by both humans and animals and its importance are explored. Visitors have the opportunity to mix coloured lights and experience strange and fascinating colour illusions. In the Colour and Textiles gallery, the interesting story of dyeing and textile printing, from the early days in Ancient Egypt through to the 21st century, is told. Modern, computerised technology also allows visitors to take charge of a dye making factory and to decorate a room. In Lister Park, the collections at the **Cartwright Hall Art Gallery** reflect the diverse cultural mix that helps to make Bradford the unique city that it has become. From Victorian paintings and sumptuous Indian silks to the challenges of contemporary art, this gallery is as interesting and far reaching as the city itself.

Bradford is the birthplace of the composer Frederick Delius, the painter David Hockney and the writer JB Priestley. Born in Mannheim Road in 1894, Priestley worked as a wool office clerk in the city before joining up to fight in World War I. It was his novel, *The Good Companions*, about a troupe of touring actors that was published in 1929, which made his name but he is, perhaps, remembered best for his play, the Yorkshire-based comedy, *When We Are Married*. When Priestley died in 1984, Bradford's City Hall's bell tolled every minute for an hour.

CLAYTON WEST

A popular attraction at Clayton West is the **Kirklees Light Railway**, a 15" gauge steam railway that runs along the old Lancashire and Yorkshire Clayton West branch line and through gently rolling farmland for about four miles with a quarter-mile long tunnel adding to the thrill. The large station and combined visitor centre at Clayton West provides passengers with comfortable, spacious surroundings in which to await for their train or take advantage of the light refreshment café and the souvenir shop. The railway operates daily during the season and every weekend throughout the year. There is also a programme of events and theme days that take place throughout the year.

DEWSBURY

This ancient town has its roots in the 7th century when, according to legend, St Paulinus baptised converts to Christianity in the River Calder. Now standing on this spot is 12th century **Dewsbury Minster** with a tower erected in 1767 to a design by the eminent York architect, John Carr. The interior has some interesting features, among them fragments of an Anglo-Saxon cross and coffin lids, but the Minster is perhaps best known for its custom of tolling the 'Devil's Knell' on Christmas Eve to ward off evil spirits with a bell known as Black Tom. Patrick Brontë was curate of Dewsbury between 1809 and 1811, his daughter Charlotte taught at Wealds

House School nearby and it was Miss Wooler, the school's headmistress, who later gave her away when she was married.

Right from the beginning of the Industrial Revolution, Dewsbury became the heart of the West Riding's heavy woollen area and the invention, by a Yorkshire man, of the rag-grinding machine in the 1830s that enabled woollen cloth to be reprocessed as 'shoddy and mungo', helped the town to develop as a manufacturer of quality blankets, coats and military uniforms. The steam powered local mills, of which there were many, also used locally mined coal. Although the textile industry has declined and has given way to modern industrial processes, many of the grand Victorian buildings, built on the back of the wealth and pride that the woollen trade brought to Dewsbury remain.

Piece Hall, Halifax

The **Dewsbury Museum** is dedicated to childhood and takes visitors on a fascinating journey back to the first decades of the 20th century, as seen through the eyes of children.

HALIFAX

Halifax boasts one of Yorkshire's most impressive examples of municipal architecture and one of the Europe's finest and most complete 18th century buildings, the glorious **Piece Hall**. It possesses a large quadrangle, where regular markets are held on Fridays and Saturdays, which is surrounded by classically styled colonnades and balconies behind which are some 40 specialist shops. On Thursdays a flea market is held here and there is a lively and varied programme of events for all the family throughout the season. There's also an art gallery with a varied programme of contemporary exhibitions and workshops, a museum and tea room. The Town Hall, designed by Sir Charles Barry, architect of the Houses of Parliament, is another notable building, while there is the attractive Borough Market, constructed in cast iron and glass with an ornate central clock. In Gibbet Street stands a grisly reminder of the past, a replica of a guillotine, whose original blade is kept in the **Piece Hall Museum**.

Halifax boasts the largest parish church in England, dating from the 12th and 13th centuries and of almost cathedral-like proportions. It has a lovely wooden ceiling, constructed in 1635, and visitors should look out for

Old Tristram, a life-sized wooden effigy of a beggar, reputedly based on a local character, which served as the church poor box and still does.

Right next door to Piece Hall lies the **Calderdale Industrial Museum**, which houses working looms and mill machinery and holds regular hand textile demonstrations. From the Great Wheel to the Spinning Jenny, from mining to moquette, from steam engines to toffee, the museum provides a riveting insight into Halifax's industrial heritage. Also among the many displays is one celebrating the town's greatest contribution to modern travel – the cats-eye! Situated next to Halifax railway station, **Eureka!** is Britain's first and only interactive museum designed especially for children between 3 and 12 years of age. With more than 400 larger-than-life exhibits and exciting activities available, Eureka! opens up a fascinating world of hands-on exploration. A team of 'Enablers' help children make the most of their visit and there are regular temporary exhibitions.

Now a vibrant complex of businesses, galleries, theatre, café and design and book shops, **Dean Clough** is housed in a magnificent Victorian carpet mill that is a reminder of Halifax's textile heritage. Built between 1840 and 1870 by the Crossley family, this mill was once home to one of the world's leading carpet factories; it ceased production in 1982.

On the eastern outskirts of the town lies **Shibden Hall and Park**, the home of the Lister family for over 300 years, although the hall predates them and was built in around 1420. A distinctive timber framed house, which has been carefully furnished to reflect the various periods of its history, the hall gives the impression that the family living here will return at any moment. The 17th century barn behind the hall is now a Folk Museum where craftsmen work in wood and iron without electricity.

Also on the outskirts of the town is the **Bankfield Museum**, the home, between 1837 and 1886, of Edward Akroyd, the largest wool manufacturer in Britain. He lavished money and attention on the building, transforming it from a modest town house into a magnificent Italianate mansion with elaborate ceilings, staircases and plasterwork. After his death, his sumptuous home became a museum and now houses an internationally important collection of textiles and costumes from around the world. Contemporary crafts are also featured and the museum hosts an interesting programme of temporary exhibitions, workshops, seminars, master classes and gallery demonstrations. Here, too, are a Toy Gallery, the **Duke of Wellington's Regimental Museum** and the Marble Gallery that sells contemporary crafts. Surrounding his house, Akroyd built a model village, called Akroydon, that, with its terraced houses, allotments, park and church, was the first 'urban' village.

HAREWOOD

One of the grandest stately homes in the country, **Harewood House** was built at a

Harewood House

Tintoretto, while family portraits by Reynolds and Gainsborough look down from the silk-covered walls of the opulent drawing rooms. Elsewhere in the house there is a display of Royal memorabilia that belonged to Lord Harewood's mother, HRH Princess Mary, the Princess Royal. Along with superb gardens, charming walks and a Bird Garden that is home to some 120 exotic species, the grounds also feature an Adventure Playground, boat trips on the lake and an extensive events and exhibitions programme throughout the season.

time when many of the most illustrious names in the history of English architecture, interior decoration, furniture making and landscape gardening were all at the peak of their powers. Therefore, in the mid 17th century, when Edwin Lascelles conceived the idea for Harewood, he was able to employ the dazzling talents of Robert Adam for the interiors, John Carr as the architect, Thomas Chippendale as his cabinet maker and Capability Brown to landscape the grounds. Edwin's son, Edward, was one of the first to patronise a young artist named JMW Turner and many of Turner's paintings are still here along with hundreds of others by numerous distinguished painters collected by later generations of the family. Many of the finest of them are displayed in a superb gallery that extends along the whole west end of the house. Among the masterpieces on show are works by Bellini, Titian, Veronese, El Greco and

HAWORTH

It was this once bleak moorland town and its dramatic setting that fired the romantic imaginations of the Brontë sisters but, today, Haworth has been transformed into a lively, attractive place, with wonderful tea houses, street theatre, and antique and craft shops, and it is very different to how it must have been in the Brontë's days. Then it was a thriving industrial town that was squalid with the smoke from its chimneys and filled with the noise of the clattering looms that were rarely still. It is, however, worth exploring the ginnels and back roads off the steeply rising high street, to get a feeling of what the place was like in the days of the Brontës.

The Parsonage, built in 1777, is the focus of most Brontë pilgrimages and it is now given over to the **Brontë Parsonage Museum**; the Brontë Society have restored the interior to be as close as possible to the house in which the sisters lived with their father and brother. There are exhibitions and displays of contemporary material, personal belongings, letters, and portraits, as well as a priceless collection of manuscripts, first editions and memorabilia in the newer extension. Here, too, visitors can see the world famous 'little books' the sisters wrote in their own minute handwriting that was made to look like printed text and there are also some of their drawings, from cartoons to copies of Thomas Bewick's engravings. The Brontë family moved to this fine Georgian house in 1820 when Patrick Brontë, the sisters' father, became the local parson.

Taking their inspiration from the surrounding bleak and lonely Haworth Moor, and from the stories they made up as children, the three sisters, Anne, Charlotte, and Emily, under their male pen names, all became published authors while Branwell, their brother, though by all accounts a scholar, sought refuge in the beer at the local inn. Then the tuberculosis that had attacked the family earlier returned and, one by one, Patrick Brontë's surviving children finally succumbed to the terrible disease. The story of the Brontë family is one of tragedy but the circumstances of their deaths were all too common in the 19th century and graphically illustrate the harshness of life just 150 years ago.

Many visitors are drawn to the area by the story of the family and the Brontë Way, a 40 mile linear footpath with a series of four guided walks, links the places that provided inspiration to the sisters. The most exhilarating and popular excursion is that to **Top Withins**, a favourite place of Emily's and the inspiration for the 'Wuthering Heights' of her novel. It is said that the ghost of Emily Brontë has been seen walking, with her head bowed, between the Parsonage and Top Withins Farm. The route also takes into account a great variety of scenery, from the wild moorlands to pastoral countryside. Brontë enthusiasts can also sit in the Black Bull, where Branwell sent himself to an early grave on a mixture of strong Yorkshire ale, opium and despair (although the last

Brontë Parsonage Museum

atmosphere of the days of steam. There are daily services during July and August and intermittent services throughout the rest of the year.

HEBDEN BRIDGE

In St George's Square, in the heart of the town, is the historic **Hebden Bridge Mill** that for almost 700 years has been powered by the fast-flowing waters of the River Hebden. For over four centuries this was a manorial corn mill before it was converted into a textile mill that was finally abandoned in the 1950s. Now lovingly restored, the mill is home to various stylish shops, restaurants and craft workshops.

The **Rochdale Canal**, which flows through the town, was completed in 1798 to link the Calder and Hebble Navigation with the Bridgwater and Ashton canals from Lancashire. Used by commercial traffic until 1939, the canal has been repaired and sections of it, including that between Hebden Bridge and Todmorden, are now open to traffic, most of it pleasure craft. Horse drawn and motor boat cruises are available from the marina.

To the northwest of Hebden Bridge lies the **Land Farm Sculpture Garden and Gallery**, a delightful woodland garden created over some 30 years from a

Haworth Moor

two are not available here these days). The Post Office from where the sisters sent their manuscripts to London publishers is still as it was, as is the Sunday School at which they all taught. Sadly, the church that they all attended no longer exists, although Charlotte, Emily and Branwell all lie in a vault in the new church, which dates from 1879: their sister Anne is buried in Scarborough.

As well as being a place of pilgrimage for Brontë enthusiasts, Haworth is popular with devotees of steam railways and the town is the headquarters of the **Keighley & Worth Valley Railway**, a thriving volunteer-run railway that serves six stations, most of them still gas-lit. The railway owns an extensive and varied collection of locomotives and everything combines to re-create the barren Pennine hillside that faces north and lies some 1,000 feet above sea level. Attached to the house is an art gallery and both are open at weekends and Bank Holidays from May to the end of August.

HOLMFIRTH

As with many towns and villages in the West Riding of Yorkshire, Holmfirth's development came with the Industrial Revolution and the advent of the textile industry. The proximity to the moorland sheep and the convenience of the town's fast flowing streams and river saw, first weaver's cottages and then more and more impressive mills built here and, today, local firms still supply materials to some of the top names in the fashion industry. As a result, this is a town with numerous narrow alleyways, or 'ginnels' that climb steeply up steeply from the valley bottom to weavers' hamlets with their cottages easily recognisable by their long mullioned windows that let in as much natural light as possible.

However, today, Holmfirth is familiar to television viewers around the world as it is the location for the long running BBC comedy *Last of the Summer Wine*. Visitors to this little Pennine town can enjoy an authentic bacon buttie in the real Sid's Café, gaze at Nora Batty's cottage and sit in the famous pub. Here, too, is the **Last of the Summer Wine Exhibition** that covers the nearly 30 years of this, the longest running television comedy series, through photographs, memorabilia and a display of some of the unusual inventions

devised by the characters. The exhibition is open daily and is located in what Compo's house in the series.

Another popular attraction in the town is the **Bamfords Postcard Collection** that displays a comprehensive exhibition of the traditional saucy seaside postcards and the patriotic World War I postcards produced by Bamfords of Holmfirth in the first half of the 20th century. The company also produced hymn sheets and, rather surprisingly, many early silent movies.

Holmfirth has a lovely Georgian church, built in 1777-8 in neo-classical style to the designs of Joseph Jagger. The gable faces the street and the tower is constructed at the eastern end against a steep hillside.

HUDDERSFIELD

This town's earliest roots can be found on the 1,000 feet high **Castle Hill** that has been occupied as a defence since the Stone Age and simple tools, flints, bone needles, combs and pottery dating back to 2000BC have been unearthed here. The much later ramparts of an Iron Age fort, built here around 600BC, can also still be seen although this fort was destroyed by a mysterious fire just 200 years after it was built. In 1147 the Normans repaired the earthworks and built a motte and bailey castle here, which gave the hill its name, which was apparently used as a base for hunting. The hill was also used as a beacon when England was threatened by the Spanish Armada, and again during the Napoleonic wars. The lofty **Jubilee Tower**, built in 1897 to celebrate Queen Victoria's Diamond Jubilee and funded by public subscription, is the most recent structure on the summit.

The Huddersfield of today dates, in essence, from the 18th and 19th centuries when the town developed rapidly, with the help of the then lords of the manor, the Ramsden family, as a woollen town, exporting worsted cloth all over the world. This booming textile industry has left a wealth of grand Victorian buildings that include the stately railway station, which was designed by James Pigott of York and was built between 1846-50, and the Italianate Town Hall. The town's **Tolson Memorial Museum** paints a vivid and intriguing picture of Huddersfield and its people from prehistoric times through to the present day. One of the most popular exhibits is the collection of vintage vehicles and motoring memorabilia in the 'Going Places' collection while other displays trace the story of the Industrial Revolution, which was so important to the growth of the town, and the political protests it engendered. **Huddersfield Art Gallery**, which holds the Kirklees Collection of British Art covering the last 150 years, has a lively programme of exhibitions that showcases contemporary art from regional, national and international artists.

The town is also home to two canals that helped to link Huddersfield not only with the national canal network but also with other industrial towns. Completed in 1780 and paid for by the Ramsden family, the **Huddersfield Broad Canal** was constructed to link the town with the Calder and Hebble Navigation. The canal's Aspley Basin was, in the heyday of the waterway, a busy area of docks and warehouses and, today, it is home to a marina, while the warehouses have been converted into offices and flats. Later, in 1794, work on the **Huddersfield Narrow Canal**, which links the town with Ashton-under-Lyne, began and its centrepiece, the Standedge Tunnel, took 17 years to complete. The longest, highest and deepest canal tunnel in the country has now reopened with its own visitor centre. The **Standedge Visitor Centre** at **Marsden** houses an exciting and interactive exhibition telling the story of the canal and the tunnel's construction and, from here, visitors can travel through the famous tunnel. Originally opened in 1811, the tunnel, one of the great feats of canal engineering, was designed by Thomas Telford and is regarded as one of the Seven Wonders of the British Canal Network. The countryside surrounding the centre offers a wide range of activities, including walking, cycling and fishing, and this area of outstanding natural beauty is also a haven for wildlife.

ILKLEY

Originally an Iron Age settlement, Ilkley was eventually occupied by the Romans who built a camp here to protect their crossing of the River Wharfe. They named their settlement 'Olicana' and so gave rise to Ilkley's present name with the addition of the familiar 'ley' that is Anglo-Saxon for pasture. Behind the Manor House is the site of the Roman fort of **Olicana** although all that remains today is a small portion of the 1st century fortification. Close to this site is the medieval **All Saints' Church** that was built on the site of a Saxon place of worship. Though the doorway dates from the 13th century and the tower from the 15th century, the most interesting feature here must be the 17th century box pew and the medieval font that is made from local stone. Now housed in the town's museum are the altars, carved in gritstone, which are dedicated to the Roman gods.

The spring at **White Wells** began to bring more visitors to the town in the 18th century and, in 1765, Squire Middleton built walls around this moorland spring so that patients could both bathe in and drink the pure cold water. The roof was added at a later date and one bath is still open for the public to view. It was the early Victorian era that saw the development of the hydros, hydropathic treatment hotels, which provided hot and cold treatments based on the ideas of Dr Preissnitz of Austria who, in 1843, became the director of Britain's first Hydro at nearby

Ben Rhydding. The coming of the railways from Leeds and Bradford in the 1860s and 1870s, during a period of growth in the Yorkshire woollen industry, saw the town take on a new role as a fashionable commuter town. Wool manufacturers and their better-paid employees came to Ilkley not only to enjoy the superb amenities but to build handsome villas.

If it was in Bradford and Leeds that people made their brass, so it was said at the time, then it was usually at Ilkley that it was spent. Even today, Ilkley sports some remarkable and opulent Victorian architecture as proof of this and Ilkley's patrons and well-to-do citizens gave the town a splendid Town Hall, Library, Winter Gardens and King's Hall and this sense of elegance is still present along The Grove. Between the remains of the Roman fort and the River Wharfe lie the **Riverside Gardens**, a favourite place for a stroll that could lead over a 17th century packhorse bridge

Manor House Art Gallery and Museum

across the river. On the side of this bridge, beside the stone steps, the flood levels of the river have been marked, along with the dates. On the opposite side of the River Wharfe is **The Lido**, one of the few surviving outdoor swimming pools in Yorkshire.

Housed in a building that dates from the 15th, 16th and 17th centuries, which is complete with mullioned windows, carved beams and an interesting wall privy, is the **Manor House Art Gallery and Museum**. The museum, on the ground floor, tells the history of Ilkley from its prehistoric routes through to its development as a Victorian spa town while, upstairs, the art gallery hosts a programme of temporary exhibitions throughout the year.

Keighley and Worth Valley Railway

KEIGHLEY

Lying at the junction of the Rivers Worth and Aire, this bustling textile and engineering town, despite its modern redevelopment, still retains a strangely nostalgic air of the Industrial Revolution of 18th and 19th centuries. It was that era of rapid growth that created the town seen today, beginning at Low Mill in 1780, when cotton spinning on a factory scale was first introduced. Reminders of hardships endured by the many factory workers of that time can be seen in the labyrinth of 'ginnels' and terraces that lie amid the many elaborately decorated mills. The centre of Keighley is dominated by impressive Victorian civic buildings, built on the prosperity the textile industry brought to the town, and

a beautifully set out covered shopping precinct, where the statue of legendary local giant, Rombald, stands. The parish church, also in the centre, is famous as the site where Patrick Brontë often officiated at marriages.

Outside the town centre is **Cliffe Castle** that, despite its deceptive name, is, in fact, a grand late 19th century mansion complete with a tower, battlements and parkland that once belonged to local mill owners, the Butterfields. It now houses **Keighley Museum**, which concentrates on the fascinating local topography and geology of Airedale as well as the history of the town. Also housed in the museum is the hand loom, complete with unfinished cloth, that was used by Timmy Feather, the last hand loom weaver in England. Part of the building is still furnished and decorated in the lavish style of the 1880s.

From Keighley southwards runs the line of the Keighley and Worth Valley Railway to Haworth. This restored steam railway line passes through some attractive small villages and some notable stations that include Haworth, the Brontë village. An award-

Leeds Town Hall

winning visitor attraction, steam trains run every weekend, and daily throughout the summer, and this is a wonderful way to explore this delightful part of West Yorkshire. Keighley station, one of the termini of the line, has a turntable, picnic area and souvenir kiosk.

From the heart of industrial Keighley, there is an interesting 5-mile walk, the **Worth Way**, which leads to the eastern edge of the Worth Valley at Oxenhope. This landscape has changed little since the time when Mrs Gaskell wrote about the area while visiting Charlotte Brontë in 1856.

LEEDS

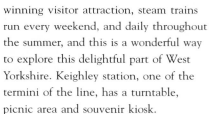

In recent years, the city of Leeds has seen something of a renaissance – its waterfront, neglected and derelict for so long, is now buzzing with new developments and abandoned warehouses have been imaginatively transformed into fashionable bars, restaurants and tourist attractions – and this is taking place less than 15 minutes walk from the shopping centre. Perhaps the most talked about store in Leeds is Harvey Nichols whose Knightsbridge emporium enjoyed a heightened reputation in the 1990s thanks to the BBC series *Absolutely Fabulous*. In parallel with these developments the Aire and Calder Navigation is being transformed to enable leisure traffic to use the waterway as well as freight. Leeds is a major European cultural centre with its own opera and ballet companies, Northern Ballet Theatre and Opera North, while the West Yorkshire Playhouse, regarded as the 'National Theatre of the North', is a showcase for classic British and European drama as well as work by new Yorkshire writers.

Situated adjacent to the monumental City Hall, the **Leeds City Art Gallery** boasts an exceptional collection of Victorian and Pre-Raphaelite paintings, French Post-Impressionist paintings along with major works by Courbet, Lowry, Sickert, Stanley Spencer and Bridget Riley. Linked to the gallery is the **Henry Moore Institute**, the first centre in Europe devoted to the display and study of sculpture of all periods.

Leeds, like much of West Yorkshire, owes much of its prosperity to wool and, found in what was the largest woollen mill in the world, Armley Mills, is the **Leeds Industrial Museum**. Here on the banks of the River Aire, visitors can explore the city's rich industrial past through displays and exhibits that include textile and clothing industries, printing, engineering and photography. At the **Thackray Medical Museum**, one of the largest museums of its kind in Europe, visitors get the chance to look at the development of medicine through the eyes of ordinary people. There are more than 25,000 extraordinary objects in its collection and they range from a surgical chain saw and Prince Albert's medical chest through to a 17th century correction frame. There are several

Henry Moore Institute

themed exhibitions here, including one that illustrates how surgery was performed in the days before anaesthetics, while another allows visitors to walk into a giant gut and explore the human body with the help of Sherlock Bones.

One of the city's most fascinating places is the **Royal Armouries**, opened by the Queen in 1998, which traces the development of arms and armour from the 5th century BC to modern times. The museum utilises interactive computer displays, videos, films, music and poetry to tell the story of arms and armour in battle, self-defence, sport and fashion while, outside, the Tiltyard features jousting and hunting tournaments daily from April to September and a bustling Menagerie Court includes displays of falcons, hunting dogs and horses. This world renowned collection includes the only surviving elephant armour in a public collection and Henry VIII's elaborate tournament armour.

Lovers of real ale may well want to take advantage of a joint ticket that gives admission to both the Royal Armouries and **Tetley's Brewery Wharf**, where visitors can learn how Joshua Tetley founded his great empire and also learn the secret of his famous brew. To the southeast of the city centre, between the River Aire and the canal, lies **Thwaite Mills Watermill**, an early 19th century mill, with two giant waterwheels, which once sustained a small, self-sufficient community. To the southwest of the city is **Temple Newsam House**, a wonderful Tudor-Jacobean mansion that is known as the Hampton Court of the North. Set in 1,200 acres of parkland landscaped by Capability Brown, the house boasts extensive collections of decorative arts displayed in their original room settings, which feature interior design styles from the 16th to the 20th centuries, and among the collections is one of the largest displays of Chippendale furniture in the country. Adjacent to Temple Newsam House is the country's largest approved Rare Breeds Centre – Home Farm. Visitors to this working farm will see pigs, goats, horses and poultry alongside interesting displays of vintage farm machinery and past farming methods.

OAKWORTH

Those visiting Oakworth may find its splendid and authentic Edwardian station, on the Keighley and Worth Valley Railway line, somewhat familiar as it not only featured in the classic children's film, *The Railway Children*, but also in episodes of the television series

Oakworth Station

Sherlock Holmes. Further up the line lies Ingrow West station that is home to the **Museum of Rail Travel** and where fascinating collections of historic railway carriages, along with elderly steam locomotives, are on display. The museum concentrates on telling the story of rail travel from the point of view of the ordinary passenger. Further along the line again lies Damems Station – Britain's smallest.

PONTEFRACT

Shakespeare alluded to this town as 'Bloody Pomfret' (the original name of this settlement) in his play *Richard II* and it featured as a place of influence and power that was often visited by kings and their retinues and, indeed, in medieval England, the town was home to one of the greatest fortresses in Yorkshire. On a crag to the east of the town stand the great shattered towers of the once formidable **Pontefract Castle** that was built by Ilbert de Lacy in the 11th century. In medieval times the castle passed to the House of Lancaster and became a Royal Castle – Richard II was imprisoned here and tragically murdered in its dungeons on the orders of Henry Bolingbroke, who then assumed the crown as Henry IV. The castle was a major Royalist stronghold during the Civil War, after which it was destroyed by Cromwell's troops and, today, it remains as a gaunt ruin with only sections of the inner bailey and the lower part of the keep surviving intact. Another ancient site worth visiting is the **Pontefract Hermitage**, a little known monument that comprises two chambers and a well and it is reached by a spiral staircase that has been cut from the solid rockface. Many of the streets of Pontefract evoke memories of its medieval past with names such as Micklegate, Beast Fair, Shoe Market, Salter Row and Ropergate. Modern development has masked much of old Pontefract but there are still many old Georgian buildings and winding streets to be discovered. For an insight into the history of this old town, the **Pontefract Museum** has displays covering the ages from the time of the Normans to the present day.

The town's most famous product is Pontefract Cakes; liquorice root has been grown here since monastic times and there is even a small planting of liquorice in the local park. The town celebrates this unique heritage with the 5-day **Pontefract Liquorice Fayre** in mid August that includes two days of jousting, archery and battle re-enactments at Pontefract Castle. Pontefract has the longest, flat, circular **Racecourse** in Europe.

RIDDLESDEN

Although parts of **East Riddlesden Hall** (National Trust) date back to Saxon times, the main building was constructed in by James Murgatroyd, a wealthy Halifax clothier and merchant. A fine example of a 17th century manor house, the gabled hall is built of dark stone with mullioned windows and retains its original centre hall, superb period fireplaces, oak panelling and plaster ceilings. The house is furnished in the Jacobean style, which is complemented by carved likenesses of Charles I and his Queen, Henrietta Maria, and an impressive collection of embroideries, textiles and Yorkshire oak furniture can also be seen within. East Riddlesden Hall also has one of the largest and most impressive timber framed barns in the north of England that now houses a collection of farm wagons and agricultural equipment. The house stands in glorious grounds, with mature beech trees, which also include lavender, herbs, mixed herbaceous borders and the Orchard Garden, home to old varieties of apple trees.

SALTAIRE

This model village was created by Titus Salt for the workers at his mill and he proved to be a very benevolent employer and was determined to provide his workers with everything essential for a decent standard of living. Built between 1851 and 1876, the facilities in the village were designed to cater for all their needs – health, leisure and education – but there were no public houses. The spiritual needs of the work force were attended to by the elegant Congregational church that has been described as the most beautiful Free Church in the north of England. A statue of Titus Salt stands in nearby Robert's Park (where swearing and gambling were banned) above the figures of a llama and an alpaca, whose wool he imported for spinning in his mills.

The **Victoria Boat House** was built in 1871 and has been beautifully restored,

River Aire, Saltaire

with an open fire, pianola and wind-up gramophone, all re-creating a traditional parlour atmosphere where visitors can enjoy cream teas and attend special Victorian Evenings in the dress of that time. Also in Saltaire is the **Museum of Victorian Reed Organs** that has a collection of more than 45 instruments, including harmonicas and an American organ, which are demonstrated from time to time, and some of which are available for visitors to try. However, this village is not completely locked into the past and the former Salt's Mill has been converted into the **1853 David Hockney Gallery** that displays the world's largest collection of paintings by the internationally acclaimed artist, who was born in Bradford in 1937.

THORNTON

This village is an essential stopping place on the Brontë trail for it was here that the three sisters were born, at 74 Market Street, which is now open to the public as the **Brontë Birthplace**. Their father was the vicar of Thornton at the time and one of the treasures of his parish church is the font, inscribed with the date 1687, in which Charlotte, Emily and Anne were all baptised. Charlotte was only 4 years old, her two sisters still toddlers, when the family moved a few miles northwest to Haworth after their father had been appointed rector of the parish.

TODMORDEN

This is another typical mill town that grew with the expansion of the textile industry but, before the 19th century, Todmorden had been a spartan place with many of the villagers eking out frugal lives by hand loom weaving. Following the building of the first mill here Todmorden began to grow and the highly ornate and flamboyant public buildings were, in the main, built by the mill owners. Firstly producing wool or worsted cloth, the mills soon turned to cotton spinning and weaving, and the proximity to Manchester, both a source of raw material and a market place for the finished product, was an important factor in the change of direction. In 1798, the Rochdale Canal reached Todmorden and along this stretch, from Manchester to Sowerby Bridge, across the Pennines, the canal has some 92 locks. One of the most unusual of which is the Guillotine Lock.

Though many towns that owe their existence to industry also bear the scars, Todmorden has retained all its charm and character and is an excellent place to visit for those interested in architecture. It boasts a magnificent **Town Hall**, designed by John Gibson and opened in 1875, which is one of the finest municipal buildings of its size in the country. As the grand old building once stood half in Yorkshire and half in Lancashire, the ornate carving in the pediment represents the farming and iron trades of Yorkshire in the right panel and the cotton trade of Lancashire in the left.

However, some buildings here predate the Industrial Revolution, notably **Todmorden Hall**, which dates back to 1293. In the early 17th century, the old timber-framed building was replaced by one built of stone that contains some wonderful panelling and a grand heraldic fireplace. Housed in an early 19th century listed building, the **Todmorden Toy and Model Museum** is ideal for all the family who will enjoy this nostalgic journey back to childhood. Open from Wednesday to Sunday, the museum also buys and sell toys and models.

One of the oldest towns in Yorkshire, Wakefield stands on a hill guarding an important crossing of the River Calder. Its defensive position has always been important and it was the Battle of Wakefield in 1460, when the Duke of York was defeated, which gave rise to the mocking song *The Grand Old Duke of York*. It is also claimed by many that Robin Hood had his origins in Wakefield and, indeed, in the Court Rolls a 'Robin Hode' is noted as living here in the 14th century with his wife Matilda before fleeing to the woods of Sherwood Forest. Also medieval in origin are the **Wakefield Miracle Plays** that explore Old and New Testament stories in vivid language. The 600-year-old cycle is performed in the cathedral precincts as part of the city's annual Festival.

There are four main streets in the city, Westgate, Northgate, Warrengate and Kirkgate, which still preserve the medieval city plan and one of the most striking buildings that survives from that time is the tiny Chantry Chapel of St Mary, on Wakefield Bridge, which dates from the mid 1300s and is the best of only four such examples of bridge chapels in England. It is believed to have been built by Edward IV to commemorate the brutal murder of his brother Edmund. The stone bridge on which it is built was of great economic importance to the town as it provided a vital river crossing for travellers who had to pay a toll when making the crossing.

Grandest by far of all the city's buildings is **Wakefield Cathedral** that was begun in Norman times, rebuilt in 1329 and refashioned in 1470 when its magnificent 247 foot high spire – the highest in Yorkshire – was added. The eastern extension to the cathedral is a 20th century addition considered necessary after the church became a cathedral in 1888. Other interesting buildings in the town include the stately Town Hall, the huge County Hall, the recently restored Edwardian Theatre Royal and many fine Georgian and Regency terraces and squares. A further cultural attraction is the **Wakefield Art Gallery**, housed in an attractive former Victorian vicarage just a short stroll from the town centre. Here, the exhibits include one of the most important collections of modern British Art, with works by Henry Moore and Barbara Hepworth along with many other major modern British artists.

Wakefield Museum, located in a 1820s building next to the Town Hall, was originally a music saloon and then a Mechanics' Institute but it now houses collections illustrating the history and archaeology of Wakefield and its people from prehistoric times to the present day. There is also a permanent display of exotic birds and animals that were collected by the noted 19th century traveller, naturalist and eccentric Charles Waterton, who lived at nearby Walton Hall where he created the world's first nature reserve. The **Steven G Beaumont Museum** houses an unusual exhibition of medical memorabilia and, in particular, it tells the story of the local lunatic asylum that was founded in 1818 and only closed in 1995.

Just south of the city centre lies **Sandal Castle**, a 12th century motte and bailey fortress that was later replaced by a stone castle that overlooks the site of the Battle of Wakefield in 1460. Such was this castle's importance that Richard III was planning to make Sandal his permanent northern stronghold when he was killed at Bosworth Field. Today all that remains are ruins as the castle was destroyed by Cromwell's troops after a siege in 1645. From here there are magnificent views across the Calder Valley and the finds made during recent excavations of the site can be found in Wakefield's museum.

A few miles to the southeast from Wakefield lies **Nostell Priory** (National Trust), one of the most popular tourist venues in the area; the term 'priory' is misleading since the building seen today is, in fact, a large Palladian building erected on the site of an old Augustinian priory. It was in 1733 that the owner, Sir Rowland Winn, commissioned James Paine to build a grand mansion; the architect was only 19 years old at the time and this was his first major project. Thirty years later, only half the state rooms were constructed and Sir Rowland's son, also named Rowland, engaged an up and coming young designer to complete the decoration. The young man's name was Robert Adam and between 1766 and 1776 his dazzling designs produced an incomparable sequence of interiors.

There was a third man of genius involved in the story of Nostell Priory, the cabinet maker Thomas Chippendale, and what is believed to be his 'apprentice piece', made around 1735, is on display here – an extraordinary Doll's House complete with the most elaborate detail. Today, Nostell Priory can boast the most comprehensive collection in the world of Chippendale's work.

To the southwest of Wakefield, at Caphouse Colliery, in Overton, is the **National Coal Mining Museum**. Along with guided underground tours led by local miners, visitors can see outdoor machinery, a working steam winder, and pit ponies and, for the children there is an adventure playground and nature trails.

West Yorkshire

THE BRIDGE INN

KEIGHLEY ROAD, SILSDEN, WEST YORKSHIRE BD20 0EA
TEL: 01535 653144

Directions: Silsden is located on the A6034, a half-mile north of the A650

Built in 1799, when it was called The Spoon and Slipper, **The Bridge Inn** is a distinguished and friendly pub set alongside the Leeds-Liverpool Canal. Here in this tranquil setting, there's a good mix of old and new, with attractive furnishings and décor throughout. Run by Kevin and Tracey Hurt, who have been here since July 2002, it's a popular place with locals and visitors alike, due to its great food and drink and warm hospitality. To quench that thirst, there are three real ales – John Smith's Cask and two changing guest ales – as well as a good selection of lagers, cider, stout,

wines, spirits and soft drinks. The menu and specials board has something for everyone. Tracy is a great cook, and uses only the freshest local produce. Specialities include the home-made meat and potato pies. The intimate non-smoking dining area seats 12, and guests can also enjoy their meal in the bar area or outside in the lovely canalside beer garden. Children are welcome right up until 9 p.m. There's occasional live entertainment and regular jam sessions, as well as disco/karaoke evenings.

The excellent accommodation comprises three guest bedrooms available all year round. There's a double, single and family room, located adjacent to the inn and with full facilities, available at room-only or bed-and-breakfast rates. Comfortable and welcoming, these guest rooms make an excellent base to explore the area.

- 🕐 Winter Mon-Thurs 16.00-23.00; Fri 13.00-23.00; Sat 12.00-23.00; Sun 12.00-22.30. Summer Mon-Thurs 11.00-15.00, 17.00-23.00; Fri-Sat 11.00-23.00; Sun 12.00-22.30
- 🍴 Mon-Thurs 11.00-17.30; Fri-Sat 11.00-14.00; Sun 12.00-15.00
- 💷 All major
- 🛏 Three rooms ensuite
- 🅿 Off-road car park, beer garden
- 🎵 Singalong/jamming Thurs night; Karaoke and disco Fri and Sat night' occasional live entertainment, pool, darts, bull ring
- @ kevandtraceyhurt@aol.com
- ❓ Walking, cycling (Ilkley cycleway less than 1 mile), boating (Leeds-Liverpool canal less than 1 mile), Skipton 4 miles, Keighley 4 miles

THE CHEQUERS INN

CLAYPIT LANE, LEDSHAM, WEST YORKSHIRE LS25 5LP
TEL: 01977 683135

West Yorkshire

Directions: East of the A656 and west of the A1, near Castleford

The Chequers Inn at Ledsham is a real treasure, well worth seeking out.

Although it is a Free House, the premises have been leased from the local estate by the Wraith family since 1984. Now personally run by Chris Wraith, who has been the licensee here since 1990, this picturesque and welcoming inn dates back to the mid-14th century. The handsome stonebuilt frontage is covered in creepers, and inside there are homely features like the stonebuilt bar, a wealth of warm wood and open fires. Made up of lots of separate rooms downstairs, with an elegant restaurant on the first floor, the ambience here is always friendly and relaxed. Outside there is an outstanding garden with mature trees and a paved area with supremely comfortable outdoor furniture, for enjoying a drink or hearty meal when the weather is fine.

Some 170 years ago the Lady of the Manor, offended by the antics of a drunken worker while on her way to church, ruled that the pub would never open on a Sunday. This ban is still in force, so that the inn is open Monday to Saturday only.

The five real ales on tap include John Smiths, Theakstons, Timothy Taylor Landlord, Brown Cow (from a local micro-brewery) and a changing guest ale, together with a good range of lagers, stout, cider, wines, spirits and soft drinks.

The restaurant seats 32, but guests can also dine anywhere throughout the inn. Choosing off a printed menu or the specials board, there's an excellent selection of delicious meals such as home-made steak and mushroom pie to enjoy. No bookings are taken and the inn is very popular for its food, so come early to avoid disappointment. Children welcome.

- Mon-Fri 11.00-15.00, 17.00-23.00; Sat 11.00-23.00
- Mon-Sat 12.00-14.15, 18.00-21.15
- All major
- Off-road parking, patio/garden areas
- www.thechequersinn.f9.co.uk
- Castleford 3 miles, Garforth 5 miles, Leeds 10 miles

THE DUNKIRK INN

231 BARNSLEY ROAD, DENBY DALE, HUDDERSFIELD,
WEST YORKSHIRE HD8 8TX
TEL: 01484 862646

Directions: From Barnsley, Denby Dale is 8 miles west on the A635. Denby Dale is also 8 miles southeast of Huddersfield, on the A629 and then the A635.

The Dunkirk Inn began life in the 1800s as a row of traditional stonebuilt cottages. In 1912 the cottages were converted into a public house, called The Junction and in 1983 it was renamed to preserve the little-known hamlet's name. This fine traditional Free House had seen some hard times before Christine Lidster arrived in February 2003 and gave it a new heart, a totally new look, and added great food and ale to Yorkshire hospitality to put this lively and friendly pub back on the map.

Recently refurbished, redecorated and restored to its old charm and character, the inn combines the best of modern-day furnishings and comfort with 18th-century elegance. Outside, the lovely beer garden is just the place to enjoy a relaxed drink or meal on fine days.

Standing proud amid breathtaking views of the surrounding countryside, the pub serves up delicious home-made meat and potato pie as one speciality, with Lynn whipping up other excellent dishes and daily specials such as mixed grills, salmon with lobster sauce, steak Dijonnaise and Thai duck, as well as traditional Sunday lunch, served in the two adjoining dining areas. All meals make use of the finest local ingredients wherever possible, including meats from the local butcher. Booking advised for Sunday lunch. There are always at least four real ales on tap, including Tetleys and changing guest ales. Other thirst-quenchers include Fosters, Stella, Kronenbourg, John Smith's Smooth, Scrumpy Jack and Guinness, together with a good selection of wines, spirits and soft drinks. Children welcome.

- 🕐 Mon-Fri 12.00-15.00, 17.00-23.00; Sat 12.00-23.00; Sun 12.00-22.30
- 🍴 Lunch Tues-Sat 12.00-14.30; dinner Tues-Sat and Bank Holiday Mon 18.00-21.00; Sunday lunch 12.00-18.00
- £ All major
- Ⓟ Off-road parking, beer garden
- 🎵 Quiz Sundays from 9 p.m
- @ www.dunkirk.co.uk
- ❓ Denby Dale, Barnsley 8 miles, Huddersfield 8 miles, Peak District 10 miles, walking, cycling

THE FOX

34 SOUTH BAILEYGATE, PONTEFRACT, WEST YORKSHIRE WF8 2JL
TEL: 01977 780619

Directions: From junction 32 of the M62, take the A639 south to Pontefract. From the centre of Pontefract, follow the Ferrybridge/Knottingley signs – The Fox is just a short walk from the centre of town, near Pontefract Castle.

Dating back to the mid-18th century, **The Fox** began life as a coaching inn, with the local smithy nearby to help when teams of horses were changed. The exterior is handsome and welcoming, with hanging baskets of flowers and pristine paintwork. The interior, too, is charming and inviting, with original features such as the stone fireplace and wealth of woodwork. Very well-decorated and furnished, the inn retains that olde-worlde feeling while providing every modern comfort. Outside there's a hidden beer garden to the rear, accessible only through the pub. Here guests will find a patio with tables and a smooth lawn with picnic tables and children's play equipment.

Licensees Janeen and David have been

tenants here since 1996. They and their friendly, helpful staff ensure that all their guests enjoy a pleasant and relaxing time here while enjoying the great food, drink and atmosphere.

Food is available every lunchtime, and the pub is well known for its delicious, freshly prepared, home-made dishes such as giant Yorkshire puddings with different fillings, steak and kidney pie, vegetable curry, burgers, salads and more traditional favourites. All meals are listed on the blackboard, as they change regularly. The roasts are justly popular. The real ale here is John Smith's Cask, and there is a range of lagers, ciders, stout, wines, spirits and soft drinks, to quench every thirst.

Entertainments here include regular quiz nights and group games such as Open the Box and Play Your Cards Right.

- Mon-Fri 11.00-15.00, 17.00-23.00; Sat 11.00-23.00; Sun 12.00-22.30
- Mon-Sat 12.00-14.00; Sun 12.00-14.30
- Beer garden, off-road parking, function room, children welcome
- Quiz night Weds, quiz and Play Your Cards Right Fri, quiz and Open the Box Sun (all from 9.30)
- Pontefract Castle, Pontefract Racecourse (flat racing), Leeds 9 miles

THE GOLDEN LION

1 THE SQUARE, FERRYBRIDGE, WEST YORKSHIRE WF11 8ND
TEL: 01977 673527

> **Directions:** From junction 33 of the M62 where it meets the A1, go 1½ miles on the B6136 (Ferrybridge-to-Castleford Road). The Golden Lion can be found ½ mile to ¾ miles from the centre of Knottingley.

Standing alongside the River Aire, **The Golden Lion** in Ferrybridge is a traditional inn in all the best senses of the term. Dating back to the early 19ᵗʰ century, this former coaching inn once housed a ferry crossing within its grounds. The exterior of this friendly inn is large and impressive, its white paint looking pristine and welcoming, with picnic tables to one side. Inside, all is light and spacious, with an attractive traditional décor and comfortable furnishings.

Tetleys Cask real ale is on tap here, together with a good choice of keg bitters, lagers, cider, stout, wines, spirits and soft drinks – something, in short, to quench every thirst.

- Mon-Sat 11.00-23.00; Sun 12.00-22.30
- Mon-Sat 12.00-14.00, 17.30-20.30; Sun 12.00-15.00
- Visa, Mastercard, Switch, Delta, Eurocard, Solo
- 8 guest bedrooms
- Off-road parking, patio
- Quiz nights Thursday and Sunday; pub games
- goldlion@aol.com
- Pontefract 1 mile

The printed menu and specials boards list a range of delicious home-cooked meals and there's a carvery at Sunday lunchtime. The tasty food can be enjoyed in the bar, lounge or in the no-smoking restaurant (children welcome). Along with bar meals and favourites such as burgers, steaks and scampi, there are filled baguettes, Greek salad platters, lasagne verdi and more. The puddings, too, are worth leaving room for!

The accommodation here comprises eight comfortable and attractive guest bedrooms. The rooms differ in size from singles and twins to triples, and are available for bed-and-breakfast or on a room-only tariff basis. Families welcome.

Mother and daughter team Heather and Haley run this fine pub with flair. They are friendly, welcoming hosts who have worked hard to ensure that the inn maintains its fine reputation.

528 THORNTON ROAD, THORNTON, WEST YORKSHIRE BD13 3NH
TEL: 01274 833400

Directions: Found on the B6145 2 miles north of Queensbury and 4 miles west of Bradford

Located on the edge of Thornton village, as its name suggests **The Great Northern** was built by the Great Northern Railway back in the 1870s, at which time the railway station stood opposite along the line that linked Bradford to Keighley and Halifax via Queensbury.

The interior is charming, spacious and light, with pale woods and a bright décor adding to the welcoming ambience. The open-plan layout also enhances the relaxed and convivial atmosphere.

Tenants Pete and Jo have been here since mid-2003, bringing their experience of running another local pub to bear on making this a success. Friendly and welcoming, they and their helpful, attentive staff offer the very best in hospitality and service. There are

usually three real ales to sample – all from the Thwaites Brewery range – together with three draught lagers, a cider, a stout and a good selection of wines, spirits and soft drinks. Happy Hour is weeknights between 5 and 7 p.m.

Meals are served at lunch and early evenings throughout the week, and for long lunches (1 to 4.30 p.m.) at weekends. Guests choose from a good variety of dishes such as filled giant Yorkshire puddings and other tempting traditional favourites like steak and ale pie, battered haddock and more. Bar snacks are available most evenings.

Thornton is an attractive village, home to the Bronte Birthplace and close to many sights and attractions at Queensbury, Bradford, Halifax and the surrounding southern Dales.

- Mon-Sat 11.00-23.00; Sun 12.00-22.30
- All day every day
- All major
- Off-road parking
- Live bands once a month, Saturday nightsplease ring for detailsKaraoke Friday evenings; quiz night Thursday; couples' night Saturdays
- Bronte Birthplace, Queensbury 2 miles, Bradford 4 miles, Halifax 6 miles

THE GREEN DRAGON

30 CHURCH STREET, EMLEY, HUDDERSFIELD,
WEST YORKSHIRE HD8 9RW
TEL: 01924 848275

> **Directions:** Off the A637, A629 and A636, 6 miles north of Denby Dale and 5 miles east of Huddersfield

Situated in the picturesque village of Emley, **The Green Dragon** is a welcoming and well-looked after inn dating back to the mid-19th century. Its handsome whitewashed exterior makes it easy to spot, while inside the décor is tasteful and traditional. The comfortable lounge boasts real fires, while the dining area is light and spacious. Superbly decorated and furnished throughout, this gracious and charming pub has bygone memorabilia on display, exposed beams and stone walls.

Robert and Julie Lodge, locally born and bred, offer all their guests warm hospitality and great service. They took over as leaseholders in 2002 , their first venture into the business, and are

making a fine go of it. Together with their superb chef, James Bolton, they have created a place well worth seeking out for its great food, drink and atmosphere.

The fully-stocked bar offers a selection of real ales including John Smith Cask and Theakston Old Peculiar, complemented by Tetley Smooth, Stella Artois, Carling, Scrumpy Jack, Guinness and a good range of spirits, wines and soft drinks. There's a tempting range of bar snacks, and guests can also choose from the a la carte menu or specials board for a selection of mouth-watering main courses on Friday and Saturday evenings. The traditional Sunday lunch is also a treat not to be missed.

A fair is held every summer in the first two weeks of August, all proceeds going to charity, with live music, games and more.

🕐 Mon-Thurs 17.00-23.00; Fri-Sat 11.00-23.00; Sun 12.00-22.30

🍴 Fri-Sat 12.00-14.00 and 19.00-22.00; Sun 12.00-17.00

£ Visa, Mastercard, Delta, Switch

Ⓟ Beer garden, off-road parking

🎵 Organist every other Thursday from 8 pm; occasional food theme nights; summer fair first two weeks in August

❓ Denby Dale 6 miles, Huddersfield 5 miles, Holmfirth 7 miles, walking, cycling, birdwatching

THE HUNTSMAN COUNTRY INN & RESTAURANT

GREENFIELD ROAD, HOLMFIRTH, WEST YORKSHIRE HD9 3XE
TEL: 01484 850205

Directions: The Huntsman Country Inn & Restaurant can be found on the A635 (Holmfirth-to-Greenfield Road) about six miles south of Huddersfield

A former farmhouse, the **Huntsman Country Inn & Restaurant** became an alehouse in the early 19th century. The olde worlde interior is brimming with character and is spacious, light and completely charming, with a relaxed ambience and welcoming, homely feel.

Local farmers and butchers prior to coming here in November 2002, owners Tony and Lorraine still farm in a smaller way. Well-known in the area, they have built up a fine reputation for good food, ale and hospitality. Four real ales are always on tap: Tetleys, Black Sheep, Timothy Taylor Landlord and a changing guest ale. In addition there's a

very good selection of keg bitters, lagers, cider, stout, spirits, wines and soft drinks. Happy Hour is Monday to Friday from 5 to 7 p.m., with specials on selected draught bitters and lagers. Guests choose from the printed menu or the daily specials board to sample the delicious and freshly prepared range of home-made dishes including steaks, tasty giant Yorkshire puddings and much more. Booking is advised at Sunday lunchtime.

The handy certified caravan site can accommodate up to five caravans, with guests welcome to use the inn's facilities. Spaces are available all year round. Plans are afoot for the creation of 14 en suite guest bedrooms, which will include ground-floor rooms and facilities for people with disabilities. There will also be a new function room for up to 150 people, and a new non-smoking restaurant seating 50.

- 🕐 Mon 17.00-23.00; Tues-Sat 11.00-23.00; Sun 12.00-22.30
- 🍴 Tues-Fri and Bank Holiday Mon 12.00-14.00, 18.00-21.00; Sat-Sun 12.00-21.00
- 💷 All major
- 🛏 Caravan site; 14 rooms en suite planned for 2004
- 🅿 Patio garden, car parking
- 🎵 Monday night quiz and 'play your cards right' from 9 p.m.; impromptu music nights
- ❓ Holmfirth, Huddersfield 6 miles, Leeds 20 miles

THE KINGS ARMS

2 CHURCH STREET, HAWORTH, WEST YORKSHIRE BD22 8DR
TEL: 01535 647302

Directions: Haworth is south of Keighley on the B6144

Here in the heart of famous Howarth, **The Kings Arms** is an impressive and venerable stonebuilt pub in keeping with the wonderful local church and Bronte parsonage. Dating back to the 17th century, it has always been an inn, offering great food, drink and hospitality.

The pub boasts a long and interesting history. The private rooms upstairs were once used as the Manorial Courts, while the cellar once served as the mortuary. Comfortable, cosy and welcoming inside, the décor and furnishings enhance the marvellous ambience at this fine pub. There are always at least four real ales on tap, including Tetleys, Timothy Taylor Landlord and two changing guest ales, as well as draught kept cider, lager and stout, wines, spirits and soft drinks. Well known for its excellent food, diners can choose from the menus or specials board from a range of traditional and creative dishes such as steaks, chicken chasseur, barbecued ribs, vegetable curry, lasagne, scampi and lamb chops, as well as a delicious all-day breakfast to keep visitors going while they explore the many sights and attractions of the surrounding area. The Duke's Bistro can seat 24; guests can also dine in other areas of the pub, or in the beer garden.

The accommodation comprises one attractive and comfortable double en suite guest bedroom, available all year round.

Licensees Kevin and Susan Duke have been here since 1999, bringing the wealth of their 25 years' experience in the trade to bear on offering the finest service and hospitality. They and their friendly, helpful staff ensure that guests have a relaxing and enjoyable drink, meal or stay.

- Mon-Sat 11.00-23.00; Sun 12.00-22.30
- Tues-Sat 12.00-20.00; Sun-Mon 12.00-18.00
- All major except AMEX
- 1 room en suite
- Car parking, beer garden, children welcome
- Curry night Tuesdays; Steak and wine nights Wed, Thurs Fri; Quiz night Sundays
- Bronte Parsonage 500 yards, Keighley 4 miles, Keighley & Worth Valley Railway 1 mile

THE LIQUORICE BUSH

MARKET PLACE, PONTEFRACT, WEST YORKSHIRE WF8 1AX
TEL: 01977 600863 FAX: 01977 780071

Directions: From junction 32 of the M62, take the A639 south to Pontefract..

Situated in the heart of Pontefract **The Liquorice Bush** takes its name from the annual Liquorice Fair held every July, and from the associations the town has with Liquorice, being a centre of production for hundreds of years. The impressive exterior has three storeys and plenty of windows making for a light and airy interior.

Dating back hundreds of years, the inn has also been known as The Tankard and The Central - but has always maintained its reputation for hospitality. It's a large, open-plan public house with raised area to the rear for diners. Recently refurbished, the décor and furnishings are very attractive and comfortable. Traditional, features such as the large brick fireplace, stained glass and wealth of wood make this a truly pleasant place to enjoy a drink or meal.

- Mon-Sat 11.00-23.00; Sun 12.00-22.30
- Mon-Sat 11.00-14.30 and special occasions (e.g. Race Days, Liquorice Fair days, occasional Sunday lunch carvery – please ring for details
- Car parking, children welcome
- Happy Hour Mon-Thurs 16.00-23.00
- Pontefract Castle, Pontefract Racecourse (flat racing), Leeds 9 miles

Two real ales are on tap – Black Sheep and a changing guest ale – together with a choice of lagers, ciders, stouts, wines, spirits and soft drinks.

Experienced licensees Shaun and Gill White took over at this fine inn in February of 2003, after running the pub next door for six years. Along with their dedicated staff, they've given the inn the popularity it deserves, with a welcome for locals and visitors.

Food is available at lunchtime Monday to Saturday, as well as on select Sundays (please ring for details), when there's a delicious carvery. Guests choose from the menu for a range of good food at good prices. On race days and during the Liquorice Fair, meal times are extended.

THE NEW DELIGHT INN

JACK BRIDGE, BLACKSHAW HEAD, NR HEBDEN BRIDGE,
WEST YORKSHIRE HX7 7HT
TEL: 01422 846178

Directions: From Hebden Bridge take the minor road out signposted Heptonstall and Blackshaw Head. The inn is a couple of miles down on the right. Alternatively, from Halifax take the A646 for eight miles northwest

Set high on a hillside overlooking Calder Water and Hebden Bridge, and dating back to the early 1700s, **The New Delight** really lives up to its name. It retains many traditional features and a has a cosy, welcoming ambience. The flagstone floors, open fireplaces, exposed beams and stonework all add to its homely comforts. The walls are adorned with paintings, usually by local artists, and the collection changes every four to six weeks.

Owned and run by a local farming family since 2002, Dan Tasker is the licensee, ably assisted by his parents Barbara and Max, along with brothers Sam and Ben. Together they have made the pub a real success, popular with

locals and visitors for its great food, drink and hospitality.

The four real ales available always include Mansfield Cask and locally-brewed Moorhouses and Newdy Light Ale, plus changing guest ales. Together with a good selection of lagers, cider, stout, wines, spirits, soft drinks and coffee, there's something for every thirst. Food is available at lunch every day except Monday, and on Thursday and Friday evenings. The menu boasts snacks, salads, sandwiches, burgers, giant Yorkshire puddings, home-made pasta, steak-and-ale pie and more.

For those wishing to stay in this beautiful part of the county, there's a self-catering family flat adjacent to the inn, available all year round. In addition there's a campsite with 12 pitches and a shower and toilet on-site.

- ◷ Mon-Sun 11.45-15.00, 18.00-23.00
- 🍴 Tues-Fri and Bank Hols 12.00-14.30; Sat-Sun 12.00-15.00; Thurs-Fri 17.00-20.00
- 🛏 1 self-catering family room; campground
- 🅿 Off-road parking
- ♪ Free pool Weds nights
- @ dan@newdelight.freeserve.co.uk
- ? Todmorden 3 miles, Hebden Bridge 2 miles, Halifax 8 miles, Huddersfield 10 miles

THE OLD STAR

1 SKIPTON ROAD, STEETON, WEST YORKSHIRE BD20 6SD
TEL: 01535 652246

Directions: 4 miles north of Keighley off the A629 and on the junction with the A6034, between Keighley and Eastburn.

Dating back to the early 18th century, **The Old Star** is a distinguished and gracious old coaching inn offering great food, drink and hospitality. In the early days, teams of horses were changed here for the Keighley–Skipton coach, and stables stood to the rear and a smithy was housed adjacent to the inn. For about 120 years it was also used as a Post House, and during the 18th and 19th centuries a local court sat upstairs here once a month.

Since those times, of course, the inn has moved on with the times, and this family-run pub is tastefully decorated and furnished throughout. Cosy and comfortable, the interior is attractive and welcoming.

The inn is run by the Foster family –

John, his wife Fiona and his mum and dad Kath and Colin – who have worked hard to give the inn a new lease of life. Through their hard work, they definitely have a success on their hands. Already very popular with locals and visitors alike, the good food, well-kept ales and welcoming ambience ensure that all guests will enjoy their time here.

Thirst-quenchers served here include John Smith's Cask together with a range of lagers, cider, stout, wines, spirits and soft drinks. Meals are served all day long, with dishes listed on the printed menu and specials board. John is a qualified professional chef, and creates a range of delicious dishes that includes bar snacks, salads, burgers, giant mouth-watering Yorkshire puds and more. No-smoking areas ensure that children are welcome.

- Mon-Sat 11.00-23.00; Sun 12.00-22.30
- All day every day
- All major
- Off-road parking
- karaoke alternate Saturdays – please ring for details
- @ fstaryeyes@aol.com
- Keighley 2 miles, Haworth 5 miles, Ilkley 7 miles, Skipton 11 miles, Harrogate 20 miles

THE OLD STAR INN

LEEDS ROAD, COLLINGHAM, WEST YORKSHIRE LS22 5AP
TEL: 01937 579310 FAX: 01937 573334

Directions: From Leeds take the A58 northeast for 10 miles, then the A659. Collingham is situated where the A58 meets the A659.

The **Old Star Inn** is a very impressive place. Once a very well-known coaching inn along the Harrogate to Leeds coach route, teams of horses would be changed here. The premises date back to the early 18th century as an inn. Charming and welcoming, the inn faces a handsome green dotted with old-fashioned street lamps, and there are tables lining the frontage where the casement windows and hanging baskets add to the appeal of this large and elegant inn.

The superb interior décor combines the traditional – flagstone floors, exposed beams – with stylish modern touches such as plush seating. The wealth of exposed wood and cosy nooks enhance the comfortable and welcoming ambience.

Well-known for its quality cuisine, food is available at lunch and dinner every day. The no-smoking restaurant seats 56. Guests choose off the printed menu or the specials board, while on Sundays there's the carvery and bar meals on offer. Booking required for Sunday lunch. Children welcome.

The two real ales served here are John Smiths Cask and a changing guest ale, together with a good range of keg bitters, lagers, cider, stout, an excellent wine list, spirits and soft drinks.

Licensees Jan and Wendy have been in the trade since 1970. Their experience shows: they and their friendly, considerate staff offer every guest great service and warm and genuine hospitality.

Popular with locals and visitors alike, this convivial pub hosts regular quiz nights (Thursdays) and cocktail nights on certain Fridays.

- Mon-Sat 11.00-23.00; Sun 12.00-22.30
- Mon-Sat 12.00-14.30, 18.00-21.00; Sun 12.00-20.00
- Visa, Mastercard, Switch, Delta, Eurocard, Solo
- Off-road parking
- Quiz night Thur from 9 p.m.; cocktail night some Fridays – please ring for details
- Boston Spa 3 miles, Harewood House 5 miles, Leeds 10 miles, Harrogate 10 milesHarrogate 20 miles

213 RICHARDSHAW LANE, PUDSEY, WEST YORKSHIRE LS28 6AA
TEL: 0113 256 4219

Directions: Pudsey is reached off the A647 out of Bradford. The Pig & Whistle can be found a short walk from the centre of Pudsey in Richardshaw Lane, close to the railway line.

From the time it was built in the 19th century until 2001, this tall and impressive pub was known as The Great Northern, taking this name from its proximity to the Pudsey–Leeds railway line. It was used in the first instance by railway workers and later by visitors to this once-industrial area. In July of 2001 it was renamed **The Pig & Whistle Hotel**. Three storeys tall, painted in pristine cream with black trim, it presents a welcoming face to the world.

Inside, the pub is traditional and elegant, with original features that include the exposed woodwork, stone walls and open fireplace. Brass ornaments hang from the beams. This rustic inn is at once spacious and cosy, with an open-plan design and plenty of intimate seating areas.

There are three real ales here –

Timothy Taylor Landlord, Tetleys and a changing guest ale – as well as a good range of keg draught bitters, lagers, cider, stout, wines, spirits and soft drinks.

There are five upstairs letting rooms, which are available all year round on a B&B rate – here standing for bed and beer rather than bed and breakfast! The superb residents' lounge boasts well-polished pannelled walls beneath an arched ceiling, while the letting rooms are attractive, clean and comfortable. Discounts are available for stays of more than one night.

Jill Pearson and business partner Richard Taylor run the premises. They and their excellent staff ensure that all guests meet with a very warm welcome, comfortable accommodation, well-kept ale and unbeatable hospitality.

- 🕐 Mon-Fri 15.30-23.00; Sat 12.00-23.00; Sun 12.00-22.30
- 🛏 5 guest bedrooms
- 🅿 Beer garden, car parking, stabling, paddocks, dogs welcome
- 🎵 60s/70s/80s disco Thurs from 8.30 p.m.; live music Fri/Sat from 9 p.m.
- ❓ Bradford 4 miles, Leeds 4 miles, Saltaire 8 miles, Halifax 10 miles, Keighley 12 miles

THE QUEENS HEAD INN

191 WAKEFIELD ROAD, SCISSETT, HUDDERSFIELD,
WEST YORKSHIRE HD8 9JL
TEL: 01484 862296

Directions: From Denby Dale take the A636 2 miles east to Scissett

Here in the lovely village of Scissett, **The Queens Head Inn** is a friendly and welcoming place. After running a restaurant in part of the premises, Nick Adamski and his partner David took over the entire inn in January 2001 when the opportunity arose. They've given it a new lease of life and it has grown in popularity with locals and visitors alike thanks to their friendly service, genuine hospitality and great food and drink. The décor and furnishings are a happy marriage of the traditional and innovative, always with an eye for taste and style, with exposed beamwork and stone walls complemented by ultra-

modern furnishings, artwork, and subtle lighting.

The real ale here is Timothy Taylor Landlord, accompanied by a good range of lagers, ciders, stout, wines, spirits and soft drinks. Food is available all day long from 12 until 8 p.m. (Wednesdays until 9 p.m.), and guests choose from the printed menu or the specials board. All the very tempting dishes are expertly prepared and presented. Children are welcome and, if you want something that isn't on the menu, if they have the ingredients to hand they are happy to prepare it to order. Wednesday night is Steak Night, where for one low price guests get two steaks (either T-bone, sirloin or fillet) plus sauces and a bottle of house wine.

The downstairs function room holds 100, and is available to hire for any occasion.

- Mon-Sat 12.00-23.00; Sun 12.00-22.30
- Thur-Tues 12.00-20.00; Weds 12.00-21.00
- Visa, Mastercard, Switch, Eurocard, Solo
- Off-road rear car park
- Happy Hour Mon-Fri 16.30-19.00; Disco Fri from 20.00, Quiz Thurs from 21.30 with free supper, pool table, darts, dominoes and cards; karaoke some Sundays from 20.00; occasional live music
- nicdavid69@hotmail.com
- Denby Dale 2 miles, Barnsley 9 miles, Huddersfield 9 miles, Clayton West 1 mile

THE RED ROOSTER

123 ELLAND ROAD, BRIGHOUSE, WEST YORKSHIRE HD6 2QR
TEL: 01484 713737

Directions: From junction 25 of the M62, take the A646 to Brighouse, then the A6025. The Red Rooster is on the edge of Brighouse, beside the Calder and Hebble Canal.

Built over 100 years ago and, until 1983, known as The Wharf, **The Red Rooster** looks more like a house than an inn. The welcoming exterior is mirrored inside, where, following a recent refurbishment, the interior is comfortable and eye-catching with a new flagstone floor, handsome pannelling, tasteful décor and good seating.Located not far from the Calder and Hebble Canal, it is surrounded by lovely countryside.

Tenants Eddie and Claire have 10 years' experience in the trade, and took over here in March of 2003. They bring enthusiasm and a conscientious attention to detail in making sure all their guests have a relaxing and enjoyable time.

A real-ale fan's dream, there are always eight available. Regulars include Deuchars IPA, Roosters Yankie, Timothy Taylor Landlord and Thwaites Lancaster Bomber, along with changing guest ales, one of which is always from the Osset Brewery range. There's also a changing dark beer, together with a good range of lagers, stout, a changing real draught cider, and a selection of Belgian and German bottled beers. These, of course, are augmented by wines, spirits and soft drinks, to quench every thirst.

Food is available from opening time until around 7 p.m., with two dishes available each day – always delicious and expertly prepared, they include such delights as stews, curries, chillies and more. Made with the freshest local ingredients, there's always something to tempt the palate.

Children are welcome at this fine pub, as are well-behaved dogs.

- 🕐 Mon-Sat 12.00-23.00; Sun 12.00-22.30
- 🍴 Mon-Sat 12.00-19.00; Sun 12.00-19.00
- 🅿 Off-road parking
- 🎵 Quiz night Weds from 9.30 pm; live band last Sun of the month (jazz, R&B) 3-7 pm; Mon-Tues night motorcycle club; Mon cycling club
- ❓ Brighouse, Halifax 4 miles, Huddersfield 4 miles

THE RISING SUN

WHITWOOD COMMON LANE, WHITWOOD, CASTLEFORD,
WEST YORKSHIRE WF10 5PT
TEL: 01977 554766 FAX: 01977 554271

Directions: Take junction 31 off the M62, then follow Whitwood/Castleford signs. The Rising Sun is on the left as you enter the village.

The Rising Sun is a handsome whitewashed inn that began life as the Miners' Welfare Institute back in 1908, designed by the esteemed architect C F A Voysey and featuring his original stone mullions and leaded glass. Long and filled with light from the numerous casement windows, this charming inn is set in the village of Whitwood, recorded in the Domesday Book as Witewood.

The décor, furnishings and hospitality at the inn are second to none. Tasteful, airy and spacious throughout, the inn boasts a restaurant, lounge bar and the Palm Court which stands behind the pub. This was formerley the Old Memorial Hall, impressively refurbished and available for morning coffee, afternoon tea and functions, with seating

for 100.

Food is available every day – booking advised for Saturday evenings and Sunday lunch – and guests choose from the menu and specials board. All meals are freshly prepared and home-cooked, with a range of delicious choices to suit every palate. The two real ales here are Tetleys and Timothy Taylor Landlord, together with a full selection of draught keg bitters, lagers, cider, stout, wines, spirits and soft drinks.

Local woman Maureen Madeley is the tenant here. She has been in the licensing trade for six years and also runs The Fourways in Castleford, some 10 minutes' walk away. Maureen and her cheerful, helpful staff ensure that all their guests have a pleasant time while at the inn. Accommodation is available just opposite the pub.

- Mon-Sat 11.00-23.00; Sun 12.00-22.30
- Mon-Sat 12.00-22.00; Sun 12.00-21.00
- Visa, Mastercard, Switch, Delta, Eurocard, Solo
- Directly opposite the pub
- Off-road parking, patio, function room
- Castleford 2 miles, Pontefract 4 miles, Wakefield 6 miles, Leeds 10 miles

THE ROSSE HOTEL

62 BINGLEY ROAD, SALTAIRE, SHIPLEY, WEST YORKSHIRE BD18 4SD
TEL: 01274 584168

Directions: Take the A650 from Bingley (south) or Shipley (north) to reach Saltaire. The Rosse Hotel is located on the roundabout on the edge of Saltaire.

Handsome and imposing, **The Rosse Hotel** in Saltaire is a grand building, its sandstone brick giving it a soft aspect that does not lessen its impressiveness. This Grade II Listed building was named after Lady Rosse, a local Edwardian lady who was one of the passengers on the ill-fated *Titanic*.

Leaseholder Hilary Burns has particular reason to be proud of the pubs superb décor and furnishings, she was hired to redecorate the interior, and put so much care and dedication into her work that the then-leaseholder asked her if she'd like to run the place. She jumped at the chance, and became the new leaseholder in July 2003. She has taken this pub from strength to strength, rebuilding the its popularity with locals and building up a faithful clientele of visitors who come to sample the excellent food, drink and hospitality on offer.

There are two keg bitters available – John Smiths and Boddingtons – together with a good range of keg lagers, cider, stout, wine, spirits and soft drinks.

Food is served at lunchtime every day but Saturday, guests can choose from the printed menu and specials board, while on Sunday the roast is well worth making a special visit for. The regular entertainment programme ensures that there's something to divert you every night: Monday is games night, Tuesday there's a jam session/open mic; live entertainment on Wednesdays, quiz night Thursday, party night and fancy dress theme Fridays, karaoke and disco Saturdays, and five-a-side football Sunday, with more karaoke to follow in the evening - along with regular weekend barbecues (weather permitting).

No children, please, as smoking is permitted throughout the pub.

- Mon-Sat 11.00-23.00; Sun 12.00-22.30
- Mon-Fri 12.00-14.00; Sun 12.00-14.00
- Off-road parking
- Weekly entertainment programme – see main text
- Shipley 1 mile, Bradford 5 miles, Keighley 5 miles, Ilkley 7 miles, Harewood House 12 miles

THE SHOULDER OF MUTTON

West Yorkshire

BRIDGE GATE, HEBDEN BRIDGE, WEST YORKSHIRE HX7 8EX
TEL: 01422 842585 FAX: 01422 845217

Directions: From Halifax take the A646 for six miles west to Hebden Bridge

Situated in the heart of picturesque Hebden Bridge, **The Shoulder of Mutton Inn** is a lovely public house, pristine and impressive. The River Calder runs right alongside the back of the building, and the surrounding village and countryside are truly marvellous. This handsome stonebuilt pub dates back to the 17th century, and in full bloom, with hanging baskets and window boxes, it presents a lovely and welcoming façade to customers.

Inside, the traditional ambience is enhanced by the classic décor and furnishings. The pub has recently been carefully refurbished, its lovely original features complemented by modern comforts. Spacious and airy, it boasts a wealth of wood pannelling and exposed beamwork.

Tenants Cath and Tony have been here since April 2003. Cath has 15 years' experience in the trade, and they offer all their guests great food, drink and hospitality that is second to none.

With four real ales – Timothy Taylor Landlord, Flowers IPA and rotating guest ales – this pub is ideal for real-ale enthusiasts, and there are also lagers, cider, stout, wines, spirits and soft drinks available, to be enjoyed in the attractive lounge, bar or outside on the patio.

Food is available every day between 11 a.m. and 9 at night. Guests choose off the printed menu or the specials board, with everything from snacks and basket meals to hearty favourites, all prepared with the freshest local ingredients.

Children are welcome at this friendly and convivial inn, which is justly popular with locals and visitors alike.

- Mon-Sat 11.00-23.00; Sun 12.00-22.30
- Mon-Sun 11.00-21.00
- Car parking nearby, front patio, children welcome
- Discos/live music between Thurs-Sun evenings – ring for details
- shoulderofmuttoninn@btopenworld..com
- Hebden Bridge, Halifax 6 miles, Huddersfield 12 miles, Keighley 10 miles, walking, cycling

MUTTON FOLD, TOWNGATE, NORTHOWRAM, HALIFAX,
WEST YORKSHIRE HX3 7EA
TEL: 01422 206229

Directions: From Halifax take the Queensbury–Brighouse road to the sign for Northowram. On the main road turn alongside the Post Office into Towngate, following this road along for 600 yards. The Shoulder of Mutton is on your left.

The Shoulder of Mutton in Towngate is a Grade II listed building and an inn of real quality. The oldest part of the premises dates to the 16th century and once housed the stables for teams that would be changed here on the Halifax-to-Bradford route. The larger building was built as a private house in the 18th century for a local landowner. This handsome and distinctive inn boasts lovely stone mullioned windows and a feature cooking range. Charming and cosy, the inn features cosy nooks and is bright and airy throughout, with a cheerful décor and original features like

the open fireplace adding to the welcoming ambience.

Tenants Chris and Sheila have been here since 1992, and have nearly 20 years' experience in the trade. They've built up a loyal local following for their great food, ales and hospitality, and have made the inn a real success. There's always one real ale on tap from an ever-changing list of possible brews, together with lagers, cider, stout, wines, spirits and soft drinks.

Food is served at lunch every day and evenings Monday to Saturday, with a menu and specials board boasting a selection of tempting dishes. Sheila is an excellent cook and prepares each dish with care and expertise. On Sundays there's a choice of four roasts. Early Bird Specials are available between 5.30 and 8 p.m. Children are welcome.

- Mon-Thur 11.00-15.00, 17.00-23.00; Fri-Sat 11.00-23.00; Sun 12.00-22.30
- Mon-Fri 12.00-14.00, 17.30-20.00; Sat 12.00-14.00, 17.00-19.00; Sun 12.00-16.00
- Visa, Mastercard, Switch, Delta, Amex, Eurocard, Solo
- Off-road parking, beer garden, patio area, function room
- Quiz night Wednesdays from 9 p.m.
- hewittchris@aol.com
- Brighouse 2 miles, Halifax 5 miles, Bradford 10 miles, Hebden Bridge 6 miles, Haworth 12 miles, Keighley 17 miles

West Yorkshire

THE SUN INN

11 ACKTON LANE, NORTH FEATHERSTONE, PONTEFRACT,
WEST YORKSHIRE WF7 6AP
TEL: 01977 702055

Directions: From Pontefract take the A645 for 2 miles; from Wakefield take the A638 then the A645; from the M62 junction 31, take the B6134 then the B6428.

Dating back 110 years, **The Sun Inn** was formerly known as The Bradley Arms after the then-Lord of the Manor. Well-recommended for its hospitality, it makes a good place to stop and enjoy a relaxing drink and meal. Close to Pontefract Golf Club, this excellent inn is cosy and welcoming. Traditional and handsome inside and out, John Smith Cask is the regular real ale here, together with Tetley Smooth, Carlsberg, Castlemaine, Stella, Woodpecker, Strongbow and regular and extra-cold Guinness along with a good selection of wines, spirits and soft drinks.

Food is available every day for lunch, and Monday to Saturday evenings.

Booking is advised Sunday lunchtimes. Jane is a superb cook and prepares fresh, delicious food every day using the freshest produce cooked to order. The menu includes liver and bacon casserole, chicken tikka, seafood dishes, spinach and feta cheese goujons, steaks and much more. Meals can be enjoyed in either the bar, lounge or in the no-smoking dining room, which seats 22. Occasionally there are barbecues on Sunday afternoons, weather permitting. Entry by ticket only.

The pub is tenants Mick and Jane's first venture into the licensing trade and they have been here since 2000. Their hard work and hospitality have ensured the success and popularity here, where locals mix freely with visitors. On Wednesday nights the pub hosts a quiz, and on some Saturday evenings there's karaoke.

- 🕐 Mon 18.00-23.00, Tues-Sat 11.00-15.00, 18.00-23.00; Sun 12.00-22.30
- 🍴 Tues-Fri and Bank Hols 12.00-14.00, 18.00-20.30; Sat 12.00-14.00, 19.00-20.30; Sun 12.00-14.00
- 💷 Visa, Mastercard, Switch, Delta, Solo
- 🅿 Beer garden/patio area, off-road parking
- 🎵 Quiz night Wednesday, karaoke some Saturdays
- ❓ Pontefract 2 miles, Wakefield 7 miles, Leeds 10 miles

THE TRIANGLE INN

ROCHDALE ROAD, TRIANGLE, SOWERBY BRIDGE,
WEST YORKSHIRE HX6 3NE
TEL: 01422 831512

Directions: From Huddersfield, take the A6026 for six-and-a-half miles northwest to Sowerby Bridge. From there, take the A58 – Triangle lies between Sowerby Bridge and Ripponden.

Built in 1760 and named after the triangular piece of land that gives the village its name, **The Triangle** offers guests great food, drink and hospitality. The exterior is large and impressive, built in the light stone prominent in the region and with a small patio to one side. Across the road there's a lovely beer garden for when the weather is fine. Inside, what were once the stables have now been incorporated into the inn, creating secluded alcoves amidst the spacious, attractive interior. Exposed beams, wood pannelling and the large stone fireplace enhance the warm and cosy ambience.

Ivan, Jayne and their son John have been tenants here since 2000. With seven years experience, they extend a genuine welcome and a high standard of service.

Along with two real ales on tap – Tetleys plus a changing guest ale – the inn also offers a variety of lagers, cider, draught Guinness, wines, spirits and soft drinks. Hearty and delicious meals are served and the menu boasts such delights as crispy fried scampi, fisherman's pie, chicken tikka masala, Cumberland sausage, roasted vegetable lasagne and lamb burgers. For smaller appetites there's a choice of light bites, and the desserts – apple crumble, spotted dick, toffee sundaes and more - are well worth leaving room for.

During the lifetime of this edition there will be accommodation available here, in the shape of three en suite double guest bedrooms, which will be available all year round.

- Mon-Weds 16.00-23.00; Thurs-Sat 11.00-23.00; Sun 12.00-22.30
- Mon-Weds 16.00-19.00; Thurs-Sat 12.00-19.00; Sun 12.00-15.00
- 3 rooms ensuite
- Off-road car park, beer garden, patio area
- Happy hour Tues-Thurs 18.00-19.30; occasional live entertainment
- Hebden Bridge 5 miles, Halifax 6 miles, Brighouse 8 miles, Huddersfield 8 miles, walking, cycling

THE WAGGON & HORSES

16 HUDDERSFIELD ROAD, MELTHAM, NR HUDDERSFIELD,
WEST YORKSHIRE HD9 4AE
TEL: 01484 850269

Directions: Meltham can be found where the B6107 meets the B6108, 5 miles southwest of Huddersfield

Right in the heart of Meltham, **The Waggon & Horses** is a sturdy, stonebuilt Victorian pub with a welcoming ambience. Run by Mike and Pam Cox, who took over in September 2001, this marvellous inn serves up a good selection of quality beers, with four draught ales to choose from – Deuchers IPA, Tetley, Timothy Taylor Landlord plus a guest ale, together with a range of lagers, cider, stout, wines, spirits and soft drinks. Mike's ales are always in top condition – so much so that he has been awarded The Cask Marque Certificate.

And it's not just the ales that make this place so popular with locals and visitors alike. The food menu at the Waggon has an extensive choice to tempt any guest. From traditional

Sunday Roasts to Giant Yorkshire Puddings, Chilli Con Carni, Jumbo Haddock and Chicken Dijionnaise there is sure to be something for everyone. The "Special Waggon Sauce" which accompanies a juicy Rump steak is a real delight. Along with the main menu and specials board a range of light snacks are available from 12 noon- 9pm everyday. The desserts are also well worth leaving room for.

It is believed that this fine old inn takes its name from the sheep market which for many years was sited to the rear of the premises – sheep farmers and buyers would arrive in their wagons to haggle over livestock prices. The interior is traditional and cosy, with a lounge bar, games room, dining room and bar area, each tastefully furnished and decorated, with bright, cheerful colours and plenty of handsome burnished wood.

- 🕐 Mon-Sat 11.00-23.00; Sun 12.00-22.30
- 🍴 Tues-Fri 12.00-14.00, 18.00-20.00; Sat-Sun 13.00-16.00
- 💷 Visa, Mastercard, Switch, Delta, Eurocard, Solo
- 🅿 Car parking, children welcome
- 🎵 Quiz night Weds, pool, darts, games, juke box
- @ m.cox903@ntlworld.com
- ❓ Meltham, Huddersfield 5 miles, walking, cycling, birdwatching

LINDLEY MOOR ROAD, HUDDERSFIELD, WEST YORKSHIRE HD3 3TD
TEL: 01422 372324

Directions: From junction 23 of the M62, take the A640 at the roundabout. After about 1 mile The Wappy Spring Inn is on the right

The Wappy Spring Inn was built in 1765, and took its name from the Wappy Spring Brewery which used to stand alongside it. Large and impressive, it's a handsome stonebuilt pub with a large feature window to the front. Inside, guests will feel immediately at home in comfortable, tasteful and attractive surroundings with traditional features that include the exposed beam ceiling, brass ornaments and plush seating.

Austin Wylie and Trevor Simpkins took over at the Inn in May 2003 as leaseholders. They bring experience and enthusiasm to running this fine inn, and they and their friendly, attentive staff make every effort to ensure that guests receive the best hospitality and service possible.

This excellent pub boasts two changing guest ales plus a good selection of draught keg bitters, lager, cider, stout, wines, spirits and soft drinks, to quench any thirst.

Food is served every day but Monday, at lunch and dinner. Guests choose off the printed menu or specials board from a good variety of delicious dishes, all expertly prepared and presented. Austin cooks at lunchtime, and children are welcome then and in the early evening. There are no-smoking areas inside, and also a large beer garden. Dishes combine the best of innovation and tradition, and are made with the freshest local ingredients. The pub hosts occasional theme nights with dishes from around the world – please ring for details.

Both Austin and Trevor are local men, and they've been in the trade for over four years. They also run another pub in Huddersfield called The Cavalry Arms, found about a mile from junction 23 of the M62 towards Huddersfield town centre.

- 🕐 Mon-Fri 12.00-14.00, 17.00-23.00; Sat 11.00-23.00; Sun 12.00-22.30
- 🍴 Tues-Sun 12.00-14.00, 18.00-21.00
- 💷 Visa, Mastercard, Switch, Delta, Eurocard, Solo
- 🅿 Beer garden, off-road parking
- 🎵 Quiz night Sundays, occasional food theme nights
- ❓ Huddersfield, Holmfirth 6 miles

West Yorkshire

THE WHITE HORSE INN

SCHOLES ROAD, JACKSON BRIDGE, NR HOLMFIRTH,
WEST YORKSHIRE HD0 1OY
TEL: 01484 683940 FAX: 01484 684142

Directions: Jackson Bridge is found 1 mile from New Mill off the A616. From Holmfirth, follow the Scholes or Hepworth sign off the A616

Built as an inn in 1830, **The White Horse Inn** will be immediately familiar to many readers as it was used for many years as the pub in the popular BBC series *Last of the Summer Wine*. This impressive stonebuilt inn is handsome inside and out and as might be expected, the comfortable lounge area is adorned with photographs of characters from the series. In every way a traditional and characterful pub, the real ale here is Tetley Cask, and there's also a good selection of lagers, stout, cider, wines, spirits and soft drinks.

Run by Terry and Claire, long a local couple, became leaseholders here in 2001. This has been their first venture into the licensing trade, and they have made a great success of it. The pub is justly popular not just for its association with *Summer Wine* but also because of the quality food, well-kept ales and, most of all, for the genuine hospitality offered all comers. Claire is a super cook, creating delicious, hearty dishes at lunch and dinner. Guests choose off the menu or specials board. Specialities include lamb, home-made lasagne, curries and fish and chips. All are expertly prepared and presented. Booking is advised for Sunday lunch.

Children are welcome and there's excellent accommodation available for those wanting a base for touring in the area. There are five en suite guest bedrooms. Three rooms have a double and single bed, one is a double with four-poster bed, and one is a spacious single. The tariff includes an abundant breakfast – just the thing to set you up for a day's sightseeing in this picturesque part of the world. Well-behaved dogs are welcome.

Apr-Sept: Mon-Sat 11.00-23.00; Sun 12.00-22.30 Oct-Mar: Mon/Tues and Thurs-Sat 11.00-15.00, 17.00-23.00; Sun 12.00-15.00, 19.00-22.30

Thur-Tues 12.00-14.30, 18.00-20.00

5 rooms ensuite

Car parking, beer garden

Occasional live entertainment

Holmfirth, Huddersfield 8 miles

THE YEW TREE

NEWALL CARR ROAD, OTLEY, WEST YORKSHIRE LS21 2AU
TEL: 01943 461330

West Yorkshire

Directions: From Leeds, take the A65 northwest to Otley. From the centre of Otley take the B6451 for three-quarters of a mile; The Yew Tree is on the left.

The Yew Tree hasn't always been a public house, but began life as a row of three cottages, becoming an inn just over 30 years ago. Its handsome brickbuilt exterior bears witness to its distinguished past and continuing elegance. The impressive interior is traditional and cosy, with a wealth of wood and exposed brick adding to the relaxed and comfortable ambience. Barry and Linda have been leaseholders here since 2000, and have personally run it since 2002. It was their first venture into the business, and they have made it a real success.

The three real ales here are Tetley Bitter, Tetley Mild and Black Sheep, and there are also keg draught lagers, cider, stout, wines, spirits and soft drinks.

Delicious food is served Wednesday to Saturday at lunch and dinner at this excellent pub. Guests can choose from the printed menu or specials board from a range of tempting dishes that include chicken in wild mushroom sauce, steak and ale pie and jalfrezi curry. Sandwiches are available on Mondays and Tuesdays. On Sundays, expertly prepared roasts are added to the menu, and meals are served between midday and 6 p.m. There's a non-smoking area in the dining room, and children are welcome.

A hub of the community, popular with locals and visitors alike, the pub's decorated float won first prize in its class in the 2003 Otley Carnival. Regular entertainments include quizzes and karaoke evenings.

- 🕐 Mon-Thur 12.00-15.00, 17.00-23.00; Fri-Sat 11.00-23.00; Sun 12.00-22.30
- 🍴 Wed-Sat and Bank Hols 12.00-14.00, 17.00-19.30; Sun 12.00-18.00. Sandwiches available Mon & Tues
- £ Visa, Mastercard, Switch, Delta, Eurocard, Solo
- Ⓟ Front patio, off-road parking
- 🎵 General knowledge quiz Sundays from 9 p.m.; pop quiz and 'play your cards right' Tuesdays from 9 p.m.; karaoke once a month
- ❓ Ilkley 7 miles, Harrogate 10 miles, Leeds 10 miles

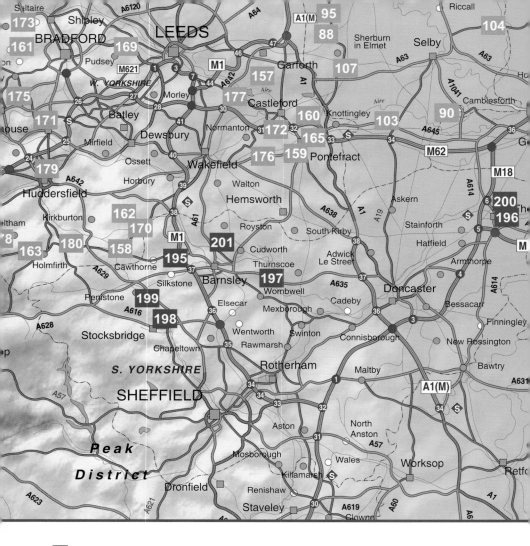

Please note all cross references refer to page numbers

SOUTH YORKSHIRE

Lacking the spectacular scenery of the Yorkshire Dales, the Moors and the Heritage Coastline, South Yorkshire tends to be overlooked as a tourist venue. However, this is a region of great age and antiquity and, in many places, the heavy industry with which South Yorkshire

Mappin Art Gallery, Sheffield

is associated goes hand in hand with farming and agriculture. This is principally a coal mining area although iron founding and smelting has taken place here for centuries. The main centre here is Sheffield that rightly claims to be England's greenest city; the wild open spaces of the Pennine moorlands of the Peak District National Park roll right up to its western boundaries.

To the north of Sheffield is Barnsley, the county town of South Yorkshire, whose prosperity comes from the rich seams of coal that have been exploited in the local area. To the east lies Rotherham, where iron ore has been mined and smelted since the 12th century. While its wealth is certainly based upon the metal, Rotherham is also the home of Rockingham pottery that was once favoured by royalty.

Further east again is the charming riverside town of Doncaster, which was established by the Romans and certainly today has the air of a pleasant market town. However, this was once one of the country's most important centres of steam locomotive manufacture and it is famous for having created the *Mallard*, which still holds the record for the top speed attained by a steam train. Today, though, Doncaster is best known as the home of the St Leger, Britain's oldest classic horse race.

Elsewhere in the county visitors can discover the delights of Roche Abbey, a 12th century Cistercian house, Conisbrough Castle, which boasts the oldest stone keep in England, and the faded Victorian grandeur of Brodsworth Hall.

BARNSLEY

The county town of South Yorkshire, Barnsley stands on the River Dearne and derived its Victorian prosperity from the rich seams of coal found in the local area. It has an appropriately imposing Town Hall although the building is comparatively recent and was completed in 1933 while, nearby, the **Cooper Gallery** is a lively centre for the arts that hosts a varied programme of exhibitions throughout the year as well as housing a fine permanent collection.

To the south of the town is the **Worsbrough Mill Museum and Country Park**, a grade II listed mill that dates from around 1625 although it is known that there was a mill here since the time of the Domesday Survey. A steam mill was added in the 19th century and, now, both have been restored to full working order to form the centrepiece of an industrial museum. Wholemeal flour, ground at the mills, can be bought here. The mills are set within a beautiful 200-acre country park, whose reservoir attracts a great variety of birds including herons.

CADEBY

Listed in the Domesday Book as 'Catebi', this pleasant little village is surrounded by prime agricultural land. For centuries Cadeby had no church of its own and its residents had to travel two miles to the parish church in Sprotbrough until, finally, in

Cooper Gallery, Barnsley

1856, the owners of the huge Sprotbrough estate, the Copley family, paid for a church to be built in the village. Designed by Sir George Gilbert Scott, the architect of St Pancras Station in London, the church resembles a medieval estate barn with its steeply pitched roofs and lofty south porch. A century and a half later, Cadeby is again without a church, since Sir George's attractive building has recently been declared redundant.

Cannon Hall Museum

CAWTHORNE

This picturesque village has many historical links with the nearby estate of Cannon Hall, the home of the Spencer family from the mid 17th century. Cawthorne's major industry at the time was a mix of farming, coal and iron and the Spencers had interests in the local iron industry and owned Barnby Furnace, just a mile to the east of the village.

Cannon Hall Museum is housed in a magnificent 18th century country house that is set in formal gardens and historic parkland. Designed by John Carr of York and the home for 200 years of the Spencer-Stanhope family, the rooms provide the perfect backdrop for the museum's fine collections of pottery, furniture, paintings, glass and Moorcroft. The Charge Gallery documents the history of the 13th and 18th Royal Hussars.

Set in the grounds of Cannon Hall Country Park is the **Cannon Hall Open Farm**, a family run farm that is home to hundreds of animals and where visitors can see a real farm at work, help feed the animals and catch up on the new animals being born. Also here is an adventure playground, a farm shop, a gift shop and a tea rooms.

Also in the village is the **Cawthorne Victoria Jubilee Museum**, which houses original collections of butterflies, moths, birds, eggs, fossils and domestic artefacts. This quaint little museum provides interest for all the family and it is open from April to end of October at the weekends and Bank Holidays.

CONISBROUGH

The town is best known for the 11th century **Conisbrough Castle** (English Heritage) that features prominently in one of the most dramatic scenes in Sir Walter Scott's novel *Ivanhoe*. The most impressive medieval building in South Yorkshire, Conisbrough Castle boasts the oldest circular keep in England, which rises some 90 feet and is more than 50 feet wide. The keep is situated on a man-made hill that dates back to Saxon times. Once the northern stronghold of the de Warenne family, Earls of Surrey, it was William, the 1st Earl, who built the original timber motte and bailey castle on this site just after the Norman Conquest but, by the times of Hamelin Plantagenet, the 5th Earl, this wooden construction was deemed inadequate for a family of such wealth and status so Hamelin ordered the construction of a stone keep, to his own designs, in 1180. After the demise of the family, the castle was abandoned as a residence and it was saved from dereliction during the Civil War as it was indefensible as a fortress. After some 500 years of neglect, the castle's keep once again has a roof to protect it from the elements, along with two new floors, and it is now safe for generations to come. As well as a series of events being held here throughout the year, the castle has a visitor centre, a presentation detailing its history and a tea room. Conisbrough Castle is open daily throughout the year.

This town is also home to the **Earth Centre**, a place of the future, which lies close to Conisbrough Station. Through a series of compelling indoor and outdoor exhibitions, the centre uses the latest technology to explain the wonders of this planet and also how they are best preserved. Set beside the River Don,

visitors can tour the unusual garden, taste the delicious organic food, go pond-dipping and enjoy the sweet smell of the environmentally friendly sewage works!

DONCASTER

The Romans named their riverside settlement beside the River Don, 'Danum', and a well-preserved stretch of the road they built here can be seen just west of Adwick le Street. A lively shopping centre today, with a market that takes place every Tuesday, Friday and Saturday, the market has existed here since Roman times although the first charter was not granted to Doncaster until 1194 by Richard I. The large triangular market place today was laid down in medieval times and here can be found the Market Hall, built in 1849, and the stately Corn Exchange building of 1866. The modern town boasts some other impressive buildings, including the **Mansion House** built in 1748 and designed by James Paine; it remains one of only three civic mansion houses in England. The parish church was rebuilt in 1858 by Sir Giles Gilbert Scott and is an outstanding example of Gothic revival architecture with its lofty tower that rises some 170 feet high and is crowned by pinnacles.

Doncaster was once one of the most important centres for the production of steam engines and, over the years, thousands were built here, including both the *Flying Scotsman* and *Mallard*. *Mallard* still holds the record as the fastest steam train in the world when it achieved a top speed of 125 mph in July 1938. For a further insight into the history of the town and surrounding area, the **Doncaster Museum** contains several exciting and informative exhibitions on the various aspects of natural history, local history and archaeology. The Art Gallery has a lively programme of temporary

Cusworth Hall

exhibitions as well as permanent displays of fine and decorative art; it is housed in the same building as the **Regimental Museum of the King's Own Yorkshire Light Infantry**, which reflects the history of this famous local regiment.

There is no-one connected with racing who has not heard of the St Leger, the oldest of England's great classic races, which has been held at Doncaster since 1776. There has been horse racing here since at least the beginning of the 17th century and, today, in the Yorkshire tradition, **Doncaster Racecourse** remains a magnet for racing enthusiasts, whether they follow the Flat or the National Hunt game.

On the northwestern outskirts of the town lies **Cusworth Hall**, a splendid Georgian mansion built in the 1740s and surrounded by a landscaped park that is home to the Museum of South Yorkshire Life. The displays of local history here, which cover the last 250 years of the area, include agriculture, mining, the

railways, crafts and costume, and show the changes in the work, home and social lives of the people of South Yorkshire over that period.

A little further northwest of Doncaster, lies **Brodsworth Hall** (English Heritage), a remarkable example of a Victorian mansion that has survived with much of its original furnishings and decorations intact. When Charles and Georgiana Thellusson, their six children and 15 servants moved into the new hall in 1863 the house must have seemed the last word in both grandeur and utility. A gasworks in the grounds supplied the lighting and no fewer than eight water-closets were distributed around the house although, rather surprisingly, only two bathrooms were installed. However, more immediately impressive to visitors are the opulent furnishings, paintings, statuary and decoration. The sumptuous reception rooms have now a rather faded grandeur and English Heritage has deliberately left it so, preserving the patina of time throughout the house to produce an interior that is both fascinating and evocative. A vanished way of life is also brought to life in the huge kitchen, complete with its original utensils, and the cluttered servants wing. The hall stands in 15 acres of beautifully restored Victorian gardens complete with a summer house in the form of a classical temple, a Target Range where the family practised its archery, and a Pets Cemetery where the family dogs and a prized parrot bearing the unimaginative name of 'Polly' were buried between 1894 and 1988. There is also a fascinating exhibition illustrating the family's obsession – yachting.

ELSECAR

This is an excellent example of an early industrial village whose economy was based on coal mining and iron working that were developed by the Earls Fitzwilliam of Wentworth Woodhouse. Along with one of the area's prettiest small parks and its attractive stone cottages built for the miners and foundry workers, there is a reservoir here that is popular with both fishermen and bird watchers. The village is also home to **Elsecar Heritage Centre**, an imaginative science and history centre that is fun and educational for all the family. Housed in these restored workshops, which were once owned by the Earls Fitzwilliam, visitors can discover hands-on science in the Power House where the amount of energy it takes to hoover a carpet or mow the lawn is calculated. At Ches, a working metalsmith uses traditional techniques to fashion numerous tools and utensils while, at Coddswallop, the National Bottle Museum, there are all manner of bottles, pot lids, Wade and Doulton pottery and numerous other collectables to see. Finally, there is also the chance to take a nostalgic journey on the Elsecar Steam Railway. The centre is open daily throughout the year.

FINNINGLEY

A unique feature of this pleasant village, which lies close to the Nottinghamshire border, is its five village greens, the main one having a duck pond complete with weeping willows. Finningley has a beautiful Norman church with a rectors' list dating back to 1293 and a post office that has been in the same family for 5 generations. Just before World War II, Finningley RAF airfield was built to the west of the village and, although the airfield is no longer in regular use, it provides the venue for an annual **Air Show** that includes some spectacular flying displays.

MALTBY

To the southeast of this village lie the dramatic ruins of **Roche Abbey** (English Heritage) that was founded in 1174 by Cistercian monks and takes it name from the rocky limestone outcrop on which it is situated. The majestic remains of this once great abbey stand in a landscape that was created by Capability Brown in the 1770s as part of the grounds of Sandbeck Park, the home of the Earls of Scarborough.

NORTH ANSTON

This village, which is separated from its neighbour South Anston by the main road, is home to the **Tropical Butterfly House, Wildlife and Falconry Centre** where visitors can see the exotic butterflies, birds, snakes and crocodiles in a tropical jungle setting and enjoy outdoor falconry displays and, at the baby farm animal area, bottle feed the lambs (depending on the season). The centre, which is open all year, also has a nocturnal reptile room, a nature trail and a children's outdoor play area.

RENISHAW

This sizable village gives its name to **Renishaw Hall**, the home of Sir Reresby and Lady Sitwell, which can be found just a mile or so to the west. The beautiful formal Italian gardens and 300 acres of wooded park are open to visitors, along with a nature trail and a Sitwell family Museum, the John Piper Art Gallery, a display of Fiori de Henriques sculptures in the Georgian stables, and a café. The grounds are open from April to September from Friday to Sunday and on Bank Holiday Mondays (and also on Thursday during July and August) while the hall itself is open to group and connoisseur tours by special arrangement only.

ROTHERHAM

There has been a settlement here since prehistoric times but it was the Romans, exploiting the local iron ore, who made the first attempts at establishing a permanent town here. A market town for 900 years, Rotherham is steeped in history but throughout the last 2,000 years it seems unable to escape from its iron roots. While the monks from Kirkstead Abbey, in nearby Lincolnshire, mined and smelted iron ore near here in the 12thh century, it was not until the Industrial Revolution that Rotherham became, primarily, an industrial town. From the mid-18th century, the Walker Company of Rotherham was famous for its cannons and their products featured,

Rotherham Centre

to lethal effect, in the American War of Independence and at the Battle of Trafalgar. The company also built bridges, among them Southwark Bridge in London and the bridge at Sunderland and, when the Walkers' Rotherham works closed in the 1820s, several of their former employees set up their own works, a move that was to place the town in the forefront of the iron founding industry in the 19th century. The Rotherham of today is still a leading site of the country's steel industry, along with glass, mining and engineering.

This rich industrial heritage can be explored at the massive former steelworks at Templeborough that are now the **Magna Science Adventure Centre**. Divided into four hands-on explorative exhibitions – earth, air, fire and water – visitors can unearth the mysteries of the natural world. In the water challenge there are pumps and locks to investigate as well as salmon to catch, while the fire centre has a larger than life size lava lamp. The subterranean playground of Earth provides the opportunity to operate a real JCB and explode a rock face and, in Air, visitors can spin in a gyroscope chair and also feel the sensations of flying. Naturally, Magna also provides an intimate insight into the lives of steelworkers and visitors can see a powerful arc furnace being brought back to life.

Though somewhat tamer than Magna, the fine collections at the **Clifton Park Museum** are no less interesting. Housed in a late 18th century mansion, whose interior has changed little since it was built in 1783 for the Rotherham ironmaster, Joshua Walker, the museum has displays of Yorkshire pottery, including an impressive collection of Rockingham made at nearby Swinton, English glass and silver, Victorian domestic items and local and natural history displays. The grounds around the house now form the borough's largest urban park. Another museum of interest is the **York and Lancaster Regimental Museum**, housed in the Central Library and Arts Centre. The regiment had strong ties with South Yorkshire and its recruits were drawn mainly from Barnsley, Sheffield and Rotherham. The displays include historic uniforms, campaign relics and over 1,000 medals, among them nine Victoria Cross. There are also sections on local militia, rifle volunteers and the territorials.

The town's most striking building, however, is undoubtedly the **Church of All Saints** and, with its soaring tower, pinnacled buttresses and battlements and imposing porch, it is one of the finest examples of Perpendicular architecture in Yorkshire. The church dates mainly from the 15th century although there is evidence of an earlier Saxon church, dating from 937, on the site. A church here was listed in the *Domesday Book* and in 1161 the monks of Rufford Abbey were granted the right to prospect for and to smelt iron, and to plant an orchard, and from that day industry has existed side by side with agriculture.

Rotherham is also home to one of only four surviving medieval chantry chapels that are situated on a bridge in England: the **Chapel on the Bridge**, now superbly restored, features a beautiful new stained-glass window that illustrates the story of the town.

Sheffield Cathedral

Along with being able to claim to be the birthplace of both the screw down water tap and the Bailey Bridge, which was said by Sir Winston Churchill to have shortened World War II by at least two years, Rotherham is also associated with several notable figures throughout its long history. Thomas Rotherham, the Chancellor of England in the 15th century, was born here, as was Ebenezer Elliot, who was influential in repealing the Corn Laws in 1846, Sandy Powell, who coined the phrase, "*can you hear me mother?*" and, finally, the former England goalkeeper, David Seaman.

To the south of the town lies **Ulley Country Park** that incorporates a reservoir, with excellent coarse fishing, and a nature reserve in a park that nestles between the surrounding hills.

SHEFFIELD

England's fourth largest city, Sheffield is best known for its manufacture of stainless steel and cutlery though, today, many people will associate it with the successful film, *The Full Monty*, which was made in and around the city. However, despite its heavy industry, its location, beside the River Don, in the foothills of the Pennines, and surrounded by a landscape of valleys and woods, ensures that there is attractive countryside right on the city's doorstep. As early as the 17th century, Sheffield was gaining a reputation for its knives and tools and, later that century, it began to make its own steel. During the Industrial Revolution, these industries expanded rapidly and by the mid-19th century Sheffield was producing 90 per cent of the country's steel. Harry Brearley's accidental discovery of stainless steel in 1913 saw the industry develop further and, today, though the workforces required in the industry are reduced, the output of steel, cutlery, surgical instruments and cutting edges has never been higher.

Despite its relatively long history, Sheffield has few ancient buildings and its only remaining medieval building is the **Cathedral of St Peter and St Paul**, whose notable architectural features include the chancel roofs; in the Chapter House are stained-glass windows that depict the city's history. Facing the cathedral is the **Cutlers' Hall**, built in 1832, an imposing building that houses the Cutlers' Company's wonderful collection of silverware and cutlery. There are guided tours of the hall and the collection and, among the unusual artefacts on display is an ornate silver galleon and a huge penknife with almost 100 blades.

For an insight into Sheffield's industrial past the **City Museum** houses the city's collection of cutlery as well as displays of archaeological finds, decorative arts and both natural and social history. The museum, located in Weston park, is open Tuesday to Sunday and Bank Holiday Mondays all year round. Also in Weston Park is the **Mappin Art Gallery**, a leading centre for contemporary arts, which hosts a major programme of exhibitions while also displaying the city's collection of traditional paintings that includes superb portraits, landscapes and still life. However, it is the **Millennium Galleries** that have helped to establish the city as a cultural force in the north of England. A remarkable building of white columns and striking glass arches, it holds four unique galleries that not only showcase Sheffield's impressive metalware collection but also provide space to show the city's wonderful collection of

paintings, drawings and natural history exhibits. Next to the Millennium Galleries can be found the recently constructed **Winter Garden** a beautiful wood and glass building which is home to more than 2000 plants made up of more than 150 species from around the world.

The **Kelham Island Museum** is a living museum that tells the story of Sheffield. Visitors can see the mighty River Don Engine, the most powerful working steam engine in Europe, in steam; reconstructed workshops; the 'Little Mesters' working cutler; and craftspeople demonstrating traditional 'Made in Sheffield' skills. For children up to 9 years old, The Melting Shop provides an interactive experience where they can 'clock on' to become a piece of steel – including being rolled and hammered! The museum is open daily all year except Fridays and Saturdays. The **Traditional Heritage Museum**, offers a unique collection of displays on life and work in the city between the 1850s and the 1950s while, at the University, the **Turner Museum of Glass** contains over 300 items of contemporary and art glass from Europe and the United States along with a unique collection of over 100 drinking glasses. Housed in an original Georgian factory, built around a central courtyard, the Butcher Works, which is now occupied by small businesses, is regularly used as a film location and the **Cultural Industries Quarter** is home to many of South Yorkshire's finest skilled artists and craftspeople.

The city's most picturesque museum is undoubtedly the **Bishop's House Museum** that dates from around 1500 and is the earliest timber-framed house still standing here. Many original features survive and the Bedchamber and Great Parlour are furnished in the style of the home of a prosperous 17th century yeoman. There are also displays on Sheffield in Tudor and Stuart times, and changing exhibitions on local history themes. A museum of a very different nature is the **Sheffield Bus Museum**, housed in the Tinsley Tram sheds on Sheffield Road. The collection includes many types of bus and other transport-related exhibits such as destination blinds, old timetables and models. The museum also houses the Tinsley Model Railway layout. Finally, the city's large Victorian Fire and Police Station is now home to the **Fire Police Museum** where not only is there a comprehensive display of fire appliances and equipment from the 18th century to the present day but it also houses an exhibition on the police force complete with some of their vehicles. The museum is open on Sundays and Bank Holiday Mondays. To the west of the city can be found the **Abbeydale Industrial Hamlet** a site for metal working since before 1200 AD and now a working museum which explains how steel was produced, how the machinery was powered and how the metal workers and their families lived their lives. The Hamlet is open daily from April to October.

However, Sheffield is not all hustle and bustle, buildings and industry and here, too, can be found numerous parks including its largest, Graves Park, that was given to the city by Alderman Graves before World War II. Perhaps, though, the city's most peaceful place must be the **Sheffield Botanical Gardens** where the collections of shrubs and trees are set within a historic landscape that was first opened in 1836. The recently renovated glasshouses, designed by the famous architect Joseph Paxton, and the attractive but informal gardens are open daily all year round until dusk.

SILKSTONE

The travel writer Arthur Mee dubbed Silkstone's parish church 'The Minster of the Moors' and it is indeed a striking building, though the present church, parts of which date back to Norman times, probably stands on the site of an older Saxon building. Most of the present church dates from the golden age of English ecclesiastical architecture – the 15th century. Outside, there are graceful flying buttresses and wonderfully weird gargoyles while, inside, the ancient oak roofs sprout floral bosses on moulded beams and the old box-pews and lovely medieval screens all add to the charm. In the churchyard is a memorial to 26 children who were drowned while they worked underground in Husker Pit in 1838.

To the southeast lie **Wentworth Castle Gardens**, a wonderful historic garden with an impressive collection of plants including the national collections of rhododendrons, magnolia and X *Williamsii camellias*. Also in the grounds are some magnificent follies including a Gothic castle and an obelisk dedicated to Lady Mary Wortley Montague.

WALES

A mile or so to the west of Wales lies the **Rother Valley Country Park** that provides excellent facilities for water sports including sailing, windsurfing, canoeing and jet skiing, as well as a cable water ski tow. Visitors can hire equipment or use their own, and training courses from beginner to instructor level are available in various water sports. Other attractions at this 750-acre country park include a lakeside golf course, a Craft Centre with craftspeople at work, adventure playgrounds, a nature trail, cycle routes and cycle hire, bridleways, gift shop and a cafeteria.

WENTWORTH

This historic village is home to the palatial 18th century mansion, **Wentworth Woodhouse**, which boasts the longest frontage in England, some 600 feet.

Although the house is not open to the public this wonderful facade can be seen from the surrounding deer park through which there are lovely walks that include a follies trail. The follies and monuments date from the 1700s and the most curious of these is the Needle's Eye that consists of a tower with a stone urn on top and is pierced by a carriageway. Legend says it was built in response to a wager by the Marquis of Rockingham, owner of Wentworth Woodhouse, that he could drive through the eye of a needle.

Another bizarre monument is the Hoober Stand, the most prominent of the follies, which stands at 518 feet above sea level and is a triangular tower some 100 feet high. There are fine views from the tower's viewing gallery that can be reached by climbing the 155 steps inside. One monument that is open to the public is the Wentworth Mausoleum that was built in 1788 in memory of the 2nd Marquis.

THE HERMIT INN

3 HERMIT LANE,HIGHAM,BARNSLEY,SOUTH YORKSHIRE S75 1PL
TEL: 01226 387661

Directions: Higham can be reached by travelling south off the A635 or north off the A628. The Hermit Inn is a short drive from junction 37 of the M1.

The Hermit Inn in Higham is a good-looking public house in an attractive village location. Believed to date back to the early 19th century, the exterior is adorned with tasteful window boxes and hanging baskets. Inside, it is well decorated and furnished throughout. The lounge, public bar and stunning dining room are all comfortable and boast a welcoming ambience. Beamed ceilings, comfortable seating and a wealth of warm reds and golds in the décor and furnishings add to the comfort and relaxation of guests at this excellent pub. Brass and copper cooking implements adorn one wall in an eye-catching and unusual display.

Local couple Vanessa and John Woodhouse have been leaseholders here since April 2003. It is their first venture

into this type of business, and they have made a real success of it. Already they've gained a fine reputation, all down to Vanessa's culinary expertise. Delicious food is available at lunchtime Tuesday to Sunday and at dinner Tuesday to Saturday. Guests choose off the printed menu and specials board from a range of tempting dishes such as chicken and mushroom pancakes, minted lamb shank, steaks, vegetable pasta bake and home-made steak and ale pie. Teatime specials featuring roast chicken, gammon, chicken curry, veggie pasta or liver and onion casserole – two meals for £8.50 available Tuesday to Friday between 5 and 8 p.m., and there are also Senior Citizen three-course luncheon specials Tuesday to Friday from midday to 1.45.

To accompany your meal there's also a range of drinks including two real ales – Tetleys and John Smiths – and lagers, cider, stout, wines, spirits and soft drinks.

- Tue-Fri 11.00-15.00, 17.00-23.00; Sat 11.00-23.00; Sun and Bank Hols 12.00-22.30
- Mon-Sat 12.00-14.00; 17.00-20.00; Sun 12.00-14.00
- Off-road parking
- Themed food evenings – please ring for details; quiz nights Friday and Sunday; karaoke Saturdays
- Barnsley 4 miles, Elsecar 5 miles, Wentworth 8 miles, Sheffield 15 miles

THE JOHN BULL INN

WATERSIDE, THORNE ROAD, THORNE, NR DONCASTER,
SOUTH YORKSHIRE DN8 4JQ
TEL: 01405 814677 FAX: 01405 817986

> **Directions:** From Doncaster take the A630 north and then the M18 to Thorne; or leave the M18 at junction 6 and follow signs.

The John Bull Inn is a Free House with a history going back to 1630. Waterside was, in its heyday, a centre for shipbuilding on the River Don, and this grand old pub once stood right by the river. It takes its name from the steamer *John Bull*, which was built in the early 19th century to ply the route from Thorne Quay to Hull. Locals and travellers made good use of the quayside inn, and still do, though the diversion of the river in the early 1940s took it away from the riverside.

Behind a distinctive beige-painted frontage, the pub has been managed since May 2003 by Jan and Derek Parker, and has enormous olde-worlde charm, with whitewashed walls contrasting with black beams, a fire with brick and beaten

copper surround, and a feature open-brick pillar in the charming function room. Open all day every day for the dispensing of John Smith's and other excellent ales along with a good range of lagers, wines, spirits and soft drinks, the pub serves food at lunchtime and evening, with Jan managing the kitchen. All dishes are listed on the blackboard; specialities include The John Bull mixed grill.

The river and the adjacent Stainforth & Keadby Canal still hold plenty of interest. Thorne has been a port since at least 1500, with ships sailing to Hull, York, London and Europe. In the builders' yards, vessels of up to 400 tons were constructed and as late as 1987 some yards were still operating. Since closing, the area has been carefully developed to preserve this heritage.

- 🕐 Mon-Sat 12.00-23.00; Sun 12.00-22.30
- 🍴 Tues to Sat and Bank Hols 12.00-14.00, 18.00-21.00; Sun 12.00-14.00
- £ All major
- Ⓟ Off-road parking
- ♪ Themed evenings once a month on a Saturday
- ❓ Fishlake 2 miles, Stainforth 3 miles, Doncaster 8 miles

THE LONGBOW

BARNSLEY ROAD,DARFIELD,SOUTH YORKSHIRE S73 9DJ
TEL: 01226 752980FAX: 01226 752047

> **Directions:** From the A633 near Wombwell, follow the sign for Darfield for about a mile, then turn left into Barnsley Road. The Longbow is a short drive up this road on your left.

The Longbow is a large, modern and stylish public house, built just about 40 years ago. Long and low with a wealth of windows letting in plenty of light, this friendly pub combines decorative touches with modern facilities and comfort. The interior includes a carvery area, lounge bar and public bar. The décor has a Georgian feel, with caramel-coloured walls above a dado rail, with salmon-red paint below this rail in the lounge. Leather Chesterfield sofas sit side by side upholstered chairs and more traditional seating. In the public bar, mint green and turquoise offset the green of the snooker table and the polished woof of the tables and chairs.

Outside there's a superb outdoor patio area – a real suntrap – and a secure children's play area with climbing frames and other diversions made from logs.

Experienced licensees Ray and Myra Hawksworth have been in the trade for many years, and their expertise shows in the high standard of service and hospitality they provide all their guests. Ably assisted by their daughter Kim and their friendly, attentive staff, they offer every guest a warm welcome.

Keg-draught drinks served here include Stones, Worthington Creamflow, Stella, Carlsberg Export and Carling, together with a good choice of cider, stout, wines, spirits and soft drinks.

Food is served every day at lunch and dinner. Myra and Kim do all the cooking, and are dab hands in the kitchen, preparing a selection of delicious dishes. The Sunday lunch is particularly popular – a carvery meal with a choice of meals available. Children are very welcome and there's a special family area.

- 🕐 Mon-Sat 11.00-23.00; Sun 12.00-22.30
- 🍴 Mon-Sun 12.00-14.00, 17.00-20.00
- £ None – cash machine on-site
- 🅿 Patio area; children's play area; off-road parking
- 🎵 General knowledge quiz Tues and Sun; music quiz Thurs
- ❓ Barnsley 5 miles, Penistone 8 miles, Sheffield 11 miles

THE MINERS ARMS

BRACKENMOOR LANE, STOCKSBRIDGE, SHEFFIELD,
SOUTH YORKSHIRE S36 2AN
TEL: 0114 288 6394

Directions: Stocksbridge lies about 4 miles northwest of Sheffield city centre. The Miner's Arms is about a mile north of the centre of Stocksbridge off the A616, towards and on the edge of the Derwent Valley.

The Miners Arms in Stocksbridge is a large and impressive inn with great food and drink. This traditional coaching inn with stables dates back to the early 19th century. Known locally for well over 100 years as The Wragg, leaseholders David and Clare have been here since 2001, and have nearly 10 years' experience in the trade between them. Friendly and welcoming, they offer warm hospitality to all their guests. Attractively decorated and furnished throughout, this fine pub is clean and gracious, with a wealth of wood and brass fittings enhancing the cosy ambience. It boasts a handsome bar and comfortable lounge.

David is a chef by profession, and applies his skills and training to preparing superb food, available at lunch Weds-Mon and at dinner Mon and Weds-Thursday. The menus comprise a mouth-watering range of creations such as fresh fish and seafood, grill selections, dishes from around the world like chicken and mushroom stir fry and home-made lasagne, and classics such as stuffed peppers and hickory chicken. Snacks available include jacket potatoes and delicious sandwiches. There's also a children's menu and a selection of tempting desserts.

To drink there are always three real ales, including Tetley, Tetley Imperial and a changing guest ale, together with a good selection of lagers, cider, stout, spirits, wines and soft drinks. Booking advised Sundays. Children welcome.

- 🕐 Mon-Sat 11.00-23.00; Sun 12.00-22.30
- 🍴 Mon, Weds-Thurs 12.00-14.00, 17.00-20.00; Fri-Sat 12.00-17.00; Sun 12.00-16.00 (roast dinner), 12.00-17.00 (menu)
- £ All major
- Ⓟ Patio garden, off-road car parking
- 🎵 Music quiz Weds from 9.30 p.m.; Fun Fortunes and Open-the-book Thurs night; disco Fri; live music first Sat of the month; karaoke Sun eves
- ❓ Sheffield 4 miles, Peak District 1 mile

THE OLD CROWN

6 MARKET STREET, PENISTONE, SHEFFIELD,
SOUTH YORKSHIRE S36 6BZ
TEL: 01226 762422

Directions: Penistone is northwest of Sheffield off the A616/A629

Situated in the heart of the popular old market town of Penistone, on the edge of the Peak District National Park, **The Old Crown** is an attractive and welcoming inn dating back in parts to the 17th century. Hosts Helen and Steve offer all their customers good food, excellently maintained ales and comfortable accommodation. The traditional home-made and freshly prepared meals and snacks are available at lunchtime and in the evenings, and the choice of quality drink includes Tetleys Cask, John Smith Smooth, Stella,Carling, Fosters, cider, wines, spirits and soft drinks.

Upstairs on the second floor of the inn, the accommodation comprises six twin and single guest bedrooms, available at competitive rates and

equipped with TV, tea- and coffee-making facilities and other amenities. Comfortable and welcoming, decorated and furnished to a high standard of comfort and quality, the rooms make a perfect base from which to explore the many sights and attractions of the region, which include not only Sheffield and the Peak District, but the many lovely and historic villages, stately homes, venerable churches and nature trails and parks in the area. A full English breakfast is included in the tariff and there are special rates for longer stays. This lively inn also plays host to a range of entertainments throughout the week, including a music and general knowledge quiz, disco (held in a separate room from the main bar/lounge areas) and live music once a month.

- Mon-Sat 11.00-23.00; Sun 12.00-22.30
- 12-2pm Mon-Fri, 7-8pm Mon-Thurs
- £ All major
- Six rooms
- Quiz Weds; Disco Fri-Sat eves; Live music one Sun a month
- Sheffield 12 miles, Peak District 1 mile, Barnsley 6miles, Huddersfield 10 miles

THE VICTORIA INN

SOUTH END, THORNE, SOUTH YORKSHIRE DN8 5QN
TEL/FAX: 01405 813163

Directions: From junction 6 of the M18, take the A614 to Thorne, following signs to Thorne South Railway Station. The Victoria Inn is opposite the station, and just a short walk from the centre of Thorne.

Dating back over 200 years, **The Victoria Inn** is a former coaching inn. Recently refurbished, it is a truly pleasant and welcoming place with comfortable and tasteful décor and furnishings. The lounge and bar are attractive and cosy, while the no-smoking conservatory/dining area is light, airy, spacious and clean. The superb patio area and lawned garden are particularly attractive and there's also a lovely fenced-off private ornamental garden with fish pond for adult guests.

The two real ales at this Free House are John Smiths and a changing guest ale. Alongside these there's a good range of lagers, cider, stout, wines, spirits and soft drinks.

Owners Tina and Mark, together with

Tina's brother Mark, run this fine pub with flair and dedication. They and their friendly staff offer a warm welcome to all their guests.

Food is served evenings only Monday to Saturday, and Sundays at lunch. Both Tina and Mark cook. Guests choose off the printed menu or specials boards from a range of home-cooked specialities that include steak and ale pie, lasagne and other tempting dishes. Booking is required Friday and Saturday night and for Sunday lunch. Children are welcome.

Recently Tina and Mark have also purchased a property next to the pub, to be available for guest accommodation from September of 2003. To be called The Victoria Lodge, the property will have five guest bedrooms that will be available on a bed-and-evening meal or room-only basis all year round.

- Mon-Sat 11.00-23.00; Sun 12.00-22.30
- Mon-Sat 17.30-21.00; Sun 12.00-14.30
- 5 rooms
- Off-road parking
- Darts and dominos Mon; quiz Thurs; karaoke Sat
- Doncaster 10 miles, Scunthorpe 13 miles, Pontefract 15 miles, Sheffield 23 miles

THE WELLINGTON

LAITHES LANE,ATHERSLEY NORTH,BARNSLEY,
SOUTH YORKSHIRE S71 3AP
TEL: 01226 284246

> **Directions:** Athersley North is just a short drive off the A61 (Wakefield–Barnsley Road). The Wellington is in Laithes Lane.

Opened as a new building in 1962, **The Wellington** took its name from an old public house in the heart of Barnsley which had been demolished.

Inside, the cream-coloured ceiling is trimmed in a soft blue-green. Deep reds and burgundies in the décor and furnishings add to the warmth and cosiness of the interior. The stone fireplace makes an interesting centrepiece.

The large lawned beer garden and patio area are real suntraps. Adjacent to the beer garden is the garden room, a lovely and welcoming place to enjoy a drink or meal.

Draught-keg beers here are John Smiths Smooth, Fosters, Woodpecker and Guinness, along with various bottled drinks, cider, stout, wines, spirits and soft drinks.

Delicious food is served every day at lunch; evening meals are served Monday to Thursday, while Friday and Saturday nights there's a range of sandwiches available. Guests choose off the menu and specials board from a variety of tempting traditional favourites. The Sunday roast is particularly popular – booking is advised. Children are very welcome. Pensioners' specials are also available – please ring for details.

Tenants Steve and Janet Garrett arrived here in 1999. Janet does all the cooking – and her care and expertise are obvious by the delicious results. The Garretts and their friendly staff offer all their guests the best in food, drink and genuine hospitality.

- 🕐 Mon-Sat 12.00-23.00; Sun 12.00-22.30
- 🍴 Mon-Sat 12.00-14.30; Sun 12.30-15.15; Mon-Thur 17.00-19.30; Fri-Sat eve sandwiches only
- Ⓟ Beer garden, patio area, garden room, function room, off-road parking
- 🎵 Disco (60s/70s/80s) Fridays; karaoke Saturdays; auctions held in the function room Monday nights
- ❓ Barnsley 5 miles, Wakefield 5 miles, Leeds 12 miles, Sheffield 17 miles

ALPHABETICAL LIST
OF PUBS AND INNS

G

H

J

K

L

M

N

O

Alphabetical List of Pubs and Inns

SPECIAL INTEREST LISTS

Accommodation

THE YORKSHIRE DALES

The Boars Head Hotel	Long Preston, Skipton, North Yorkshire	26
The Clarendon Hotel	Hebden, Grassington, North Yorkshire	28
The Elm Tree Inn	Embsay, Skipton, North Yorkshire	29
The Farmer's Arms	Catterick Bridge, Brompton on Swale, North Yorkshire	30
The Fox & Hounds Inn	West Burton, Leyburn, North Yorkshire	31
The Golden Lion Hotel	Leyburn, North Yorkshire	32
The Greyhound Inn	Hackforth, Bedale, North Yorkshire	33
The Half Moon Inn	Fellbeck, Pateley Bridge, North Yorkshire	34
The Lister Arms Hotel	Malham, Skipton, North Yorkshire	36
The Old Horn Inn	Spennithorne, Leyburn, North Yorkshire	37
The White Lion at Kildwick	Kildwick, Skipton, North Yorkshire	38
The White Lion Inn	Cray, Buckden, North Yorkshire	39

THE MOORS, THE HERITAGE COAST AND THE VALE OF PICKERING

THE CITY OF YORK AND CENTRAL YORKSHIRE

All Day Opening

THE YORKSHIRE DALES

THE MOORS, THE HERITAGE COAST AND THE VALE OF PICKERING

THE CITY OF YORK AND CENTRAL YORKSHIRE

THE EAST RIDING AND NORTH HUMBERSIDE

WEST YORKSHIRE

All Day Opening

SPECIAL INTEREST LISTS

Childrens Facilities

THE MOORS, THE HERITAGE COAST AND THE VALE OF PICKERING

THE CITY OF YORK AND CENTRAL YORKSHIRE

WEST YORKSHIRE

SOUTH YORKSHIRE

SPECIAL INTEREST LISTS

Credit Cards Accepted

THE YORKSHIRE DALES

THE MOORS, THE HERITAGE COAST AND THE VALE OF PICKERING

THE CITY OF YORK AND CENTRAL YORKSHIRE

THE EAST RIDING AND NORTH HUMBERSIDE

WEST YORKSHIRE

SOUTH YORKSHIRE

Garden, Patio or Terrace

THE YORKSHIRE DALES

THE MOORS, THE HERITAGE COAST AND THE VALE OF PICKERING

THE CITY OF YORK AND CENTRAL YORKSHIRE

Garden, Patio or Terrace

SPECIAL INTEREST LISTS

Live Entertainment

Restaurant or Dining Area

Restaurant or Dining Area

PLACES OF INTEREST

Order Form

ORDER FORM

To order any of our publications just fill in the payment details below and complete the order form. For orders of less than 4 copies please add £1 per book for postage and packing. Orders over 4 copies are P & P free.

Please Complete Either:

I enclose a cheque for £ [   ] made payable to Travel Publishing Ltd

Or:

Card No: [   ]   Expiry Date: [   ]

Signature: [   ]

Name: [   ]

Address: [   ]

Tel no: [   ]

Please either send, telephone, fax or e-mail your order to:

Travel Publishing Ltd, 7a Apollo House, Calleva Park, Aldermaston, Berkshire RG7 8TN   Tel: 0118 981 7777   Fax: 0118 982 0077 e-mail: karen@travelpublishing.co.uk

	Price	Quantity		Price	Quantity
Hidden Places Regional Titles			**Hidden Inns Titles**		
Cambs & Lincolnshire	£7.99	....	East Anglia	£5.99	....
Chilterns	£7.99	....	Heart of England	£5.99	....
Cornwall	£8.99	....	Lancashire & Cheshire	£5.99	....
Derbyshire	£8.99	....	North of England	£5.99	....
Devon	£8.99	....	South	£5.99	....
Dorset, Hants & Isle of Wight	£8.99	....	South East	£7.99	....
East Anglia	£8.99	....	South and Central Scotland	£5.99	....
Gloucs, Wiltshire & Somerset	£8.99	....	Wales	£7.99	....
Heart of England	£7.99	....	Welsh Borders	£5.99	....
Hereford, Worcs & Shropshire	£7.99	....	West Country	£7.99	....
Kent	£8.99	....	Yorkshire	£7.99	....
Lake District & Cumbria	£8.99	....			
Lancashire & Cheshire	£8.99	....	**Country Living Rural Guides**		
Lincolnshire & Notts	£8.99	....	East Anglia	£9.99	....
Northumberland & Durham	£8.99	....	Heart of England	£9.99	....
Sussex	£8.99	....	Ireland	£10.99	....
Yorkshire	£8.99	....	Scotland	£10.99	....
			South of England	£9.99	....
Hidden Places National Titles			South East of England	£9.99	....
England	£10.99	....	Wales	£10.99	....
Ireland	£10.99	....	West Country	£9.99	....
Scotland	£10.99	....			
Wales	£9.99	....			

Total Quantity [   ]

Post & Packing [   ]   Total Value [   ]

The *Travel Publishing* research team would like to receive reader's comments on any visitor attractions or places reviewed in the book and also recommendations for suitable entries to be included in the next edition. This will help ensure that the *Hidden Inns Series* continues to provide its readers with useful information on the more interesting, unusual or unique features of each inn or place ensuring that their visit to the local area is an enjoyable and stimulating experience. To provide your comments or recommendations would you please complete the forms below and overleaf as indicated and send to:

The Research Department, Travel Publishing Ltd,
7a Apollo House, Calleva Park, Aldermaston, Reading, RG7 8TN.

Your Name:

Your Address:

Your Telephone Number:

Please tick as appropriate:

Comments ☐   Recommendation ☐

Name of Establishment:

Address:

Telephone Number:

Name of Contact:

READER REACTION FORM

Comment or Reason for Recommendation:

READER REACTION FORM

The *Travel Publishing* research team would like to receive reader's comments on any visitor attractions or places reviewed in the book and also recommendations for suitable entries to be included in the next edition. This will help ensure that the *Hidden Inns Series* continues to provide its readers with useful information on the more interesting, unusual or unique features of each inn or place ensuring that their visit to the local area is an enjoyable and stimulating experience. To provide your comments or recommendations would you please complete the forms below and overleaf as indicated and send to:

The Research Department, Travel Publishing Ltd,
7a Apollo House, Calleva Park, Aldermaston, Reading, RG7 8TN.

Your Name:

Your Address:

Your Telephone Number:

Please tick as appropriate:

Comments ☐   Recommendation ☐

Name of Establishment:

Address:

Telephone Number:

Name of Contact:

READER REACTION FORM

Comment or Reason for Recommendation:

READER REACTION FORM

The *Travel Publishing* research team would like to receive reader's comments on any visitor attractions or places reviewed in the book and also recommendations for suitable entries to be included in the next edition. This will help ensure that the *Hidden Inns Series* continues to provide its readers with useful information on the more interesting, unusual or unique features of each inn or place ensuring that their visit to the local area is an enjoyable and stimulating experience. To provide your comments or recommendations would you please complete the forms below and overleaf as indicated and send to:

The Research Department, Travel Publishing Ltd,
7a Apollo House, Calleva Park, Aldermaston, Reading, RG7 8TN.

Your Name:

Your Address:

Your Telephone Number:

Please tick as appropriate:

Comments ☐ Recommendation ☐

Name of Establishment:

Address:

Telephone Number:

Name of Contact:

READER REACTION FORM

Comment or Reason for Recommendation:

READER REACTION FORM

The *Travel Publishing* research team would like to receive reader's comments on any visitor attractions or places reviewed in the book and also recommendations for suitable entries to be included in the next edition. This will help ensure that the *Hidden Inns Series* continues to provide its readers with useful information on the more interesting, unusual or unique features of each inn or place ensuring that their visit to the local area is an enjoyable and stimulating experience. To provide your comments or recommendations would you please complete the forms below and overleaf as indicated and send to:

The Research Department, Travel Publishing Ltd,
7a Apollo House, Calleva Park, Aldermaston, Reading, RG7 8TN.

Your Name:

Your Address:

Your Telephone Number:

Please tick as appropriate:

Comments ☐   Recommendation ☐

Name of Establishment:

Address:

Telephone Number:

Name of Contact:

READER REACTION FORM

Comment or Reason for Recommendation: